MW01039493

More Conversations with Walker Percy

Literary Conversations Series

Peggy Whitman Prenshaw
General Editor

More Conversations with Walker Percy

Edited by
Lewis A. Lawson
and Victor A. Kramer

University Press of Mississippi
Jackson

*Publication of this book
has been made possible in part by a generous grant
from the John N. Palmer Foundation.*

Copyright © 1993 by the University Press of Mississippi
All rights reserved
Manufactured in the United States of America
96 95 94 93   4   3   2   1
The paper in this book meets the guidelines for permanence and durability
of the Committee on Production Guidelines for Book Longevity of the Council
on Library Resources.

Library of Congress Cataloging-in-Publication Data

Percy, Walker, 1916-1990
    More conversations with Walker Percy / edited by Lewis A. Lawson
and Victor A. Kramer.
        p.   cm. — (Literary conversations series)
    Includes index.
    ISBN 0-87805-623-8. — ISBN 0-87805-624-6 (paper)
    1. Percy, Walker, 1916-1990—Interviews.   2. Novelists,
American—20th century—Interviews.   I. Lawson, Lewis A.
II. Kramer, Victor A.   III. Title.   IV. Series.
PS3566.E6912Z47   1993
813'.54—dc20   92-44968
                                                              CIP

British Library Cataloging-in-Publication data available

Books by Walker Percy

The Moviegoer. New York: Alfred A. Knopf, 1961.

The Last Gentleman. New York: Farrar, Straus and Giroux, 1966.

Love in the Ruins: The Adventures of a Bad Catholic at a Time Near the End of the World. New York: Farrar, Straus and Giroux, 1971.

The Message in the Bottle: How Queer Man Is, How Queer Language Is, and What One Has to Do with the Other. New York: Farrar, Straus and Giroux, 1975.

Lancelot. New York: Farrar, Straus and Giroux, 1977.

The Second Coming. New York: Farrar, Straus and Giroux, 1980.

Lost in the Cosmos: The Last Self-Help Book. New York: Farrar, Straus and Giroux, 1983.

The Thanatos Syndrome. New York: Farrar, Straus and Giroux, 1987.

Signposts in a Strange Land. [Edited with an introduction by Patrick H. Samway, S. J.] New York: Farrar, Straus and Giroux, 1991.

Contents

Introduction

By 1970 Walker Percy was besieged by his own success. The voice that he had created in *The Moviegoer* (1961) and *The Last Gentleman* (1966) convinced many readers that he was talking directly to them. Thus they responded by writing to him—it quickly became a marvel among college students that he would answer their letters—or by coming to Covington, Louisiana, to visit him. Not all of them were as persistent as a later couple from Chicago, who parked their camper on Percy property for three days, "hoping for a chance to talk to the writer," according to Linda Hobson.[1] But there were even those readers who moved to New Orleans or Baton Rouge to be within audible range.

In his excellent biography *Pilgrim in the Ruins* (1992), Jay Tolson graphically describes one tribe of the siege-horde, the interviewers. During 1970–72 Percy was visited by Alfred Kazin, Philip Carter, Charles Bunting, John C. Carr, Martin Luschei, and Robert Coles.[2] And these are only those who succeeded. But, however much the stream of interviewers may have constituted a distraction to the author, it was most beneficial to his readers, for the publications by Kazin, Luschei, and Coles were the first all-encompassing profiles of Percy's life. And the other interviews were published in newspapers and journals and then reprinted in *Conversations with Walker Percy* (1984) by the present editors, who would be churls, indeed, now to repine of their existence.

All the same, to Percy it may have seemed too much of a good thing, especially as the requests for interviews did not diminish. If he did refuse some solicitations, perhaps in 1972, he then relented, to give some of his most informative statements to Zoltán Abádi-Nagy, Barbara King, Bradley Dewey, and Marcus Smith. But by 1977 he may have decided to try to stop the procession of mendicants to his door by granting the Ultimate Interview, to himself. "Questions They Never

---

[1] Linda Hobson, "Man vs Malaise, In the Eyes of Walker Percy," *Louisiana Life*, 3 (July-August 1983), 57.

[2] Jay Tolson, *Pilgrim in the Ruins: A Life of Walker Percy* (New York: Simon & Schuster, 1992), pp. 369–75.

Asked Me So He Asked Them Himself" was futile as a defensive
strategy, but, as Jay Tolson observes,

> the self-interview proved to be one of Percy's most successful literary
> gambits, a self-portrait of the artist that is every bit as ironic and
> unsettling as Kierkegaard's *Point of View for My Work as an Author*.
> What Percy revealed in this piece was something that no interviewer had
> ever managed to reach, the persona of the artist, a much less sweet and
> agreeable figure than the usual interview subject, fiercer, more smart-ass,
> far more troubling, and, in certain ways, more honest.[3]

There is more honesty here than in anything else Percy ever wrote, but
even here honesty comes with a veil. Readers of Percy have not yet
sufficiently attended his confession that his "knack" for writing has a
trinity of "components," "theological, demonic, and sexual."

In response to the unabating pressure Percy acknowledged his
connection to common mortality. He adopted two opposed tacks, either
of which seemed to be initiated by chance. In 1978 Carol Andrews
observed the contradiction:

> Percy had rather ask than be asked questions; in fact, he began an
> interview the day before his reading by stating emphatically, "This is the
> last interview I'll ever give." Then he talked cordially and willingly
> about his work, including his plan for the new book [*The Second
> Coming*].[4]

Yet the next year he granted a home interview to Mrs. Dorothy
Kitchings, to be used in her master's thesis. Perhaps his guiding passion
had been earlier discovered by Bruce Cook[5]; as a gentleman he could
not ordinarily refuse a person the hospitality of his house.

Honoring the code of gentility might explain the discrepancy that
William Starr caught in 1980: "[Percy] does not quite shun interviews,
but he does not seek them out and in fact has rejected some requests
because they are too consuming of his time. But he did agree to talk a
few weeks ago."[6] If a face was attached to the request, Percy could not
seem to refuse it.

Some such convoluted reasoning might explain Percy's relationship

[3] Tolson, p. 417.
[4] Carol Andrews, "The Last Interview," *Vanderbilt University Graduate English Newsletter*, 5 (May 1978), 7.
[5] Bruce Cook, "To Walker Percy, Man's Prognosis is Funny," *National Observer*, May 23, 1971, 17.
[6] William Starr, "Interview," *The State* (Columbia, South Carolina) November 5, 1980, 1B.

with the French in the 1980s. Percy had always credited contemporary
French writing—especially Camus, Sartre, Marcel, Maritain—as one of
the chief influences upon both his fictional technique and his aesthetics;
the French, in return, had been his most enthusiastic foreign audience.
Earlier he had welcomed Gilbert Schricke to his home. And in 1981 he
welcomed Peggy Castex for an interview which was published at the
Sorbonne. But Professor Castex might have gotten her acceptance from
the fact that she was a native of Gentilly; if so, she surely delighted
Percy when she confirmed that in *The Moviegoer* he had "told it just the
way it was."[7]

Then began the semi-embargo against the French—or even something
that sounded French. *The Paris Review* had asked Percy for an interview
before and been refused, but, apparently hearing of Percy's threat to
abandon interviewing, it asked for the honor of the Last Interview.
Percy revealed that he had refused that request in a letter to Ms Robin
Leary, a New Orleans journalist, to whom he had given an interview in
1983: "What they want is a very long, talky interview baring one's soul.
As I told you, I've had enough of interviews."[8] He suggested that Ms
Leary will the interview she had received to the Percy Papers, in the
Southern Historical Collection, University of North Carolina, putatively
as the Last Interview. It is being spared that fate by being published
here. Perhaps because the proposed *Paris Review* interviewer was
Zoltán Abádi-Nagy, an earlier visitor to Covington and a Hungarian,
Percy relented, to conduct a mail interview, from May to October 1986,
which was published in 1987. Percy was equally initially uncooperative
with the French ministry of education, which invited him to tour French
universities, to discuss *The Moviegoer*, one of the texts to be assigned
for close analysis by French majors in English literature in 1986. Yet he
relented, to give a satellite interview, from New Orleans, with a panel
of French scholars, being delighted when he learned that one of them
was Simone Vauthier, who had written about his work with insight and
had impressed him when she had visited his home.

The word *home* is a significant key to Percy's behavior about
interviews in the 1980s. Jay Tolson concludes that, after a period of
wandering away from faith and home in the 1970s, Percy came home in

[7]Peggy Castex, "An Interview with Walker Percy," *Noveaux fragments du puzzle Americaine*
(Paris: Presses de l' Universite de Paris Sorbonne [Paris IV], 1983), 26.
[8]"Percy declines to talk," *The Times-Picayune/States-Item*, January 7, 1985, B2.

the 1980s. This movement of homecoming is beautifully reflected in *The Second Coming* (1980), the novel which completes the theme in Percy's fiction of the successful quest for the religious and romantic objects that comprise the restitution for the lost maternal object. The novel thus prefigures the final phase of Percy's life.

For all his threats, Percy gave many interviews in the 1980s, such good interviews as those by Kenneth Holditch, Linda Hobson, Jan Gretlund, Malcolm Jones, Elzbieta Oleksy, and Phil McCombs. But it is significant that almost all of them were given at home, even if they began somewhere else. By 1977 Percy was talking in interviews of the need to have a public place,[9] in some way approximate to a European cafe, in which he and likeminded persons could eat and talk informally. Jay Tolson indicates that Percy and several friends had found the place even earlier, Bechacs, on Lake Pontchartrain. Percy would take an interviewer to a Thursday meeting at Bechacs, then repair to his home for the interview, in effect situating his artistic life within the larger context of his domestic life. Percy met Linda Hobson at Bechacs, though in this case not by his instigation. When she was introduced to Percy, he asked "somewhat stiffly" where she was from. That close reader of *Love in the Ruins* (1971) replied, "Well actually, Dr. Percy, I am a chickenshit Ohioan."[10]

Once through his front door, Percy lost whatever reservations he might have had about yet another interview. Robert Cubbage, whose work is included in this volume, said that he made almost ten hours of tape. He met Percy in mid-morning; began taping; turned the recorder off only while they went out to lunch; couldn't resist turning the machine back on in the restaurant; and then returned to that "Cajun cottage" on Bogue Falaya River to talk still more—Percy finally stretched out on his back, still bemused, talking and questioning, often questioning more than talking. Percy developed the habit of doing as much as he could flat on his back when he was in the sanatorium in the 1940s. It was not a bad habit on which to rely in the interviewing '80s.

One reason Percy was willing to speak more was that, in a sense, he had become much more than a novelist. He liked to describe himself as

[9]John F. Baker, "PW Interviews Walker Percy," *Publishers' Weekly*, 211 (March 21, 1977), 7; David Chandler, "Walker Percy's Southern Novel has a Lunatic Hero and other Gothic Touches," *People Magazine*, 7 (May 2, 1977), 96.
[10]Tolson, p. 435.

a story-teller, a bemused novelist. He was, though, becoming a moralist, too. As a cultural critic and a Christian he felt that he had to speak out. The radical change of tone in his final novel, *The Thanatos Syndrome* (1987), marks his willingness to confront those ideas which he deplored. As he remarked to Phil McCombs, "even a novelist has a right to issue a warning."[11]

But always, even when meditating on the worst side of human behavior, as does Father Smith in the last novel, Percy strives to maintain a perspective from which to see God's plentitude. Thus Percy always remains cautiously hopeful. His wary optimism is reflected in the various searchers in his fiction. Open and always willing to take time, to keep on talking if it seemed necessary, Percy was by his writing and other kindnesses drawn out of himself; giving himself in this manner, he was able to accomplish the intersubjective moment that benefited both the other and himself. One example, easily multiplied, is the magic meeting in the Atlanta Delta concourse remembered by Kathleen Parker: "During our conversation, he never let go of my hand, but held it gently cupped between his two. He never took his eyes from mine, but held me captive in a gaze that can only be described as hypnotic."[12]

Another example of Percy's need to give is offered, poignant because it celebrates not a gift of excitement to a young person, but a gift of solace to two stricken people. In remarks made after Percy's death, an acquaintance of many years, Cleanth Brooks, fondly remembered how Percy had generously offered to come to New England, to drive Brooks and his wife, who was fatally ill, to country inns so that they might seek respite from their routine. Brooks had to decline the offer, but he inquired if it might be possible for Percy to send a copy of *The Thanatos Syndrome*, then not yet published. Immediately Percy sent a copy of marked page proofs. It was the last book that Brooks was to read to his wife.

As his own fatal illness ravaged him, Percy became more concerned about a culture in which "twentieth century man is deranged, literally deranged."[13] Agonizing over a world in severe trouble, he was now willing to make connections between his judgments and the institutions

---

[11] Phil McCombs, "Century of Thanatos: Walker Percy and his 'Subversive Message'," *Southern Review*, 24 (August 1988), 816.

[12] Kathleen Parker, "A Warm Encounter with Walker Percy," *Orlando Sentinel*, November 2, E1.

[13] Scott Walter, "Out of the Ruins," *Crisis*, 7 (July-August 1989), 16.

of contemporary society. When *The Thanatos Syndrome* was given an initial press run of 75,000 copies, Percy realized that he had attained a state of fame not previously accorded him by many Americans. He decided, therefore, to mount his fame as a hill from which to speak, as another convert had long ago done. During the period 1986–1988 he seems to have taken every opportunity to speak to the religious press— *The National Catholic Register*, *Notre Dame Magazine*, *Our Sunday Visitor*, *Crisis*, *Sojourners*, among others—and to the secular book reviewers, even collapsing from exhaustion during a reading tour associated with the publication of his last novel. His testament to the world was given in the Eighteenth Annual Jefferson Lecture, which he delivered at the invitation of the National Endowment for the Humanities, on 3 May 1989. To that Washington audience—many of them so intellectual that they did not realize that they were the object of his attack—he eloquently described the alienation from God that has befallen humankind since it adapted Cartesian measures and values for human concerns and relationships.

From this summit it is a pleasure to descend steeply for two final glimpses of Walker Percy. One is of him at the Fellowship of Southern Writers Fifth Biennial Conference, at Chattanooga—a much smaller mountain—in April 1989. Surely by then the Jefferson Lecture was written and he felt back among his roots, for in one of his last interviews, with Rebekah Presson, he spoke only about his craft, confessing his lingering infatuation—after all these years—for Sharon Kincaid, Binx Bolling's Aphrodite. Thus he shows solidarity with all the males who have read *The Moviegoer* in the last thirty years. The other glimpse is of Percy in the summer of 1988, in his pickup in the drive-through line at Wendy's, to get a bacon cheeseburger and "ice' tea" (Southerners would say). There he was boarded by the college-age son of a Baton Rouge Episcopalian minister, who had learned Percy's habits enough to hang around Wendy's, waiting to ask for an interview. Like Sutter's Edsel, the pickup stopped. Percy took the young man home and talked to him for an hour.[14]

In our earlier *Conversations* we gathered twenty-eight interviews or profiles, some rather informal and some not. Here, surprisingly, for all

---

[14]Tolson, p. 476.

his talk about not talking, we offer about the same number. It seems clear now that his willingness, despite his pronouncements, to let thought flow was a fundamental act of his contemplative nature. Percy puzzled over the wonders of language, telling stories, raising questions, using words to get closer to the other and to the Spirit. We are delighted to be presenting four previously unpublished interviews, by Dorothy Kitchings, Kenneth Holditch, Robin Leary, and Jan Gretlund. We are delighted to present the previously unpublished transcription of the Worldnet interview with the representatives of *Agrégation d'anglais*. We are delighted to bring two interviews home: Peggy Castex's, from Paris, and Elzbieta Oleksy's, from Lodz, Poland. We are delighted to make all the other pieces easily accessible to all Percy readers. We are not delighted that we must omit the interview by the young man from Baton Rouge, praying that his resemblance to his Biblical counterpart stops with his desire to hear the word.

In a collaborative effort such as this we have the happy responsibility to acknowledge a great indebtedness to the many writers, interviewers, and librarians who have enabled us to provide yet another encounter with Walker Percy. Above all we thank him.

LAL
VAK   1992

Chronology

1916	28 May, birth, in Birmingham, Alabama
1929	9 July, death of father, by his own hand
1930	Residence in Athens, Georgia, with mother's family
1931	Residence in Greenville, Mississippi, with father's first cousin, William Alexander Percy
1932	2 April, death of mother, in an automobile accident
1937	Graduation from University of North Carolina, with a major in chemistry; beginning of three years of psychoanalysis.
1941	Graduation from Columbia University with M.D.
1942	21 January, death of William Alexander Percy from stroke; onset of three-year bout with tuberculosis.
1945	Residence in New Mexico with Shelby Foote
1946	7 November, marriage to Mary Bernice Townsend
1947	Conversion to Catholicism; residence in New Orleans, Louisiana.
1950	Residence in Covington, Louisiana
1954	Beginning of publication in learned journals
1961	Publication of *The Moviegoer*

1962   National Book Award for *The Moviegoer*

1966   Publication of *The Last Gentleman*

1971   Publication of *Love in the Ruins*

1975   Publication of *The Message in the Bottle*

1977   Publication of *Lancelot*

1980   Publication of *The Second Coming*

1983   Publication of *Lost in the Cosmos*

1987   Publication of *The Thanatos Syndrome*

1989   Delivery of Eighteenth Annual Jefferson Lecture, National
          Endowment for the Humanities, Washington, D.C.

1990   10 May, death of Walker Percy, of cancer, Covington,
          Louisiana

1991   Publication of *Signposts in a Strange Land*

More Conversations with Walker Percy

An Interview with Walker Percy

Dorothy H. Kitchings/1979

From the Mississippi Department of Archives and History; unpublished, 29 June 1979. Reprinted with the gracious permission of
Dorothy H. Kitchings.

Kitchings: Do you believe that the Southerner of the late twentieth
century is likely to be more aware of his lostness, his alienation, than
our Yankee neighbors are?

Percy: As of now? This period?

Kitchings: Yes.

Percy: No, I don't think so. Maybe even less so, because of the great
economic revival of the Sunbelt, the Southern Rim. Really they are the
Yankees of the country now. It's the Northeast and New England that
are in the difficulties the South used to be in after the Civil War. For
instance, this is the fastest growing parish economically and population-
wise in the state, and one of the fastest in the South. In that sense it's
like Texas. So there's not too much alienation where there's a great deal
of economic growth and prosperity.

Kitchings: Not much awareness of it.

Percy: Not much awareness of it, no. Well, in the epigraph of *The
Moviegoer*, there's a difference between a kind of despair and the
consciousness of despair.

Kitchings: Yes. My question comes out of my own interest. Perhaps
we should go back twenty-five years. Do you think that the kind of
idealism that Emily Cutrer comes forth with in *The Moviegoer*, that kind
of thing that most of us Southerners were reared on, do you think that
has contributed to Southern alienation and our awareness of it? Or to
what extent has it?

Percy: I don't think it contributes much to anything these days. I
don't think it's much in evidence. It represents a point of view which
I was brought up with, which I'm familiar with, maybe you too?

Kitchings: Yes.

Percy: Mainly through my uncle, William Alexander Percy. I am

3

trying to think off-hand of anybody nowadays who represents it, and I can't; except people who get it in a very derivative and in a second-class way. For instance, there are many people who are fans and admirers of *Lanterns on the Levee*, mainly because of what they take to be its racist overtones. They say, "Well, your uncle was right." Many people have told me about *The Moviegoer*: "I sure do like this book because I like the way Aunt Emily told him off at the end. You know, she was absolutely right."

Kitchings: They miss the point.

Percy: Well, they sort of miss the point. Of course, you know, she was partly right and Binx was partly wrong, but they do miss the point.

Kitchings: It seems to me that from *The Moviegoer* to *Lancelot* your heroes, protagonists, become more and more troubled, less able to cope, by normal standards. Your vision of American society becomes more pessimistic. You become more specific about the ills of society. I wondered if when you wrote *The Moviegoer*, you had any such canon in mind, a body of work in which this would happen? Or is this just something that happened to you?

Percy: I guess it's just accidental. It's the result of the natural progression of my writing. Well, they're very different. I suppose in a way *Love in the Ruins* is more pessimistic than *The Moviegoer*; although it's so different. It's much more cataclysmic. It's much more fantastic, a sci-fi fantasy sort of thing. But in a way, maybe the ending of *Love in the Ruins* . . . maybe it ends in true hope?

Kitchings: I agree.

Percy: There's a true sense of community there.

Kitchings: I have to confess I thought of it today as I sat in line for thirty minutes to get gasoline. I thought about those abandoned automobiles.

Percy: Yes. Maybe there was a sense of starting all over again in *Love in the Ruins* which is not true in either *The Moviegoer* or *The Last Gentleman*.

Kitchings: The openness to possibility seems to me to be present in *The Moviegoer*.

Percy: Yes, that's right. Really, *The Moviegoer* is much more modest in its scope. It really had to do not with society so much as the relationship between two people, between Binx and Kate; both of whom existed in their different modes of despair, and both of whom at the end

see some possibility of a way out, you know, through each other. It is
really about love. It involves two people in modern society . . .

Kitchings: Robert Coles has said that you would scoff at words like
community, and . . .

Percy: That's a good word, a good word.

Kitchings: It seems to me that the first time I read *The Moviegoer*
what struck me about it was that Binx seems to find that relationship,
that Marcellian intersubjectivity—he calls his brothers "his brothers,"
and he commits himself to Kate. I had a little trouble with that in Coles'
statement.

Percy: Yes. I have no trouble with the idea of community.

Kitchings: You do believe it's possible?

Percy: Sure.

Kitchings: Certainly between two people, but you would say in a
larger group of people.

Percy: Yes. That's what was going on at the end of *Love in the
Ruins*. It was an incipient community. It was taking place in the slave
quarters below the bluff, you know. It was a very small beginning
community of Catholics and Protestants and blacks and Jews; people
who'd been kicked out by the revolutionary, upper-class blacks up in
the country club.

Kitchings: The outcasts, starting over.

Percy: Yes, I thought that was an appropriate place for a community
to begin, in the slave quarters.

Kitchings: You talk a great deal about the individual retaining his
sovereignty, and the individual being an individual and not being able to
be compared to other members of the species. You talk about our giving
up our sovereignty to the experts. Does that give you any problem at all
with Roman Catholicism and the authority of the church and the Pope
and so forth?

Percy: No. It never has. In the first place, just in point of actual
experience, it doesn't happen. I don't know whether it's the present
disarray of the church. Maybe it was at different times. There's no one
to tell you what to do. There's no longer any Index. No one tells you
what to read. I feel like Flannery O'Connor when Flannery said that far
from finding the Catholic Church confining or in any way oppressive,
she found it liberating. It puts you in touch with, first with the mystery,
and that, in truth, religion has to do with mysteries. It addresses the

nature of man. And secondly, the whole Catholic view of man is man as a pilgrim, or on a search or on a pilgrimage—man as a wayfarer, which is what a novel is about, you know; which is probably why Buddhists don't write good novels, or Freudians don't write good novels, or Marxists don't write good novels. They don't see man that way. So the idea of a bishop or a priest, or even a pope looking over my shoulder bothering me is absurd.

Kitchings: Never occur to you?

Percy: No.

Kitchings: In *The Last Gentleman* you have a priest called in to baptize Jamie Vaught at the last of the novel. You describe him as a fairly indifferent sort of fellow.

Percy: You're being kind. I made him downright unpleasant, as unpleasant as I could.

Kitchings: Yes, you did. But apparently he is, in that case, the newsbearer.

Percy: Yes.

Kitchings: Right. That has to say something.

Percy: Sure, because it doesn't matter what he's like.

Kitchings: He represents the church?

Percy: Yes. The point is that it would've been a mistake to make him very sympathetic, sensitive, intellectual, warm-hearted; somebody like Teilhard de Chardin, you know, a priest like that. I think it works much better to have him as a very mediocre, ordinary man.

Kitchings: Seem to be sort of caught up in the everydayness of his job.

Percy: Why sure. But nevertheless, the doctrine of the church is that the sacraments are transmitted regardless of the character of the priest. So here's this guy . . . I think I describe him as looking something like an American League umpire, a baseball umpire. You can imagine some big guy, red-faced.

Kitchings: Yes, the picture was well drawn. He kept looking at his hairy hands.

Percy: And he's giving the straight doctrine sure enough. It may sound sort of canned and packed like out of the *Baltimore* catechism, but it is the straight doctrine.

Kitchings: And he puts the purple ribbon on.

Percy: Sure, he sort of slings the stole around his neck and picks up a dirty hospital glass for the baptism, which is okay. I was going out of my way to avoid an edifying scene, to avoid all the aesthetics of a proper conversion.

Kitchings: Yes, you sought to avoid that. You have sought to avoid that at every point because modern man can't hear it.

Percy: That's something that is well known to me, to Flannery [O'Connor], to Graham Greene and others.

Kitchings: I just read *The Power and the Glory* for the first time.

Percy: Really? That's one of his early ones.

Kitchings: He is doing something like the same thing with the whiskey priest. Representative of the church no matter what he's like.

Percy: That's the idea.

Kitchings: He has this commitment.

Percy: All his priests are very flawed people.

Kitchings: This is my son's question. He asked me to ask you this question, which was provoked by your *Esquire* "Questions They Never Asked Me": Why does Christianity seem a better thing to you than accepting with resignation and courage, if you will, the fact of our aloneness and end at death?

Percy: Well, because it is better. It's better to have good news than bad news. If it's true it's good news indeed. To be in a situation of a hero in a Camus novel or a Sartre novel, alone, in despair, however heroic or stoic he is about it, he's not as well off as a man who has actually received the good news. Of course, the question is not altogether congenial to me because the novel I'm now writing has to do with a man who finds himself in an extremely Christian environment and makes a kind of joke of it. He's retired. Well, this is Will Barrett and he's retired and it's twenty years later. He has married a very rich girl. She's dead. He's retired to a very plush resort in North Carolina, which I say is the most Christian state in the most Christian country in the world, and in the county close to Montreat . . . you know, where the Billy Graham thing is. Here he is and everybody's a Christian. Kierkegaard talks about that. Will Barrett still doesn't believe it. He's an unbeliever. I can honestly say that Will Barrett will sympathize with your son's question. He's surrounded by 100% so-called Christian society and would almost rather be like Sartre, or a Camus agnostic. This present book, if I ever get it right and finish it, will probably be understood as an anti-Christian statement in that sense.

Kitchings: The second part of his question, which you may have already answered, is can a man teach himself to tie his greatest hopes to this life, to the life that we know?

Percy: I think he would have to, if he's not a believer. God knows I have the greatest respect for a great many people who're humanists, non-Christian humanists, who've done an extraordinary job with their own lives and are absolutely heroic, as far as what they make of themselves; much more so than most Christians I know. So the answer's yes. One can think of any number of examples of heroic and wonderful people who accomplish a great deal with their own lives and for other people, who're not believers.

Kitchings: His other concern is, to use Kierkegaard's metaphor of the house image . . . my son wants to know if it is not possible for man to inhabit the aesthetic sphere and the ethical without taking the leap to the religious?

Percy: Sure. Of course.

Kitchings: Kierkegaard talks about inhabiting one's own whole house.

Percy: Yes. And Kierkegaard also said that nobody lives altogether in one sphere; they are always overlapping and intermingled. Most people, I imagine, live in a combination of the aesthetic and the ethical.

Kitchings: Well, those are his questions, which leads me to one of mine which has to do with your female characters.

Percy: Uh-oh, this is where I get it. This is where I always get it; except that a girl yesterday told me for the first time, for once, she said something nice about my female characters. She said she liked the character of Anna in *Lancelot*. At first I'd forgotten who Anna was because I hadn't read *Lancelot* in a long time.

Kitchings: She didn't say a word. That tells us something.

Percy: Yes. I said, "Oh, yes, I remember now. She was the girl tapping on the wall." "Right." I said, "Why did you like her?" and she said, "Well, because she knew that even though she'd been raped, violated, still she knew it was not herself who was affected—she was still herself."

Kitchings: No man can violate that.

Percy: No man can do that. I was pleased when she said that.

Kitchings: Tom More's first wife was, as you put it: "A lusty Shenandoah girl." He was very happy with her for a while, and then she became corrupted by these heathens, these Englishmen and ran away with this cultist. As she became more religious she became less lusty. And you've got him ending up, most unpredictably I thought, with Ellen Oglethorpe, who comes off as a Puritan almost.

Percy: Yes. She's a Georgia Presbyterian, right?

Kitchings: Yes. And she doesn't go to church, doesn't have much to do with church, but she is very ethical.

Percy: That's right. That's my mother's family.

Kitchings: I see. Would you ever envision writing about a woman who inhabits her whole house, who is at the same time ethical and religious and lusty?

Percy: Sure, if I ever get good enough I could do that.

Kitchings: You do believe that there is a possibility that a woman can be all those things?

Percy: Oh, yes. You look like one to me.

Kitchings: Thank you, that is a compliment. I have done some study about female characters in American literature. You know what Leslie Fiedler says.

Percy: I remember reading his books.

Kitchings: He particularly jumps on Faulkner and Hemingway.

Percy: What does he say about them? I've forgotten.

Kitchings: He says that Faulkner's women are monsters of virtue or just whores.

Percy: Yes.

Kitchings: He says there's no nice, whole woman like, he says, Madame Bovary. He says the European has no trouble with this whole woman, but the American male novelist really does.

Percy: He does.

Kitchings: Do you think there's some merit in that statement?

Percy: I really do. I think the Americans, and maybe Southerners even more than most people, have got hung up on the myth of what they take to be the dichotomy in women, what they take to be the lady and the whore.

Kitchings: If she's virtuous then she can't be warm.

Percy: That's right. I was brought up in a male tradition which is very commonplace in the South in which it is very hard to get the two together; to get the sexual woman together with a "lady."

Kitchings: And also a woman with a little intellectual toughness?

Percy: Correct.

Kitchings: Who thinks anyway.

Percy: I think Southerners have a lot of trouble with that. Maybe less so these days. I think probably less so in your son's generation.

Kitchings: I see some hope there. I don't read any novels by my son's generation. In *Lancelot*, does Percival's final "yes" mean that he is just about to give Lancelot the good news? Is Lancelot ready?

Percy: Maybe. Maybe.

Kitchings: That's as good a guess as any about that last "yes."

Percy: Sure. It's time for Percival to speak. Lancelot's been spouting for 200 pages, and he says, "Well, what do you think of all this? Do you have anything to say?" I think he says something like, "Do you agree with me that it's got to be one way or the other? It's either got to be your way or my way? What we can't stand is the way it is now. We either have to have a classical, broadsword revolution—"kill our enemies, destroy evil, have a third revolution beginning in the Shenandoah Valley, or it's got to be your way. It can't be in between." And so Percival says, "Yes, that's true, it's got to be one or the other eventually." I forget what his last question was.

Kitchings: "Is there something more you want to tell me?"

Percy: Is that what it was: "Is there something more you want to tell me?" And so he says "Yes." And presumably Percival gives him a similar version of the orthodoxy, of the Judeo-Christian tradition, which can't be done in a novel. You can't do it.

Kitchings: I hope I didn't imagine this, it's been a few months since I reread *Lancelot*, but it certainly seems to me that you have Percival changing throughout the book. Even his dress. In the last chapter, doesn't he have his priest's collar on?

Percy: I'm glad you noticed that.

Kitchings: Is he giving up the psychiatry business . . . well, he says he's going back to the church.

Percy: He's giving up his psychiatrist, his business, and his girlfriend.

Kitchings: Yes.

Percy: I'm glad you noticed that because I was trying to do something in *Lancelot* that not many people picked up on. I was trying to delineate the character of Percival indirectly simply by what Lancelot was saying. I was noticing what he was wearing, what he did when he was walking across the cemetery.

Kitchings: And how distressed he is with this scientific/humanistic approach that he's forced into as the doctor/priest.

Percy: Yes. I'm glad you noticed he was changing. At the end he said a prayer in the cemetery, so presumably he's changing. He was going to a little church in Alabama, my Lord.

Kitchings: That's right back to the roots of the faith.

Percy: Yes. If you can stand to locate in South Alabama you've got to believe in something, right?

Kitchings: I would think so. In *The Moviegoer*, toward the end, Binx sees a man go into a church on Ash Wednesday on the corner of Elysian Fields and Bons Enfants, and he asks the question, "Why does he go in there? I don't know. Is it part of coming up in the world, or does he believe that God is present here on the corner of Elysian Fields and Bons Enfants. Or is it both: coming in for one reason and receiving the other as God's importunate gift—bonus," I believe you say. "God's importunate bonus." Is this all we can know about church and the sacraments, that for whatever reason we're there, we open ourselves to the grace of God and therefore get it?

Percy: Yes, something like that. I was thinking particularly of how it happens . . . he was probably there for the wrong reasons and the right reasons. He was there because he was probably an upwardly-mobile, middle-class black, who maybe just started going to a middle-class Catholic church for the first time. You know how middle-class blacks can be. You know, there're more black debutantes in New Orleans than there are white debutantes.

Kitchings: I was just reading about that. Antithesis to the Boston Club in New Orleans.

Percy: Oh, yes, I read about that in *Figaro* you know? And, you know, he'd be somebody like Ernest Morial, the mayor, an upper-class creole. So here's this guy going to maybe what's a fashionable church, like Holy Name. It's the thing to do to be married in Holy Name church. You wouldn't think of getting married at Mater Doloroso. That would be socially lower class. The same thing is double true with blacks. So here's this guy going to church, maybe coming up in the world, maybe moving into a new middle-class neighborhood. And yet, the strange thing is that he will receive the sacraments; that the sacraments work nevertheless. You have this strange admixture of the inauthentic living by social status; and yet who are we to say that the sacraments are not operative? That he's not receiving grace along with it? That's the mystery.

Kitchings: Do you still go to movies?

Percy: Sure. I was supposed to go to one last night, an opening. I had been at L.S.U. all day and was too tired to go.

Kitchings: What were you going to see?

Percy: I've forgotten. A friend of mine just made a new movie, and it had to do with a man who buys one of these plastic blow-up women and has relations with it. He wrote a letter to me and Bunt. It's a very erotic movie, but very good, he said.

Kitchings: I would say from what you said, it must be something.

Percy: Yes. I don't know how good it was. I'm sorry I didn't get to see it.

Kitchings: Do you have a favorite movie of the last year or two?

Percy: I'm trying to think of some offhand.

Kitchings: Do you like the Woody Allen movies?

Percy: Yes, I liked *Interiors* and *Manhattan*. Before that I can't think of anything since *Five Easy Pieces* or *Chinatown*, which I liked. I haven't seen many good ones.

An Interview with Walker Percy

W. Kenneth Holditch/1980

Reprinted by permission of W. Kenneth Holditch

Conducted on 13 May 1980, by W. Kenneth Holditch, who
was joined in the conversation by Elizabeth Mullener.

Holditch: First of all I want to ask you about movies. Have you always
been a moviegoer?

Percy: As long as I can remember. The first movie I ever saw was a
cartoon in Birmingham, Alabama, called *Krazy Kat.*

Holditch: You still go to the movies?

Percy: I still go, but either I've gotten a higher threshold or they're
not as good as they used to be. There was a time when I'd go to see any
movie. I even remember a movie which was possibly the worst movie
ever made, *Nix on Dames.* It might have been with Gene Kelly, a sailor
dancing. I even enjoyed that.

Holditch: Does it trouble you that movies are too message-laden now?

Percy: Some of them are pretty heavy with message, and I think the
trouble with movies is that movies have to beat television, and that
the only way they can do it is by [being] either bigger or better or
more violent or more explicitly sexual. The temptation is just to have
too much. Like *Apocalypse Now*—the main thought was the thought of
excess. *The Deer Hunter*—I think of it as a kind of pornography of
violence—the business with the revolver and Russian roulette, over and
over again. A heavy message, and I think that can be distracting for a
good movie. The trouble [with explicit sex] is not so much the morality
of it; it's that I find it downright embarrassing to be sitting in the theater
next to strangers, with all that's going on up there. I was trying to
remember the last good movie I saw, I mean a really good movie.
Kramer versus Kramer was o.k., but it was a rather small thing.

Holditch: I really just don't go.

Percy: You don't go? We went to New York last week, and when
you go to New York, it's almost obligatory to go to a play or an opera

13

or something. So you know what we did? We didn't even go to the movies. The best movie in town was playing on television; it was *Breaking Away*, about these high school kids in Bloomington, Indiana, the Cutters. It was well done.

Holditch: Are you an opera fan?

Percy: Some operas.

Holditch: *Don Giovanni*, of course, figures in *Love in the Ruins*.

Percy: *Don Giovanni* and Strauss's *Rosenkavalier*.

Holditch: Is *Don Giovanni* your favorite opera?

Percy: That and a couple of Strauss operas. *Rosenkavalier*.

Mullener: You didn't answer your own question. What was the last good picture you saw?

Percy: You're right, Betsy. Two I thought of. Both them were Jack Nicholson. One of them was *Five Easy Pieces* and the other was *Chinatown*. I really liked both of them, as much as I used to like movies a long time ago.

Holditch: Well, *Chinatown* was kind of old-fashioned.

Percy: It's kind of like Raymond Chandler.

Holditch: What about other musical influences on your work? I mean, do you see the opera as an influence on your work, or is it just the story of the character Don Giovanni?

Percy: Well, not so much the opera or the story as music itself, which, I think, has a relation to writing, at least to my writing. When I get lucky and occasionally write a good paragraph, it should—or I aim for it to—have a singing quality. I think good writing sings, should have a cadence to it.

Holditch: I asked you this once before, a long time ago. Did you ever write poetry?

Percy: Shelby Foote and I went to high school together, and in those days public high schools were pretty tough. You were required to write sonnets and lyrics and ballads, and I got very proficient writing sonnets and I would sell them, fifty cents a piece. I could toss out a Shakespearean or an Italian sonnet. It was cheating, actually.

Holditch: Did you start writing fiction in high school?

Percy: No. No.

Holditch: You told me about that first novel that you wrote that you submitted to Caroline Gordon.

Percy: Oh, yes.

Holditch: When was that?

Percy: That must have been when I was in my thirties.

Holditch: Had you thought about writing seriously before that?

Percy: Not really. I always wanted to be a writer. I had written in college, I had written in high school. But it never crossed my mind to undertake it as a profession, even though my uncle had been a writer. But in the South you didn't set out to become a writer. One had to be a lawyer or a doctor or a businessman.

Holditch: Well, with your uncle, it was just sort of a gentleman's pursuit on the side.

Percy: He was a lawyer, a planter, and a . . . poet. So I went into medicine by default. Eventually I took up writing because I got sick.

Holditch: You were a student at the time?

Percy: I was an intern.

Holditch: So you never practiced medicine.

Percy: No. In those days they had what they called the rest cure, two years of enforced idleness, like Hans Castorp in *The Magic Mountain*. That was when I began to read for the first time, after having been in science and completed that education. I think I wrote a couple of reviews. The first thing I ever wrote was a review of Susanne Langer's *Philosophy in a New Key*. I read that and got excited about it, wrote a review and sent it off and got it published. I got paid in reprints; I still have some reprints from that.

Holditch: You once said something that has always puzzled me, that you didn't really understand the short story, so you never wrote them. When you started writing fiction, you started with the novel.

Percy: Is that what I told you? I understood them all right.

Holditch: I gave you a short story to read and you told me, there's something wrong with it, but I don't really understand the function of a short story.

Percy: Particularly the writing of it. I would never undertake to write a short story. I think part of that comes from a secret megalomania. The secret hope in the back of the mind of every novelist is that he is going to make an ultimate discovery in a novel, some ultimate truth that's going to become clear. That can't happen in a short story, which is like the sonnet, it has its form, and it's limited, but in a novel anything can happen. I think it's a question of possibilities; all possibilities are open in a novel.

Holditch: So you see each one of your novels as being like an experimental novel.

Percy: I see every novel as an adventure in discovering. It's an exploration, and I don't know exactly which way it's going. It's an adventure to me, exploration of a territory where I haven't been before. Otherwise it wouldn't be enough fun to undertake. I have to be entertained while writing it. You know, it's a miserable enough profession as it is. Doing this day after day, three or four hours a day, alone, and no rewards, no feedback, there has to be some self-pleasure, and the pleasure for me comes from the exploration. A novel is big enough, formless enough, and open enough so that it is always open, something will turn up, and occasionally something does turn up. Never the ultimate truth, of course, but sometimes some good things happen.

Holditch: [Whom] do you read and admire and look forward to? John Updike, I know you told me.

Percy: Well, I hate to make a list because I'm afraid of leaving somebody out, but I can tell you that I'm very fond of Bellow, Updike, Cheever, Malamud, John Barth . . .

Holditch: You like Barth? I find Barth very difficult.

Percy: He is, he is, in fact his last novel is, for me, unreadable.

Holditch: What about Philip Roth?

Percy: Some things. Bellow may be the best around, to tell you the truth. I think he has a tremendous reach. He takes on the whole culture: urban, midwest or New York, mostly Jewish but not altogether, and he does it by creating his own speech, a kind of lingo, street slang, street talk. Most of the people are real street people. Yet using these rather humble materials, he gets at some very profound truths. He doesn't mind taking on the big subjects. Course that may be the failure of most of the American novelists, this philosophical voraciousness. Saul Bellow really does it and gets away with it. He's also extremely funny. My favorite may be the only non-Jewish one he's done, called *Henderson the Rain King*, which he did, I think, as a joke. I think he got tired of the reviewers saying that he could only write about Jewish subjects, so he wrote a real Gentile, goyish novel, about a pig farmer.

Holditch: I told you about Tennessee Williams at a dinner party leaning over to ask me if I liked any of the "northern writers," and I said, "Well, yes, some," and I named some, and he said, "Well, I can't read Saul Bellow," and I had to agree with him.

Percy: You don't like Bellow?

Holditch: I can understand your liking him. You're both philosophical novelists. Would you agree with that categorization?

Percy: Yes, although it's almost the kiss of death. It's almost a contradiction in terms, because it almost implies a novel with a thesis; however, the French, who were my teachers, were able to get away with it. People like Camus and Sartre and Marcel, who could somehow or other combine art and philosophy without the one killing the other.

Holditch: What about your method of writing? Do you write five days a week usually, when you're writing?

Percy: Yep. Except since I've finished [*The Second Coming*] I've been disoriented, and goofing off, and I have something in mind vaguely, but the worst thing about writing a book is finishing it, it's awful. Writing a book is bad enough in itself, but finishing it is even worst.

Mullener: You mean it's hard to finish or the reaching of the end is hard?

Percy: [It's] like I imagine a woman would feel who's been pregnant for three years and who gives birth, then goes into a post-partum depression.

Holditch: Faulkner went on binges.

Percy: I just get depressed.

Holditch: I think you said that you don't really sort of plan your novels or outline your novels. When I was a student at Southwestern, Shelby Foote came to talk to our creative writing class, and he said that he made a scenario that was about a third the length of the novel and then when he sat down to write the novel he didn't have to revise.

Percy: That is literally true. He outlines just the way that he used to do in sophomore English. You know how you write a theme with the Roman numeral and a big A and a little 1 and a little a. To me that would be fatal. I'd be bored stiff. But on the other hand he's probably doing a better job structurally, building a better house.

Holditch: So in other words you don't know necessarily what's going to happen?

Percy: I have a general idea. I start out with one or more persons— in a certain situation. In [*The Second Coming*] I knew the two people I wanted to get together, and I thought some interesting things would happen if they got together. One is Will Barrett, who is the same character as the protagonist in *The Last Gentleman*, Will Barrett about twenty years later. He has, quote, achieved all his goals, as they say. He has gotten rich, married a rich lady who died, and he's become a lawyer, been very successful, taken what they call early retirement, has built a perfect dream house in North Carolina. Cultivated man, books and music, and he and his wife retire to North Carolina and he immediately goes to pieces, goes into a real depression, has spells, falls down on the golf course, spends most of his time playing golf. He is the main character, and the other is a girl, who is schizophrenic, maybe.

One nice thing about psychiatry is that they don't know enough about it so that I'm restricted. I can make up my own cases and call them anything I like. Anyway, she's that type. She has been in a not very good private sanitarium for two or three years, and the book opens with her having escaped. She had been undergoing shock treatment and they propose to do shock treatment again, and she says the hell with that, I'm breaking out. She's shrewd enough to arrange her escape, and so the scene opens with her sitting on a bench in a town in North Carolina, a resort town, amnesiac; she can't remember who she is or where she's been or what's happened to her. She's written a journal to herself to remember what's happened after the shock treatment. So on the one hand you have Will Barrett, who's a middle-aged man to whom everything has happened, who has everything, who remembers everything—that's one of his symptoms, incidentally. Unlike having amnesia, he remembers. He sees a hawk while he's playing golf and thinks about a hawk he saw when he was hunting with his father thirty or forty years earlier. So he remembers everything and she remembers nothing. It's almost as if she was starting new in the world. It's also as if she were Rip Van Winkle, who comes into the mountain village after being asleep for twenty years. She sees American culture of 1979 or 1980 with completely fresh eyes. People are acting differently, talking differently, saying things like "What are you in to?" or "Getting your head together," and she doesn't understand it. So, he's having difficulty with his golf game, and he slices into the woods one day. She has inherited a piece of property from her aunt and [is] living alone in an abandoned greenhouse and he meets her in the woods, and that's the beginning of the story. So to answer your question, I thought it would be interesting to start out with these two types, one a young girl of a certain sort. Incidentally, both people are drawn slightly after people that I know. She is a girl who is very smart in school, made straight A's, but she didn't work out right. She disappointed her parents, who wanted what most American parents want, for her to succeed. They wanted her to graduate, wanted her to get a boyfriend, get married or get a job, get a vocation or something, and move on, move out of the house, [but] she fails, she flunks out of school—or rather she becomes emotionally disturbed and has to leave school. [For] a concert, she's learning to sing Schubert *Lieder*, [but then] forgets the music and has to leave the stage. She doesn't get married, she doesn't get a job, doesn't graduate, and she ends up back at home, which in her father and mother's eyes is the worst possible thing. She meets her father in the hall, he's on his way to work and he looks at her like "Well, what are you doing here?" As she puts it, she's flunked ordinary living.

She's a very nice girl, a very attractive girl, [but] she's failed. So, for one reason or another—which the book gets into—she retreats into something you could call schizophrenia. She is really starting out again anew in the world, a new life. And he has, in a sense, finished his life and doesn't know what to do. I know somebody [to whom this happened], who took early retirement, who had everything, achieved all his goals, beautiful house, perfect view, and then just went to pieces. And I thought, what would happen if two people like this got together? So that's what happens.

Holditch: In *The Last Gentleman*, he suffers attacks of amnesia.

Percy: He has it from the beginning, yes.

Holditch: I don't know how much criticism you read, but most critics and most readers and most students find *The Last Gentleman* the most difficult of your novels. They clearly are puzzled about what it means, and I wondered if this might be the reason why you went back to [Will Barrett].

Percy: Yeah, because he was left more unresolved than anybody else. It's strange, though; I was writing this book for several months, maybe a year [and] he had a different name. I realized suddenly that he was Will Barrett, and so I backed up and changed his name and hooked him up with his past. It didn't take much hooking up, because Will Barrett ends rather inconclusively in *The Last Gentleman*. I think that [*The Second Coming*] solves the problems.

Holditch: You also said that you were interested in telling a story in which a woman was a protagonist.

Percy: Did I say that? Where did I say that?

Holditch: Over at Hammond, year before last.

Percy: I'll be darned. The main reaction I've gotten to this book [is] that this girl is the most likable [I've created].

Holditch: I think Kate's an extremely likable woman. That brings me to a question I wanted to ask you about *Lancelot*, because I find that some very intelligent readers have, I think, misread it and they insist on identifying you totally with Lancelot [Lamar].

Percy: I haven't burned any houses down.

Holditch: You've noticed that they don't seem to be able to separate the author . . .

Percy: That's true. I have had that reaction.

Holditch: For example, I have had colleagues at [the University of New Orleans] tell me that *Lancelot* is an anti-feminist book, an attack on women.

Percy: It is strange. Talking to students about it, what disturbed me was not that they identified Lancelot with me but that they approved of Lancelot—which bothered me because Lancelot, of course, is a madman.

Holditch: But if the world is mad, then a madman is at home in the world, right?

Percy: True, but you don't go around burning houses down around people.

Holditch: Would you say that you agree with Lancelot with what's wrong with the world, but that you disagree with his solution?

Percy: I suppose some would agree partly with him, and the world is in pretty bad shape, sure enough. I think I would probably be more sympathetic or would find myself more identified with the man who was listening to him, the priest. There's where I located myself. His attitude was different, and his solution was not genocide or murder. You don't take revenge on the world.

Holditch: Do you envision the possibility of ever writing Percival's story?

Percy: No. It's funny how many people ask me that.

Holditch: Well, he obviously has a story. You want us to figure out from what's seen through the window what happens to him?

Percy: Right. When I first started to write that I wrote it from the point of view of these two men, Lancelot and Percival the priest. They grew up together. But all this business about Percival becoming a priest and going to Biafra and all that, how he got into difficulties with his vocation and all that, it didn't work, it just didn't work, and I had to back up completely and just do it from Lancelot's dramatic monologue.

Holditch: You have an office where you work. You have any little gimmicks that help you work? You don't keep rotten apples under your desk?

Percy: No. One thing I discovered, maybe the only thing of any value I ever discovered is that with me the worst times can be the best times. What I learned was that if you don't fight that, go with it, something good often happens. I think it was Carl Jung who said there's gold buried in those depths somewhere.

Holditch: You think place is important? You said several years ago in *Southern Review* that you sometimes did your best writing in a motel. Was that one of your whimsical remarks?

Percy: I understand completely what Flannery O'Connor did. Have you seen her writing room? She faced a blank wall, literally. I think it's very simple; you just have to wipe out current stimuli in order to make up your own stimuli.

Holditch: Leaving yourself open to possibilities?

Percy: Yeah, if you get in a Holiday Inn, at the junction of I-12 and 55 or anywhere, anything could happen to you, you invite the muse.

Holditch: You mentioned Flannery O'Connor. We talked a little about Southern writers before, and I know that you've heard this fifty times, so pardon my asking it again, but everyone agrees that you are not in the Faulkner tradition. You do not think of yourself as a Southern writer. But of course I do think of you as a Southern writer and have written an article to prove that you are.

Percy: Well of course you're right, I am a Southern writer. I could not possibly write the way I write unless I was born and raised and living in the South. Maybe what I was trying to do was to distinguish myself from Faulkner and Welty and O'Connor, who I think are more Southern in one sense than I am, who depend more on the Southern scene than I do. Certainly Faulkner makes heavy use of Southern legend, Southern story, family history. Welty the same way, in a different way. O'Connor, of course, uses her Georgia types, backwoods types. I think I have more of a distance than they do. My scenes are middle-class, more urban or suburban, and therefore closer to American suburbia.

Holditch: Consequently [you use] less local color? Also you only use the Gothic and grotesque in sort of a satirical way.

Percy: Either comic or satirical.

Mullener: What do you mean, you couldn't have written the way you do [if you had not been born and raised in the South]?

Percy: I would not be able to create the characters that I do. For instance, in *The Moviegoer*, a character like Aunt Emily, who is a Southern type. You wouldn't find her in the midwest; possibly [in] New England, but I doubt it. And you wouldn't find certain Catholic types anywhere except New Orleans, or certain black types like Mercer or two or three blacks in *Lancelot*, also one in [*The Second Coming*]. Maybe it's the function of time and distance, coming after Faulkner and Flannery. I'm dealing with their people but also with an interaction between them and much more standard American types. For example, someone like Binx Bolling is so detached that he is almost unsouthern; I mean he's outside of it, he's outside of the Southern scene. He might just as well be in San Francisco or Newark, and yet he's very much aware of the Southern heritage and the different traditions, the Gulf Coast Catholic tradition, the Mississippi WASP tradition. What he's interested in and what I'm interested in is what happens when the two get together.

Holditch: You said in the creative writing course at Loyola that Covington and all along this line is a very interesting place to live because it is the conjunction of two cultures, and in the *Esquire* article, to some degree you suggest the same thing. Does that [juxtaposition] inspire you? Do you think you'd be less productive living in New Orleans?

Percy: The trouble with New Orleans is that it's too pleasant a place. I'm very fond of New Orleans. I like living there, but I would find it very easy to live there and do very little, if I had the money, but have a good time, listen to music, talk to people, drink, and so forth. New Orleans . . . have you ever heard the expression "The Big Easy"? I just heard that recently.

Holditch: James Conaway has a novel called *The Big Easy*.

Percy: I think I know what that means. But I couldn't do what Faulkner did. Faulkner had to go back to his roots. I had to go to a place without roots. He had to go back to where he came from. I wasn't about to go back to where I came from, which was Birmingham, Alabama, or

Mississippi. It's maybe a difference in time, a difference in the evolution of American literature. Maybe Faulkner came along at a time when Southern regional literature was on the point of being discovered or on the point of creating itself, which is simply what Faulkner did. The famous Southern Renaissance lasted for a generation or so and is, I think, pretty well over. Now, for me, the value is not to soak myself in a Southern place or a Southern region or a Southern atmosphere, but to be in the South, which I like very much, and yet be sufficiently detached so that I can be in it and yet out of it. And that's what I like about Covington. It's right on the boundary line between the Anglo-Saxon Protestant South and the Creole-German, Italian-French Catholic Louisiana, and the interaction between the two fascinates me.

Holditch: In "New Orleans, Mon Amour," you said that you saw New Orleans as maybe being the hope for American cities. You said first of all that in New York if somebody fell down on the street, people would step over him, but in New Orleans they might drag him into a bar and give him a shot of Early Times.

Percy: I guess I don't feel as hopeful now as I did then. What's happened is what we all know, a large number of teenagers and younger kids who are mostly black, mostly unemployed—forty-five percent unemployment among blacks, young blacks—and terrible schools—the schools have gotten worse since I wrote that article. So maybe I'm a lousy prophet; it seems that things have gotten worse and not better since then. Which is not to say that New Orleans still doesn't have a quality to it and a chance that maybe a place like Cleveland or Newark doesn't have.

Holditch: You think that there is any way out of all this mess that we've gotten ourselves into with the schools? And it's not just in New Orleans, but all over.

Percy: Kenneth, it's hard enough just to write novels, without being asked to solve problems like that.

Holditch: But we read your novels and then think that you have the answer.

Percy: I have to draw Kierkegaard's distinction between an artist, which is one of the lowest forms of life, and the prophet, which is one of the higher; and I belong to the former.

Holditch: Do you think that New Orleans would ever become or is moving toward becoming Americanized to the point of being like

Cincinnati or Cleveland or Dubuque, Iowa, or do you think that there is a distinctive quality that it will retain?

Percy: I think it's remarkably resistant to Americanization, [although] I'm not saying that it is immune. [John Kennedy] Toole's book, *A Confederacy of Dunces*, shows the very distinctive quality, the ethnic quality of New Orleans life, which very few books and writers have touched on. He may be one of the first really to do it.

Holditch: He does a wonderful job.

Percy: He did it in a way that Cable and Hearn did not do it. They picked up the chic, quaint, picturesque sides of New Orleans life which the other people have always been interested in. But not Toole. He did the very solid ethnic types that we all know about in New Orleans. I think they are quite resistant, but I don't know. I hope they're around twenty years from now. It seems to me the danger is not so much homogenization of New Orleans as a gradual conversion of the French Quarter into the French Quarter in Disney World.

Holditch: I want to talk about William Alexander Percy. It must have been a real experience growing up in his house. You went there when you were how old?

Percy: I guess I was fifteen, no, wait, thirteen.

Holditch: You have two brothers.

Percy: [Yes.] Our parents died when we were fairly young, and we moved in with [Uncle Will] and later he adopted all three of us. So we lived there until he died in 1942, which was about ten or fifteen years. It was the most important thing that ever happened to me as far as my writing is concerned. I never would have been a writer without his influence. I've never met anybody like him. He was the sort of man who listened to music all the time. He had one of the first automatic record players I ever saw. You could play [an entire] Beethoven symphony. You'd put on ten 78s, on this old Capehart record player that dropped one after another. It was always going out of whack; he would get mad at it and curse it, and he would break records, throw records around. He was the first person I ever knew who became actually excited by music or poetry. He would read poetry aloud with great pleasure, you know, which was a revelation to a fourteen- or fifteen-year-old.

Holditch: It was fairly rare in the South in those days.

Percy: Right. It was amazing the way he talked about [his love of music, art, literature]. He must have been a tremendous teacher. He taught at Sewanee for a while. But you know how rare a good teacher is. He must have been one of these very few who could communicate this enthusiasm.

Holditch: He started you reading, or were you already reading before you went there, I mean seriously.

Percy: Well, I guess he did. I remember the first time I really got enthusiastic about a book, a big book, an important book, a serious book, he gave me Romain Rolland's *Jean-Christophe*, a big, thick book, not considered now, I think, one of the great novels, but it made a tremendous impression on me. It showed me how exciting it could be to enter the world of a book, to get lost in a book, and then I don't know whether he did it or not, but I can remember reading *Gone with the Wind*, which I suppose is not a good novel, but can remember being, at the age of thirteen or fourteen, totally absorbed in it. In fact even, I remember asking Caroline Gordon about it, telling her how much I enjoyed *Gone with the Wind*, and she sneered and said [it] set back literature for a hundred years. I asked her about Steinbeck's books, [and] she reared back even higher and said, "I spit on Steinbeck." After that I decided to stop asking critics about my reading, to go ahead and read what I like.

Holditch: You told me once before that you thought you had met Faulkner?

Percy: Shelby Foote claims that I met Faulkner.

Holditch: You told me that you thought you had met him earlier in Greenville.

Percy: No.

Holditch: Wasn't he a friend of your [Uncle Will]?

Percy: Not a friend. He came to play tennis a couple of times. Uncle Will told me about Faulkner coming there and playing tennis and falling down, being drunk, missing the ball. I don't think he and Uncle Will got along too well.

Holditch: Well, of course your uncle sort of was suspicious of all those hill people.

Percy: Also, Faulkner didn't like his poems much. He reviewed Uncle Will's poetry one time and said it was too old-fashioned or nineteenth-century.

Holditch: It wasn't really a bad review though. It seems to me that

Faulkner would have been very responsive to *Lanterns on the Levee*, though I don't remember reading anything he ever said. Were you conscious of the book's being written? Did you hear part of [*Lanterns on the Levee*] or read part of it in manuscript?

Percy: I was very conscious of the time he wrote it. I remember [that] the first chapter he wrote was not the first chapter in the book. It was the chapter on Sewanee. He wrote that with great enthusiasm. I could tell that he was really into something which excited him, and I think he read it aloud to us or let us read it, along with friends, and everybody liked it very much. I think he went down to the Gulf Coast, to Fort Walton Beach for a while and did some writing there, and he did some writing at Sewanee and Brinkwood. We were very much aware of the times he was writing it. He died shortly after it was published. But he lived long enough to get a reaction to it, which was an interesting reaction. It got an awful lot of fan mail. I remember how much he enjoyed getting letters from people who read it and enjoyed it. And he got some pretty hostile reviews from the liberal press, like *New Republic*. They called it reactionary and so forth.

Holditch: People still do. My students still respond to it very well. They like it.

Percy: How do they respond to it?

Holditch: Both times I've taught it, it's been to an honors class and they liked it very much. One of the most interesting comments I've ever heard made about it [was by] Helen Wagner: she said that she'd never understood her father until she read *Lanterns on the Levee*.

Percy: That's interesting. It's curious that that book was published the same month, the same year, by the same publisher, as [W. J.] Cash's *Mind of the South*. You couldn't imagine two more different books about the South, and yet both of them legitimate in their own right.

Holditch: But you know, even Cash sometimes, despite his sort of critical and objective portrayal of the South, sociological portrayal, will occasionally lapse into that sort of adoration of the old South, when he talks about the Confederate soldiers.

Percy: Oh, yes. He talks about the old captains, their great protection.

Holditch: I have always believed that *Lanterns on the Levee* had an influence on your writing, as you say, but I've always thought that the end of *Love in the Ruins* directly reflects *Lanterns on the Levee*. Are you conscious of that?

Percy: I hadn't thought about it.

Holditch: The garden. Tending the garden. The concluding chapter of *Lanterns on the Levee* [has] that sort of garden.

Percy: I see what you mean. I think the main difference is [that] I thought that scene was very sad. It was a cemetery, and [Uncle Will] was thinking about death, whereas in *Love in the Ruins* Thomas More was thinking about his new life, running a catfish line, pulling out the gaspergous, living in that old slave quarter . . .

Holditch: Going back to Southern writers, somebody said about Flannery O'Connor that in order to understand her you had to try to put yourself in the attitude of medieval Catholicism. Do you understand that comment?

Percy: I don't know what that means. She wrote as a militant Catholic, and was aware of it every minute, even though she was writing about all sorts of redneck types, but I don't see it as especially medieval. The interesting thing about Flannery O'Connor is whether being the militant Catholic that she was [is] a defect or an asset in [her work]. I've heard some critics say that they are bothered about it because they think, number one, that she's trying to evangelize, trying to preach, and, number two, unless you share her radical view of the world, the presence of God, the devil, it doesn't make any sense. I tend to think that she's one of the best writers that we have and that her faith is certainly an asset, not a defect.

Holditch: I would think so. Her following grows, and her status is increasing, critically and in terms of her readership. The students always like to read her, but they like to read her because they are drawn to the grotesque and Gothic aspects, and I'm not sure that she would approve of that reason for liking her.

Percy: I would imagine that they would like her because of her humor, too.

Holditch: Did you see the television dramatization of "The Displaced Person"?

Percy: Yeah, I think I did, the first one, about a year ago.

Holditch: I thought it was very good. And there's a movie of *Wise Blood* now.

Percy: I tried to find it in New York. Well, John Huston deserves a

lot of credit for taking that on. He must have known that he couldn't
make money on it.

Holditch: What's your favorite Graham Greene novel?

Percy: Probably *The End of the Affair*. What's the one about Africa?
The Heart of the Matter?

Holditch: Do you know *Brighton Rock*?

Percy: I remember reading it a long time ago. I think that was one of
his first, wasn't it?

Holditch: That's still my favorite.

Percy: Is that an entertainment or a novel?

Holditch: He first listed it as an entertainment, and then later he
moved it into the category of the novel. It reminds me of Flannery
O'Connor a great deal. [Greene] talks about the priest at the end of the
novel [using] the phrase, "the appalling strangeness of the mercy of
God," which I think is the best way in the world to sort of explain
Graham Greene and Flannery O'Connor and sometimes to explain some
of your novels, too.

Percy: I have a high opinion of Greene; in fact, I think it's a scandal
that he has not gotten the Nobel Prize, whereas people like John
Steinbeck have.

Holditch: I was interested in this article, about what you said about
the Agrarians, that they all had moved off to the North and left
everything. What's your response to *I'll Take My Stand* and the whole
Agrarian movement?

Percy: I went through a phase when I read that and I was reading
Freeman's life of Lee. It was a Confederate phase. I would read about
the Civil War, and hope during the reading that it might come out
differently, that we might win this time. You know, give it a lot of body
English, hoping that if such and such had happened at Chancellorsville,
we could have won. If Jackson hadn't got killed, and all that . . .

Holditch: That wonderful phrase in *Intruder in the Dust*, for every
Southern boy at least once it's still that afternoon in July and Pickett still
hasn't started his charge.

Percy: Or if that Yankee sergeant hadn't found Lee's battle orders for
Antietam, wrapped around three cigars in a ditch. If that hadn't happened, we'd have won the first invasion of the north. I went through all
that, and *I'll Take My Stand*. I think it's a good thing to do, to identify
with your region. What happens is, you discover where you come from
and reach passionate allegiances to it, and I don't mean to say you grow

out of it or you ever give that up. What you do is you retain affection
for your country, your region, but you begin to see how there are more
important things now than who won that war.

Holditch: Do you think that William Alexander Percy was an
Agrarian?

Percy: If you could have seen him riding around his plantation, you
wouldn't have thought of him as an Agrarian. All he wanted to do was
get in there and get out as fast as he could.

Holditch: Well, I don't think the [the Agrarians] really wanted to
stay there on the land.

Percy: What has happened in most cases is when a Southern writer
becomes successful, he leaves. Not many Southern writers stayed.
Except for Eudora [Welty] and Faulkner and O'Connor. Most of them
got out, like William Styron, Willie Morris, and all the Agrarians. Long
Island and Nantucket and Martha's Vineyard are full of Southern writers.

Holditch: I'm not quite sure I understand why that's true.

Percy: I like to live in Covington because it has this peculiar sense of
being in the South and yet in between different places in the South. I
could not see living in a small Southern town, like Monroeville, Alabama. It would be too much. I would be overcome by history, by aunts
and uncles; I can't see staying in the same neighborhood. One of the
things my Uncle Will said [was that] he could only write well about the
Mississippi Delta if he was in New York or Paris. I'm saying you require
a certain distance, a certain abstraction from what you are writing about.

Holditch: Then Faulkner's the exception.

Percy: Maybe he did it by drink, or by Hollywood; he did get out.
Eudora may be the real exception, because she just goes about living a
serene, peaceful life with no great Dionysiac frenzies or ecstasies or
depressions and is a very nice lady, and also a first class writer.

Holditch: She doesn't write about Jackson though, interestingly
enough.

Percy: That's true. When you meet her, she's such a delightful
person with no literary airs or anything.

Holditch: She is very timid about her . . . the first time I met her I
told her I thought she wrote the most marvelous dialogue I'd ever read,
and she said, "Oh, I always think that's my weakest point."

Percy: I heard her say once when somebody asked her to sign a book
and say something special, "Well, I just can't think what to say."

Holditch: She's said almost all of it and said it very well for a long time. The last thing was the collection of essays called *The Eye of the Story*. In your books you always mention writers. One of my colleagues came into my office the other day with [the] great discovery that the opening of *Love in the Ruins* came directly from Dante.

Percy: That's true.

Holditch: And the end of *The Moviegoer* has an allusion to Dante.

Percy: I'd forgotten that.

Holditch: I think it's the end of *The Moviegoer*. Somewhere he talks about "my thirtieth year toward heaven."

Percy: I think that was an allusion to Dylan Thomas, who has a poem "My Thirtieth Year to Heaven."

Holditch: He must have gotten it from Dante.

Percy: From Dante by way of Dylan Thomas. It's true [that] *Love in the Ruins* opens with a very conscious allusion to Dante, at the beginning of the *Inferno,* losing his way in the midst of his life and finding himself in a woods. [Tom More] finds himself in a pine woods on the side of an interstate.

Holditch: [A] colleague has a theory that you satirize the Great Books Program, that the allusions to authors in [your books] are designed as a sort of parody and satire on the Great Books mentality.

Percy: Well, if so I shouldn't do it, because I'm in a Great Books group right now and enjoying it.

Holditch: The Stedmann *History of World War I,* how did you happen to . . .

Percy: I made that up. There's no such [book].

Holditch: I never looked it up. You sounded so convincing. Let's see if I can remember the quotation [about the Battle of Verdun] correctly: "Here began the hemorrhage that ended in the death of the western world, western civilization." Do you think it's an influence of *Lanterns on the Levee*?

Percy: It may be, unconsciously.

Holditch: For [William Alexander Percy] says: "The Yankees destroyed my South and the Germans my world."

Percy: True. But there's a difference. I find the Battle of Verdun a convenient way of drawing a borderline between the end of what I call the modern world, with the nineteenth and the beginning of the twentieth century when everybody thought science was going to work out and the world was going to constantly improve and things were

going to get better and better and then the First World War begins
without too much incident and then the Battle of Verdun happens and
a million [French and German soldiers] get killed in one [year-long]
battle. And at the end of it, only a few hundred yards of ground have
changed hands. So it's almost a complete subversion of the old ideas of
enlightenment and progress. Uncle Will saw it as the sure enough
decline and fall without much hope for the future. Of course, I don't see
it in such dark terms.

Holditch: I know in the introduction to *Lanterns on the Levee* you
comment on his pessimism as opposed to your view.

Percy: I suppose my typical protagonist or hero or anti-hero is a
fellow to whom a great deal has happened, who sees all the dark things
that we are talking about, who's more or less dislocated like a Sartrean
or a Camus character, but who, nevertheless, despite everything, sees a
certain hopefulness, has a certain resilience and reserve, and a feeling
that there is something around the bend, like Huckleberry Finn.

Holditch: And remains a watcher and a wayfarer and a wanderer?

Percy: Right. And he has the possibility of making his own life.

Holditch: I think it must have been very difficult on men of his
generation. [William Alexander Percy] was how old when he died, 57.
He was my grandfather's generation, because my grandfather died in
1963 and he was 93. He was so cynical and distressed about what had
happened to the world. He didn't see much hope left for anything. Have
you read *Sophie's Choice*?

Percy: I didn't like it as much as you did. You gave it a big rave
review. I liked the beginning. I thought the first hundred pages were as
beguiling and as entertaining and as readable, as well written as anything I've read in a long time, [that part] which is simply Styron's
career as a young writer in New York, and his job in the publishing
house and moving to Brooklyn and meeting these people. I began to get
in difficulty with the flashbacks, switching back and forth between
Brooklyn and Auschwitz, you know, or Virginia and Auschwitz. I have
to admire his nerve for tackling the Holocaust; the thing is so big, the
evil is so incommensurate, that it defies getting hold of esthetically. The
Holocaust has ruined [many] writers; maybe [Styron] comes as close as
you can get.

Holditch: I think he found the perfect symbol for the evil in the
choosing between the two children. I may look back upon it and reread

it someday and not be as moved as I was at the time. One of the things I liked about it so much, though, was the method of narration, because it reminds me so much of the method of narration in *Absalom, Absalom!*

Percy: I admired the first half of the book. I began to have reservations about the end of it.

Holditch: What about *Nat Turner*?

Percy: I liked that better. It was shorter, and it was well done. He also had his nerve to do that. He got in trouble for that. I think he's earned his credentials. He's paid his dues. To take on the black thing, being a white Southerner. To take on a black man for a hero, and then take on the Holocaust. He's got more nerve than I do. I wouldn't take on either one of them.

Holditch: What do you think about the future of the novel?

Percy: You always hear the death of the novel prophesied. And sure enough it does look bad from time to time, what with the state of publishing, what with television, most people prefer to watch television than buy a good book, what with the fact that publishers, paperback publishers particularly, spend all their money on *Princess Daisy* and books like that, *Scruples,* which are bad books, and what with it being more and more difficult for good, promising young novelists to get published. But good novels continue to get written. And I think if something is good, if something is first class, it will find a publisher.

Holditch: Who are some of the newer writers that you [read]?

Percy: Who comes to mind? I'm thinking of Harry Crews. Tom McGuane. You ever read any of him? He's done a couple of good things. He did a couple of novels about Key West. I think he was born and raised in Key West and he's now writing for Hollywood. A guy named Cormac McCarthy. He's probably influenced more by Faulkner than is for his own good, but he's a good writer.

Holditch: You like Reynolds Price? Of course Price is not that young.

Percy: No, he's not that young. But he's good, I'm very fond of him. I got a book yesterday from a young writer in Birmingham named Charles Gaines. I liked his first novel; I think it was called *Pumping Iron* or something like that. I can't think of many really exciting young writers. I don't know why that is.

Holditch: Well, maybe someone will burst forth.

Percy: It's rather depressing that the most exciting book that I've come across in manuscript form [in the last ten years] is by Ken Toole.

Holditch: Do you have any idea yet for your next book?

Percy: I know it's not going to be fiction. It's going to be in the vein of *The Message in the Bottle*. It's going to be "Son of Message in the Bottle" or "Message in the Bottle Goes to Hawaii," I haven't decided yet.

Holditch: Are you ever going to collect the essays like "New Orleans, Mon Amour," the essay on Mississippi, and the *Esquire* article on bourbon?

Percy: I don't think [they're] really collectible, Kenneth.

Holditch: I know a lot of people who swear by that article on bourbon.

Mullener: You're always talking about Early Times.

Percy: Well, that's just because of the name. I like it. It's not a very good whiskey, actually. After that article I got a letter from the president of Brown Foreman Distillery, [which] makes Early Times, telling me how great it was and he really appreciated it, [so] I wrote him back and said, well why don't you send around a case. But he didn't do it.

Holditch: When you're working on a novel, you ever have writer's block and go for stretches . . .

Percy: It's funny, I've never understood that, never known [a block]. As I said earlier, the one thing that I know is that [the] worst times turn out to be the best times.

Mullener: I was rereading that *Esquire* piece last night and all of a sudden something struck me from *The Moviegoer*. You kept talking about the "ghostliness" of the North in the *Esquire* article and I remembered the scene where Binx and Kate first hit Chicago and I just made the connection. Do you really have that kind of allergic reaction to the North?

Percy: Chicago . . . I was only there as a boy, passing through going to camp. I didn't have a feeling of ghostliness. [In the novel] I was talking about something I've noticed. It's a peculiar kind of switch, come to think about it. Southern writers have a tendency to go north and end up in the northeast, Long Island or northern universities, whereas northern writers often go to exotic places, Latin American places, Mexico, Italy, France, Spain. I was thinking of ghostliness in that respect. We were talking about Queens earlier; I suppose there's no reason why a good book can't come out of Queens. As a matter of fact, I read a good book by Mary Gordon. But just going through Queens and spending time in Queens, it does not have the sense of tradition and place that, say, Monroeville, Alabama [does]. I couldn't stand to live in a place that had no roots at all, that was a complete non-place, like Queens would be for me.

Mullener: Do you feel uncomfortable up North?

Percy: I would feel a little like a ghost wandering around. I wasn't just talking about American cities either or northern cities. I was thinking of European cities, north European, thinking how often English writers end up in Italian places or Spanish places. There's something about the great successful northern cities of western civilization which [is] ghostly for a writer. He doesn't ever figure out where [he] belongs. American writers have never solved that question, where do they belong? And they're forever going, trying one place and then another. Should they be connected with a university? Should they be in a small town, like Faulkner, tending to his business? I don't know whether it's the fault of the society that the writer does not fit in, as I'm told a writer does fit in in France. A writer maybe feels more at home in France, in Paris, than he does in New York.

Holditch: That might be true of all artists, not just writers. Twenty-five years ago, Gian Carlo Menotti wrote an article about the sense of being outcast that artists have in America, as opposed to an artist like Ravel, whose family supported him so that he could compose.

Percy: One happy thing about it, though, that this very feeling of dislocation that the American writer has always felt is very useful now because dislocation is the name of our civilization. Nobody knows where we're going and what's happening and the dislocated Southern writer is right at home.

Holditch: Did you read Robert Penn Warren's *A Place to Come to*?

Percy: He's a remarkable guy, you know. He [has] tremendous staying power, tremendous vitality.

Holditch: *A Place to Come to* deals with that same idea, because it's about a boy who was born in Tennessee and his mother sends him away as soon as he's old enough to leave and tells him never to come back to this town because it's awful. His father was sort of the town drunk and died in a scandalous accident. He goes to Vanderbilt and [then] to the

University of Chicago. And he goes on to become a well known professor and writer. Warren says it's not autobiographical, but it seems [so]. He has the sense of rootlessness, because his mother never let him identify with the town, so he's in search always for a place to return to.

Percy: You know, I got a call from Willie Morris, who's come back to Mississippi to live. He's living in Oxford.

Holditch: I knew he was teaching there this semester.

Percy: Writing a novel. And feeling very good about it. I can remember [that] I only spent one night in my life in Tupelo [your hometown, Kenneth]. I think it was the same trip that [Shelby Foote and I] stopped to see Faulkner. We went through Oxford and then Tupelo and then up through Tennessee on the way to Chapel Hill. We stopped in Tupelo to spend the night and saw a movie. Guess what the movie was? *Birth of a Nation. Birth of a Nation* was brought back for years and years and it was the first time I'd ever seen it. Have you seen [it]?

Holditch: Yes, I saw it.

Percy: I have a peculiar memory about movies. I can remember where I saw them. I'm perfectly clear about seeing *Birth of a Nation* in Tupelo and what the movie theater looked like.

Holditch: Probably in the Lyric Theater or the Strand.

Percy: We stayed in an old downtown hotel, maybe across the street from the Strand or the Lyric.

Interview

William Starr/1980

From *The State* (Columbia, South Carolina), November 5, 1980,
1B. Reprinted by permission of The State-Record Company, Inc.,
Columbia, S.C. and William W. Starr.

In his uncommon uniting of philosophical conviction with the novelistic art, Walker Percy has emerged as one of the most provocative and powerful writers of this age.

Once a physician who diagnosed human illness, he is now a writer who diagnoses the malaise of the human spirit. He is a rarity: a writer with something serious to say who can say it with great storytelling craft; he wields a pen now as skillfully as he once manipulated a stethoscope.

He is as comfortable with the substance of science as with the humanities; he has written five novels and produced dozens of thoughtful essays on subjects ranging from language to philosophy to religion.

He is also—incredibly—critically undervalued and, until his most recent novel *The Second Coming,* a stranger to most best seller lists.

That may be due, in part, to his own reluctance to become a public figure. He has lived with his wife and children for many years in the small town of Covington, La., content to be away from the spotlight of attention and welcoming the quiet waters of the bayou as a stimulus to his writing.

Percy was born in Birmingham, Ala., in 1916, and was orphaned at the age of 13. Percy and his two brothers were taken into the Greenville, Miss., home of their father's cousin William Alexander Percy. It was "Uncle Will"—a poet, author and man of strong intellect, who proved an enormous influence on the young Percy.

Percy did some minor writing in high school in the Mississippi Delta and again at Chapel Hill where he received a degree from UNC in 1937. Determined to study medicine, he received an M.D. from Columbia University in New York in 1941 and did his internship at Bellevue Hospital in New York City looking to a career in psychiatry.

36

But there he contracted tuberculosis which forced him to abandon his medical career. It was during the long period of recuperation that he began to read heavily in the philosophy of the French existentialists— Heidegger, Kierkegaard, and others—which still influence his work today. He also converted to Roman Catholicism (and can now describe himself accurately and amazingly as a "Southern philosophical Catholic existentialist").

His first published book was *The Moviegoer,* which appeared in 1961. Though it received little critical attention initially, it surprisingly won the National Book Award the next year (the competition included Joseph Heller's *Catch-22* and is now regarded as an exceptionally well-done first novel.

Five years later his second novel *The Last Gentleman* appeared, followed in 1971 by his third, *Love in the Ruins.* A collection of non-fiction essays, which Percy himself has acknowledged has not been widely understood, *The Message in the Bottle,* was released in 1975.

His fourth novel, *Lancelot* (1977) achieved his largest popular success to that date, perhaps because of its bold Southern gothic elements. But it was not until this summer with *The Second Coming* that Percy achieved best-sellerdom, and that novel—a gloriously optimistic, affirmative book—is certain to be high on the list of the year's best fiction.

He does not quite shun interviews, but he does not seek them out and in fact has rejected some requests because they are too consuming of his time. But he did agree to talk a few weeks ago, and the conversation took place at his large, comfortable home at the end of a dead-end road in Covington.

The interview was conducted on a warm, humid afternoon in the screened-in porch at the rear of the home overlooking the dark Bogue Falaya River, with his small dog running about as he relaxed on a lounge chair with his shoes off.

The conversation opened with Percy talking about his writing efforts in high school in Greenville with boyhood chum Shelby Foote (still a close friend and a highly respected Southern novelist and historian who lives in Memphis) and the influence of William Alexander Percy on both youths:

"I think Shelby and I got interested in reading and writing at the same

time. I can remember sitting in study hall in Greenville (Miss.) High
School. I believe I was one grade ahead of Shelby: I was a sophomore,
14, he was a freshman. In those days the English teacher would give us
an assignment to write a sonnet. And I got very facile at writing
sonnets. I could write one in about 30 minutes. They were terrible, no
good, you know. But I got good at it and I could sell them to my fellow
classmates.

Then I got interested in writing poetry, or what I thought was
poetry. One day Shelby was sitting in front of me in study hall. He
turned around to me and said, 'What are you doing?' I told him I was
writing a poem, and he said, 'Why?' Well, I said, I just like the idea.
I can even remember the name of that poem. It was a long poem: "In
Somnium In the Manner of Poe" which I thought was very high class
and literary. It sounded like Poe, all about death with a lot of dark,
gloomy things in it. Shelby read it and . . . well, I'm not saying that
I'm the one responsible for Shelby's literary career, you understand,
but . . .

It was really the fact that we were both excited by talking to my uncle
William Alexander Percy, and as a result we talked to each other a lot
about writing: and too we began reading at about the same time. I mean
reading avidly and with pleasure, which is unusual, though in this case
the reading was serious. In fact, I was talking to Shelby the other day
about William Alexander Percy and we were speculating; I wonder
whether either of us would have ever gotten interested in writing if he
hadn't been there? I can't answer for Shelby, but my conclusion is that
we probably would not have.

So it was really two things. It was the man, William Alexander
Percy, who spent a great deal of time with us talking about books; and it
was also the fact that Shelby and I, maybe Shelby more than I, turned
into avid, serious readers. Shelby's always been the best reader I know.
He'll go back and re-read all of Browning one year. He wrote me last
week that he had just finished re-reading the Dickens' books *Little
Dorrit* and *Bleak House* for the umpteenth time. It would never cross
my mind to do that, but he's an inveterate reader.

But to answer your question; I think it was the two things: we began
to read together and to talk about books, which is a good thing to do.
It's better than being a solitary reader, though Faulkner may have been
that way. But he had Phil Stone to talk to, didn't he?

Q. Shelby started writing and publishing his novels in the 1940s. Because of your close relationship with him did you feel any extra pressure to write yourself?

A. No, because I was heading in a different direction. I was going to medical school intending to be a doctor at the time he was writing. I can remember him writing and being absolutely astounded myself when he was published. I had never known a published writer except for my uncle. So when Shelby, who was about my age, came over one morning and told me he had sold a story to the *The Saturday Evening Post,* that sounded wonderful! It was for over $1,000, I think, and that was a large amount of money for the time; I believe it was 1938. But no, it never crossed my mind that I could write and publish. I was busy in medical school, even though I had written some at Chapel Hill for the literary magazine. But in spite of that, it didn't occur to me to pick up writing as a profession until later.

Q. Were you writing on your own a great deal prior to the time of the publication of *The Moviegoer*? Maybe some short stories?

A. Yes, but not short stories. I've never written a short story. I don't intend to write a short story. It's my temperament; it's too challenging a form. It's like writing a sonnet. I wouldn't do that again. Every word has to count, you have to be very much aware of the whole action and to plot it like building a house. I need much more room, I need more freedom, more space for things to be allowed to happen. My novels allow that. They have allowed exploration, novelty. No, I wouldn't dream of undertaking a short story; it's too difficult.

Q. What sorts of things did you write before you were published?

A. Some of the first things I wrote were articles on philosophy. My first publication was in a philosophical journal. It was a review of Susanne Langer's book *Philosophy in a New Key.* Curiously enough, it was an important event. The book was very important to me. Later I kept coming back to that subject, the subject of symbol-using, semiotics, sign functions and the like.

Q. Those are matters you covered in *The Message in the Bottle*?

A. Yes, exactly. Most of those articles in *The Message in the Bottle* were written long before *The Moviegoer.* I wrote *The Moviegoer* about 1959 or 1960 and I'd been writing for at least ten years before that.

Q. Then that first novel hadn't been incubating in you for a long period of time?

A. No, it came all of a sudden, in a flash. I'd written two other unpublished novels which were much more traditional sort of apprentice novels. One of them was heavily influenced by Thomas Wolfe, and the other was influenced by Thomas Mann. But *The Moviegoer* came out of nowhere. It was the first thing I wrote that I felt was my own voice.

Q. Did you try to get those first novels published?

A. Yes, sure. The first one went the rounds of a lot of publishers. There were the usual comments on it, too long and things like that. But I'm very grateful now that it wasn't accepted. I would be embarrassed to have it in print. The second one was a little better. It was a sort of "mini" *Magic Mountain.* It was better constructed, better written, but I'm just as glad it wasn't published. I was fortunate not only that they were never published but also I got some good advice from some people who were very kind to me including Caroline Gordon and Allen Tate.

Q. I didn't know you wrote a novel under the influence of Wolfe. Was that a product of your Chapel Hill days? Was Wolfe still an influential figure there and among young people?

A. Oh yes, Wolfe was THE writer when I was a young man. I almost thought it was in the nature of things that if a young Southern male wrote a novel in the 1930s, 40s or maybe 50s he would write a Thomas Wolfe novel: growing up in the South, coming to terms with life, school, in the same slightly inflated style of perhaps "A stone, a leaf, a door" or "O lost by the wind grieved" and that sort of thing, which sounded great at the time, but which doesn't sound quite so good now.

Q. It's very difficult to associate your prose with that of Thomas Wolfe. They're quite apart from each other.

A. Well, maybe *The Moviegoer* was more or less a conscious revolt, or turnabout, an attempt to do something completely different, to get away from Southern rhetoric, the Wolfe-like concern with self, to do something much more abstracted, much less to do with the traditional novel's emotions. Of course in connection with that, I had been reading French novels and plays, which I think on the whole were a good influence on me. But for anybody who has been brought up on Faulkner and Wolfe, even though Faulkner was a great writer, the antidote of people like Camus and Sartre is very valuable. Maybe it takes Camus or Sartre to get you out from under Faulkner. Maybe all Southern writers ought to have to read them to keep from being overwhelmed by Faulkner, which is the worst fate to befall a Southern writer.

Q. Were you at all surprised by the success of *The Moviegoer* in winning the National Book Award?

A. Yes, but not as much as you might think. I should have been astounded. I mean, a man, 45, a Southerner, a first novel. But first, the book was accepted right off by Knopf. I didn't know anything about the literary scene or publishing or agents, therefore, I didn't see anything remarkable about the way it was handled. I did think it was a pretty good novel, a good story, but it didn't seem out of the ordinary for it to be accepted. I felt a little like, 'Why shouldn't they accept it,' and when it won the National Book Award I thought that was nice, but not really astounding. I was a little surprised that it beat *Catch-22*, which I thought would win the award. But the truth is I didn't have anything to compare it against. I didn't have a record of twenty years of struggles, disappointments, and knowledge of the publishing business. Maybe when I wrote *The Moviegoer* I knew I was on to something I hadn't been on to before, but strangely enough I've never been worried about that. I've always felt that . . . I have anxiety about other things, but not about writing. It all comes out in the wash. If you're supposed to be a writer, it'll all work out.

Q. How about *The Second Coming*? Any anxiety associated with it?

A. No. I was curious to know whether it would sell or not. And my publisher (Farrar, Straus and Giroux) said they were sure it would sell, but they've been wrong before. They said *Lancelot* would be a runaway best seller, and I said it wouldn't. I had a bet with my publisher Roger Straus. It turned out to do pretty well, but it was no best seller.

But *The Second Coming* has done very well. That's a little surprising, I guess. I've never had a real bona fide best seller before. I've made a living at writing, but yes, I'd have to say I've been surprised by *The Second Coming;* I don't pretend to know what makes a best seller, however. I do know that for several weeks this summer *The Second Coming* was the only book on *The New York Times* list that wasn't about spies or sex.

Q. You obviously don't write for fame or money or things material. Why, then, do you write? Surely it isn't to preach or moralize?

A. No. God forbid. If that were my reason I'd be a preacher. Of course, some people say I am. But I write because . . . it's a vocation. You discover what you can do and you do that. It's a small range of human endeavor which I can do, but there's more to it really. I write because I can do it and I can do it well when I put my mind to it. But I also have the feeling that I have something to say, that I have something to say that most people don't know. Or that they know it, but they don't know that they know it.

My theory of literature and art is that the best transaction that can take place is when the reader or viewer is told something he doesn't know he knows. The good thing that happens is that the reader has the shock of recognition. He says, 'Oh yeah, that's the way it is.' It's a curious combination. My medical career has something to do with it. When I was an intern at the hospital in New York I was a pathologist, and my whole set of mind was directed toward a searching out of the diagnostic. It was a diagnostic search I made, to find what had gone wrong, and I found unconsciously I transferred that mind-set to writing novels and other kinds of writing where there is something wrong in the world, something wrong with society, something wrong with the times. And in that sense, without the medical experience maybe I wouldn't have made the connection. It's a set of mind not uncommon to most writers; they're not thinking in terms of pathology. They're not thinking of the novel, of fiction, as an exploratory method of figuring out what in the hell has gone wrong.

I'm very much aware of that. For me it wouldn't be worth the trouble. What makes it really exciting is that I'm exploring in the novel for myself as well as the reader.

Q. How did *The Second Coming* come to you? Did you deliberately start out to write about Will Barrett, to carry out his story forward from *The Last Gentleman*?

A. No. When I started that story I wasn't thinking of Will Barrett. I started it about a man, in fact I know a man like this so there's a germ of a real incident here, but of a man who achieved everything he wanted in life—all of his goals—and retired too early and went to pieces. And I thought, what would it be like to have such a man and have him encounter a girl who is, as Allison says of herself, "she made good grades but she flunked ordinary living:" a grade-A student who didn't know how to live. What happens if you get these two people together; a man who has lived his life, in a sense, known everything, won everything, made money, has everything the world can offer; and a girl who has nothing to offer, a total failure.

Q. Are you working on another novel now?

A. Oh no, Lord no. When I finish something like *The Second Coming* the last thing I want to do is write another novel! It took me four years to write it. At the end, the only thing I'm certain of is that I don't want to write any more fiction right now. So what I want to do is almost routinely to go back and pick up where I left off with my non-fiction. It's about the use of language, the use of symbols, the use of signs. The way I started out, the Langer book, was reviewing, but that book was important.

An Interview with Walker Percy

Peggy Castex/1983

From *Nouveaux Fragments du Puzzle Américaine* (Paris: Presses de l'Université de Paris Sorbonne [Paris IV], 1983), 19–33. Reprinted by permission of Peggy Castex and Presses de l'Université de Paris, Sorbonne.

The following interview is composed of excerpts from a long conversation with Walker Percy which took place in August of 1981. Mr. Percy had graciously invited me to his home on the banks of the Bogue Falaya River in Covington, Louisiana where he and his family have lived for over thirty years.

The substance of our talk revolved around his latest novel, *The Second Coming,* with references to other fictional or non-fictional works of his.

There were also digressions far afield, for the encounter soon eased into a rambling chat rather than a formal question and answer session.

May I here express my gratitude to both Mr. Percy and his wife for their most cordial welcome.

Peggy Castex: Mr. Percy, there are a number of questions I would like to ask you about the tie-ups between *The Last Gentleman* and its sequel, *The Second Coming.* I say sequel, and yet you have inserted so much new material in the second novel which doesn't seem to grow directly out of the first that I wonder if it is quite so simple. What is, in fact, the genesis of *The Second Coming?*

Walker Percy: Well, it comes from an incident. In fact, I think it is the only thing I ever wrote that came from an actual incident. It's something that happened when I was living in the house next door. I was standing at the window and I saw a man walking down the driveway and he looked like a bum. He was unshaven, but I recognized him. I even remembered his name which is unusual for me; I hadn't seen him in thirty years. He was someone I had known in school who had done very well after college, had been a big business success up North, had risen to sub-senior position in management rank. He had then taken

44

what they call early retirement and come back South in his early fifties with plenty of money, having realized all his goals, to build a dream-house in the mountains of North Carolina where he and his wife settled down to lead the good life.

Peggy Castex: The country club life?

Walker Percy: Well, not just the country club life. He was a culti-vated man, a reader, very religious, a music-lover, a bird-watcher, and he had built the perfect house with the perfect view and everything was arranged according to what he though his goals were. This lasted about a year or two and then he went into an acute depression. It is a strange story, but I've heard variations on it before. One Sunday after church, he went back to town to get some cigarettes and first thing he knows he has caught a bus, the first bus out—anywhere.

So, I got to thinking about what it would be like to have a fellow like this—this is the male character—a middle-aged man who has done very well and is going through an acute crisis and then what would it be like to have a young girl, a schizophrenic young girl . . . I have also known young girls who are like that. I did some teaching at LSU and Loyola.

To get back to the first part of your question, I didn't start out writing about Will Barrett. I had the male character placed as a Carolinian going to New York. He had a different name. I had written about a hundred pages and suddenly it crossed my mind that—My God! this is what happened to Will Barrett, this is Will Barrett's story! Then I backed up to synchronize him with Will, changed his name, put him back in Alabama and Mississippi, and made the dates more or less right. Though they didn't come out exactly right, it still worked better for him to be Will Barrett.

There are a lot of stories like this. For instance, just now as I was driving home, I had the radio on WWL. They have a resident psycho-therapist on a talk-show who listens to people's problems and what do you think the problem of the fellow who was phoning in over the air was? "Doc, I have a problem of lack of motivation. I am thirty-five years old. I have a successful business and a good family and all that and I'm just not interested in anything that I am doing . . . "

Peggy Castex: And yet, at the end of *The Last Gentleman*, I got the impression that Will Barrett was back on the tack of normalcy, of everyday living, and was very happy about it. Now, twenty some-odd years later, we find him copping out . . .

Walker Percy: You're right. That was my intention, although the ending of *The Last Gentleman* has been much disputed—a lot of people have different ideas about it. My intention was to have Will make a kind of separate piece in his life. He was going to go back South and marry Kitty.

Peggy Castex: He would live him a life and marry him a wife and they would feed the chickadees together. That's why I found it puzzling when I picked up *The Second Coming* to learn he was married to someone from up North. Did this switch have anything to do with the real incident?

Walker Percy: No, it had nothing to do with that. I decided I didn't want him to marry Kitty and go back South and have him stuck there. He is a grade above that. He can do better than that.

Peggy Castex: Better than being stuck in the South . . .

Walker Percy: Well, sure. Remember where he was going. He was going to marry Kitty and work for Confederate Chevrolet in Birmingham. But then he decides to go to Harvard Law School and does very well. The idea was to make him do as well as I possibly could and how can you do better than that: going to Harvard and having a good practice in New York? You see, if I'd made him general manager and owner of Confederate Chevrolet, it wouldn't have made much sense. Anybody would want to cop out of that. But here he has got the best of the American life even by the standards of the Northeast. He's got it made—the best of the South and the best of the Northeast. He has the best of educations. He marries a nice, rich Northern girl and then returns to the best of the South. So everything is just right. He couldn't marry Kitty. You know what she was. A cheerleader.

Peggy Castex: Yet there was something as formless and unfocused about Kitty as there was about Will in the first book. She is certainly different in *The Second Coming* . . .

Walker Percy: No, Kitty goes to pot. In fact, my friend Shelby Foote said to me, "Why did you have to do that to Kitty? It was a terrible thing you had happen to her."

Peggy Castex: Having her turn into the country club type: sexy and suntanned and selfish? Money-grubbing too. It is significant that you cast Allie, the schizophrenic girl, as Kitty's daughter.

Walker Percy: Why do you think I did that?

Peggy Castex: Well, I suppose it has something to do with the theory

of return or repetition that you develop in "The Man on the Train."
Perhaps he is re-enacting his aborted experience with Kitty to a certain
extent, but better and leading somewhere. Out of the artificial life of the
country club into the greening life. Back to nature and a fresh start in
the greenhouse with Allie, the natural girl. She is almost the newborn
child who doesn't know how to speak or relate.

Walker Percy: Right. She is starting from zero. The structure of the
novel is having Will, who has gained "everything in life there is to
gain," on his way down—a breakdown, a depression. She has nothing.
She has not had a life. She has been to school—Sweet Briar, Hollins or
something like that—and then to the sanatorium. Her only experience
was that she made straight A's in college and then flunked life. She had
to give a senior recital—her mother had pushed her, forced her, into
music as mothers do—and she blew it, probably on purpose. She had a
peculiar family situation. Then she walks out and goes into a break. So
she starts from zero and he starts from 100%, but she is full of hope and
he is not.

Peggy Castex: You also have them on opposite ends of the scale as
far as memory goes. Allie remembers nothing and Will remembers
everything—the opposite of amnesia. Total recall or Hausmann's
syndrome as you call it.

Walker Percy: Well, that's curious. I made up that name.

Peggy Castex: I didn't know that. I gave you credit for it as a
physician. Though I must admit that I often had the impression your use
of medical terms and frames of reference was something of a put-on,
because you tend to reduce some of the deepest, most searching
questions, the problems and mental anguish in your character's lives to
trivia by treating them—ironically?—as medical syndromes. Is it
because most people would consider it safer for their behavior to be due
to some physical or psychosomatic disease? For instance, Will's
improper acid balance, his faulty PH which produces delusions and
abnormal longings, is that true?

Walker Percy: No. That's purely out of my head too. I made up the
syndrome which involves Will's peculiar behavior. He will be standing
in a place and something will remind him of things that happened thirty
years earlier. He'll be overcome, overwhelmed, by memory and fall
down wherever he is, on the golf course, in a bunker. He'll see a bird
and the bird reminds him of a bird he had seen when he was hunting

with his father. The syndrome is total recall, a kind of nostalgia, and also sexual dysfunction—satyriasis . . .

Peggy Castex: Which is the way most people would view his behavior with Allie. Kitty sees it that way.

Walker Percy: Well, it means behaving like a satyr or just the opposite—impotency. But—would you believe it?—after the book was published, I got letters from several neurologists and a psychiatrist who said that this is not Hausmann's syndrome, but another one that is well known: temporal lobe epilepsy.

Peggy Castex: So that explains the petty mall . . .

Walker Percy: Yes, *petit mal.* A North Carolina doctor would call it, of course, petty mall. So it turned out to be a real thing with all the same symptoms.

Peggy Castex: What about Allie? Is she amnesiac because she has nothing to remember or because she refused to remember?

Walker Percy: She simply withdraws into a schizophrenic break which wipes it all out. Amnesia also occurs after excessive EST (electric shock treatment) which she was subjected to in that crummy sanitarium.

As far as memory goes, *The Second Coming* is a continuation of the theme of *The Last Gentleman,* which shows Will trying to get his memory back. He ends up remembering only part of what happened, his father's suicide. *The Second Coming* shows him coming to the whole awful truth that his father had also tried to kill him.

Peggy Castex: You play on the idea of "second comings" in so many ways: the fact that Will returns in the first place, his second coming when he is born again into Allie's greenhouse, or Will's notion that Armageddon, the Last Days, are at hand . . . Not to mention the sexual connotations of coming as orgasm. There are "second comings" all through the book.

Walker Percy: Well, Will, in his own nutty way, is, like most of my characters, supposed to be on to something, whether he is crazy or not. He sees signs of the Apocalypse and thinks we are in worse trouble than most people think we are in. He picks up on theological signs of Armageddon such as his idea that the Jews are leaving North Carolina and even sends Sutter on a mission to Israel where the real thing is going to happen. He tells him to watch for the return of the Jews and let him know . . .

Peggy Castex: But later on, you have him discard the notion. You seem to be fond of toying ironically with your character's search for the secrets of life. You skip from discovery to revelation; sometimes you immediately drop them or move on to some altogether new discovery. The reader is not really sure whether the character is on the right or the wrong track, whether he is deluded or has got part of a message which may lead him to a whole truth . . .

Walker Percy: You ought to know as a displaced American, latter-day French lady that a writer cannot get away with theological revelations. It doesn't work in a novel and maybe it never did. So what you do is suggest something and then you back off from it and you have an interplay between an inkling that such and such may happen and that such and such is the way you discover who you are, who Will is and who Allie is and the relationship between the two. Of course the key is at the end of the novel. It involves Will's relationship with Allie and with the nutty old priest who is out of his mind, but may be saner than the younger priest.

Peggy Castex: Than Curl? He seems to be a real swinger, into all the modern fads, even the born-again business, and pretty well removed from the old essentials. In conjunction with this, what do you think about the new wave of born-again Christians in America?

Walker Percy: Well, it confuses me because I thought all Christians were born again . . . in baptism. I don't know what to make of it.

Peggy Castex: You were just speaking of the problem of identity, of knowing who you are. It struck me that when you dealt with loss of or lack of identity in *The Last Gentleman* and in *The Moviegoer* as well, you spoke of "entropy," or "reality dissolving into ravening particles," of "worlds spinning apart." It reminded me of Wylie Sypher's *Loss of the Self in Modern Literature* in which he relates the phenomenon to the physics of our aging universe which is gradually spinning down, losing its cohesion and its dynamism. Yet the theory of entropy is absent from *The Second Coming*.

Walker Percy: No, I didn't have that in mind in *The Second Coming*. I was thinking more in terms of Yeats, of what he says about the center not holding.

Peggy Castex: You mention Yeats, I was more conscious of the many references to Blake. The sabre-toothed tiger involved in Will's cave experience is a way to God, an animation of His existence—"What immortal hand or eye", etc. . . .

Walker Percy: That's true.

Peggy Castex: You also associate the tiger and its burning eye with the stove Allie hoists out of the cellar. Now the symbolism of the cave and the tiger is obvious enough, but what do you mean by that big black stove?

Walker Percy: You don't like the stove? (He laughs at this).

Peggy Castex: On the contrary, but what I like is the realness of it. Along with the block and tackle Allie uses to hoist it up, it is one of the most concrete things in the book—something tangible for her to relate to and function with.

Walker Percy: You were talking about poetry a moment ago. What about Gerard Manley Hopkins' line, "Glory be to God for dappled things" where he talks about block and tackle and trim, about the ordinary commonplace things in the hardware store, how that can be something sacramental. You see, it is the way she gets back into the world, with the thingy-est kind of things, dense, commonplace, everyday, quotidian things. Well, what could be more commonplace than a block and tackle, a rope, and a stove?

Peggy Castex: It gives her a monumental task to perform and is good practice for hoisting Will, the faller, later on. Also it, like Will, survived what one might call its own private last days . . .

Walker Percy: Then, too, what about her getting this monstrous ugly thing out of the ground? It comes out like an abcessed tooth and what does she do with it? She works on it; she polishes it. You don't have to be a Jungian or a Freudian to grasp what else is going on besides the stove.

Peggy Castex: We're isolating the main symbols, but one thing I found most significant about them was how naturally you wove them into the story. There's nothing contrived about them.

Walker Percy: That's true. You know I hadn't thought about it until some critics and reviews called attention to the most obvious. Of course, the best symbols are those that you come by naturally without thinking that they are symbols.

Peggy Castex: Those that grow from the story . . .

Walker Percy: For instance, the greenhouse. When I put Allie in the greenhouse, I wasn't thinking about rebirth or new life. I was thinking about an old greenhouse that I remembered. I thought it would be a nice place for her to be, but, in fact, it was a nice place precisely because it was a greenhouse.

Will had a thing about greenhouses too. It turns out that when Will was wandering around in *The Last Gentleman,* he once worked, or was it lived, in a greenhouse. So it was a very good symbol because it was unconscious.

Peggy Castex: Speaking of Will and things symbolic, you have him flunk his experience in the cave, at least ostensibly so, because of a toothache which gives him nausea. This is what I meant when I talked about your often reducing his searching to something ludicrously trivial.

Walker Percy: Right, but maybe that's the way it should be. In fact, it couldn't be any other way. It's exactly what he deserved for going in there. He goes in there with a question to God which God cannot refuse to answer because Will has pinned him down. After all these years of stupid and fruitless theological discussions which lead nowhere, Will has devised the perfect question which must be answered by yes or no and no maybes. If God exists, He has to do such and such. If God doesn't exist, then Will will know. But let me turn the question around and ask you: was his challenge to God answered or was his toothache an absurdity?

Peggy Castex: Of course it has been answered. Obliquely at first since part of the deal was that if Will dies then God does not exist. But Will does not die, so . . . God must exist. In fact with all the commotion of his falling from the cave into Allie's greenhouse because of the toothache, we lose sight of the main question. He and we piece the truth together bit by bit after other discoveries and revelations which, I guess, are all part of one whole. At the end he says that Allie is a gift and therefore sign of a giver and he must have both her and Him.

Walker Percy: Right.

Peggy Castex: Speaking of the greenhouse and the womb/tomb of a cave, you seem to have quite an attachment for unusual and paradoxical places. At the beginning of *The Second Coming,* when Will falls down because of the smell of rabbit tobacco, you have him remember the weedy spot, the triangular public pubic place—"a place for loving and a place for dying," as you say—where he first felt the pangs of love for a long forgotten classmate. These places are symbolic but you also make them very real. One cannot help but relate this to what critics and the writers themselves call the importance of place in Southern fiction. Do you think this is more typical of Southern literature than of other fiction?

Walker Percy: Maybe so. That's the way it seems to have worked out. You always hear about Eudora Welty and her sense of place. There must be half a dozen articles about it. Place certainly is important. It has to do with the Southern experience, small towns . . . The Northern population is more mobile; they live in suburbs and apartments.

But it also has something to do with the general condition of being a novelist. Unless a novelist can attach himself to a certain place, he's sunk. And not just Southern novelists. My God, what about Camus? Who had a better sense of place than Camus in Algeria? He also talks about the damp, dank, gray sense of place he saw Paris as.

Peggy Castex: It is.

Walker Percy: (Laughs). I'm also thinking of his novel *The Fall* in which he spends the first ten pages of a very short novel pinning down the very particular sense of smell and feel of the place which is Amsterdam. I don't have to go to Amsterdam. I know just what it's like after reading that.

Peggy Castex: Well, you did the same thing with the atmosphere of Elysian Fields in *The Moviegoer*. I grew up in Gentilly and you had Binx Bolling living right in my backyard. I couldn't get over the way you, not originally from New Orleans or even Louisiana, told it just the way it was.

To tell the truth, place is perhaps the only thing that is immediately identifiable as Southern in your writing. With the exception of *The Last Gentleman,* you make little or no use of Southern history—the old clichés of guilt and the weight of the past which shape, or warp if you like, Southern being. The Blacks are there, but you don't harp . . .

Walker Percy: I guess my protagonists or heroes or anti-heroes are in a sense post-Southern as far as the typical Southern novel goes. They are not hung up on the Black question. As far as they are concerned that is already resolved. Now, we in the South are in the same kind of trouble the rest of the country is in. Southerners are no longer stuck on the back porch like Faulkner, nor are they in the town-square in front of the courthouse talking to the old timers. Nobody does that anymore. They are creatures of a suburban civilization.

Peggy Castex: Just plain Americans?

Walker Percy: No, they are brought up in a country club, yet with a Southern flavor. You see, it is different. It may look just the same as the country club in Ohio or Massachusetts, but it's not. The memories are there. They remember their fathers and their grandfathers so that the Southern ambience is still there; there is still a mystery.

Peggy Castex: While we are on the subject of mysteries, could I ask you something about the ending of *The Second Coming,* not the essential part which links Allie and the old priest in Will's discovery, but about Will's Utopian scheme for building a new world on Allie's latter-day Treasure Island, using as a cast the legless old man from the Old Folks' Home and his cranky cronies, with mental cases from Allie's sanitarium to do the accounting, and a work force of various and sundry teen-age drop-outs. You tell it so well, that, in the reading, we suspend disbelief and even get all enthused about what is depicted to be the real thing, the authentic life, but which is nonetheless a preposterous enterprise.

Walker Percy: Well, it sure beats being stuck in the Old Folks' Home. Maybe it will work and maybe it won't. I have a feeling that old fellow *can* still build a good log cabin and I have a feeling that the contractor—remember how those two old guys were always fighting—and he just might do something together, something better than just sitting there rotting . . . The only reason they couldn't before was circumstance. There was a third old fellow who had had a green-house . . .

Peggy Castex: The one who waters the pine trees all day long?

Walker Percy: (Laughs). Sure. The only reason he lost his was because he couldn't afford to pay his electric bills. He can be of use in Allie's greenhouse.

Peggy Castex: The paradox of building a brave new world with all these old fossils is a kind of statement on your part . . .

Walker Percy: Right. Another thing that I don't think anyone has noticed so far is that Will and Allie start off their new life in a GER Go[l]d Medallion Home which ain't exactly your old Southern homestead . . .

Peggy Castex: No, it's anonymous and anywhere.

Walker Percy: But that doesn't matter. Once they have figured out what is going on and who they are, they can live anywhere—in a log cabin or a cave or a greenhouse or a GER Gold Medallion Home or in a Holiday Inn, for that matter.

Peggy Castex: On the technical side your use of point of view is much more complex in the last novel than it is in either *The Moviegoer* or *The Last Gentleman,* or even *Love in the Ruins.* Unlike the structure of the other books, the story is told from the point of view of two different characters. You also come in with quite a bit more Omniscient Narrator. You prophesy about Will's future and give us glimpses of his past which are not of his own finding, but relate more directly to his father . . .

Walker Percy: That's true. For some reason I felt free to do that, to hop around anywhere I liked. One thing is that Will's own state of mind was such that I could shift him around. He could become his father, for instance.

I guess what I am most pleased with in the novel is that girl. I think that I succeeded more with her than I have ever done with a woman in a novel.

Peggy Castex: How did you get so much of a feel for Allie's age group?

Walker Percy: Having daughters, I guess. And doing some teaching with young people. In fact, maybe the best part about the response to my books is that people my age don't like them nearly as much as the young people do. Young people are more ready to understand the characters and sympathize with them.

Peggy Castex: Perhaps because your books speak their language. By the way how did you go about working out Allie's own very special language?

Walker Percy: I know enough about schizophrenics to know how they talk and I borrowed from clinical studies—the rhyming and getting the words not quite right.

Peggy Castex: Malapropism in a serious key?

Walker Percy: Yes, I used it deliberately as a metaphor. Getting the words wrong is sometimes better than getting them right. It has a sort of metaphorical space, so it works better in Allie's case than ordinary speech. But Will can understand it and that's the important thing.

Peggy Castex: He even adopts it at times. At the end of the book, when she gradually drops the schizophrenic patterns, he teases her with it.

Walker Percy: Unfortunately Allie is going to end up being normal. (Laughs).

Peggy Castex: You don't think she is going to end up being another Kitty, do you?

Walker Percy: Well now, that's a good question.

Peggy Castex: Let me ask you something else. Now that Will has come again, what's going to be the next step?

Walker Percy: You mean *The Son of the Second Gentleman?* Why not? . . . No, I can promise you there won't be any more of those people. I've had it with all of them. In fact, I'm so sick and tired of making up stories that I haven't thought of another novel since then.

Peggy Castex: From what you have said so far, I gather that you draw quite a bit from your experience in teaching and in medecine. How consciously do you use your medical training?

Walker Percy: A good bit, I guess, in the most obvious sense of describing various syndromes. The good thing about psychiatry—I guess I would have become one if I had stayed in medicine—is that not enough is known about it for anyone to correct you. You can make up a syndrome and nobody can say it can't happen . . .

It was even more important in a deeper sense, because my whole stance, my whole set of mind in writing novels, is unlike that of most American novelists. It is the attitude of a doctor which is diagnostic—maybe therapeutic in the end—but still mainly diagnostic in my case. It is the attitude that there is something wrong. Something wrong with the character or wrong with the world, something wrong with where he finds himself, with his home, family, society, America, the West? . . . The whole attitude is diagnostic: What's wrong?

Peggy Castex: What's the prognosis?

Walker Percy: Well, it may end up in Armageddon for all I know. (Laughs.) Seriously though, I think that is where my medical training is most influential. I couldn't possibly write novels the way most people write—portrayals and narratives and plots and all that.

I'm always writing on the narrow edge between psychosis and neurosis and "the norm." My characters always have something apparently wrong with them and apparently they are living in a "normal" world. The question is always that delicate balance: who is crazy and who is not? Who is right? The inkling is that the so-called neurotic or crazy person is on to something that "normal" people are not.

Peggy Castex: Does this have something to do with what you say about alienation in "The Man on the Train"? That alienation is, in fact, less of a predicament when you are conscious of it than when you are not?

Walker Percy: Of course, I have to give the French credit for this.

Using alienation novelistically is a French invention. Sartre and Camus were the first.

Peggy Castex: I notice that, like Sartre's, some of your characters have a tendency to retch with nausea when they come to grips with reality.

Walker Percy: Well, you take Roquentin sitting there in a café. He's out of it. He doesn't belong. But, because he doesn't belong he is able to see this bourgeois society around him very clearly. They are "normal," going about their everyday market-place jobs or going to church and so forth, while he is wandering around like a ghost. His is a valuable point of view because there are a lot more people more like Roquentin now than there are like the happy French bourgeoisie, especially among the young and the educated.

Peggy Castex: They are looking for ways out, but you don't seem to approve of their outlets, suicide, drugs or even becoming a born-again Christian. Is the way out the old way . . . ?

Walker Percy: In *The Moviegoer*, Binx Bolling has arrived at some sort of solution. He has probably, to a degree, resolved it all. He says "I don't feel like talking about it anymore." He says, "I feel like the great Danish philosopher"—meaning Kierkegaard—"I don't have the authority to talk about such things," in other words about God and the good news, the Gospel. He says, "After all I am just a character," and he tells the reader, "Anyway it's none of your business . . ." (Laughs.)

I am a Catholic, a Catholic novelist.

Peggy Castex: A convert.

Walker Percy: Yes, but I've been a Catholic ever since I've been writing, so the whole framework is, I suppose, Catholic.

Peggy Castex: There is a kinship with some of the feeling in Flannery O'Connor.

Walker Percy: As Flannery O'Connor says, it is important for me to be a Catholic because my whole way of looking at things is informed by a certain philosophy. It has to do with the flawed state of man. There is something wrong with man to begin with.

Peggy Castex: The Fall . . .?

Peggy Castex: But that's a dirty word. You can't use that word in a novel. If you do, everybody will close the book.

Peggy Castex: On the other end of the scale, what about the Bomb as some sort of Last Reckoning? You say several times that the problem is not what if there is the Bomb, but what if there is no Bomb . . .

Walker Percy: That is a simple observation. As you know, people love bad news . . . as long as it doesn't happen to them. They love headlines about disasters, assassinations, catastrophes, earthquakes, and movies and stories about the Bomb. I'm not speaking only of the bombs being made, but of the big Bomb, the ultimate Bomb—the end of the world. People love stories about the end of the world . . . and the survivors. Two survivors—there have to be two. What do the French say? *La solitude à deux* . . . (Chuckles).

There is also a vividness attached to being close to death. Anyone who has been near death—in war or illness—knows that. You get it around hospitals.

Peggy Castex: Another related image you often refer to is that of the vines growing back over the rubble and ruins after the Bomb, after the world has been destroyed. Something old and yet renewed. Is that some sort of return to pristine purity and vitality?

Walker Percy: Well, that's the good part of it, you see. That's when things are good—when the vines grow back or when Allie recovers language which is also part of renewal. Her language is fresh. She rediscovers, almost reinvents language. I did the same thing in a different way with the girl in *Lancelot* who was mute and who invented a language. The inference, of course, is that something has happened to our language. It is worn out. It is supposed to communicate and convey, but it doesn't. It too often disguises and blocks communication and is a series of trite superficial things.

Peggy Castex: "Concealing and revealing," as you have Allie say . . . Does everything have to be destroyed before it can be renewed? Must there be a *tabula rasa?*

Walker Percy: No. In *The Second Coming* renewal took place through the most obvious and commonplace of all devices—the love between a man and a woman. They encounter one another, a very unlikely pair going in opposite directions, yet something happens. You don't have to have the end of the world. You can fall in love.

Peggy Castex: Since you have given up on novels for the time being, are you working on non-fiction right now?

Walker Percy: I've been writing a series on *la sémiotique,* on language. I do it from the point of view of a woman I started with, an American woman philosopher named Susanne Langer and of a German philosopher, Ernst Cassirer. He wrote *Philosophy of Symbolic Forms*. I also use another American philosopher, a very difficult philosopher

named Charles Peirce, who is now recognized as the biggest of
American philosophers. He is the one who really discovered semiotics;
he put it on the map. It is a very amorphous, wide open, confused field
and everybody does more or less what he likes. The French do straight
textual analysis, structural analysis. They work in the direction of Lévi-
Strauss. Americans do it more along the lines of behavioral science.
They worry about whether chimpanzees can talk. (Laughs.)

I was interested in language from the point of view of Helen Keller
and how the world opened for her when she discovered that the symbol
of water meant water. All of a sudden it was an epiphany, a revelation.

That's what happened to Allie—a revelation. She renamed the world.
You don't have to destroy the world. It's the other way around.

The underlying theme of *The Second Coming* and other novels that
I've written is that the world is already destroyed. The world is already
dead.

Peggy Castex: The death-in-life Will rants against?

Walker Percy: Yes. There is something really bad wrong. You don't
have to be a prophet or a seer to know that. Why are eighteen year-olds
committing suicide? Why do I hear on the radio of a thirty-five year old
man in New Orleans who has everything and life means nothing to him?
What has happened? Where is it? What do I do now?

So I start with the premise that the world is already dead . . . for
some people, while for others it is blooming and the sky is blue and
everything is fine. That is much tougher than the Bomb falling.

Surviving His Own Bad Habits: An Interview with Walker Percy

Robin Leary/1983

Unpublished, September 1983. Reprinted with the gracious permission of Robin Leary.

Leary: Why are you so critical of the sciences of man, e.g. psychology?

Percy: I am not critical of social scientists when they are dealing with man as man, a fellow human. Psychotherapists who do this have the most difficult job in the world and I admire them for it. What I object to is the social scientist—what I would call a "triadic" creature, which is what all men are—demoting his subject to a "dyadic" creature. For example, a Skinnerian professing to understand other men as bundles of conditioned reflexes. Or Margaret Mead professing to understand Samoans by making them conform to her theory of culture which she had in her head before she got to Samoa. Therefore, it is more interesting to me to study people like Margaret Mead and B. F. Skinner—scientists with a certain set of mind—than it is to study rats in mazes or Samoans.

Leary: You write a lot about the upsidedownness of life: is there, do you suppose, any remedy for the human condition?

Percy: Probably not. As the saying goes, we're probably not going to get out of this alive. The problem then becomes: what do you do about a "human condition" which is essentially a terminal illness?

Leary: Freud defines anxiety as the product of intrapsychical conflict. Skinner defines it as a learned behavior. In Zen philosophy, Nirvana is the goal located somewhere between tuned-in and dropped-out: that is, anxiety is an evil to be removed. Heidegger, on the other hand, defines anxiety as ontological, in that it tells us about our humanness—[anxiety] is the human condition. Not a by-product or a learned behavior—or something to be avoided. To which of these definitions do you most closely subscribe? Why?

Percy: Check Heidegger. In the sense that I would agree with him

59

that we do a lot better treating anxiety (some forms, at least) as a kind
of beckoning of the self to a self rather than as a symptom of illness.
This is why in writing novels, I often find that it works to turn things
upside-down and to set forth a character, say a woman with severe free-
floating anxiety, as more interesting, more hopeful, possessing greater
possibilities than, say, another perfectly adjusted symptom-free woman.
To say this is to say a good deal more than that illness is more
interesting than health.

Leary: The work of G[abriel] Marcel has had a tremendous impact
on your philosophy. For Marcel, hope, real hope, lives only in the face
of near impossibility or real despair. Is your hope of this variety? For
what do you hope? Does your hope equal the search? And how does
hope differ from faith?

Percy: I would agree with Marcel that even in the worst of times, for
example in the 20th century, when man is behaving at his most perverse, apparently intent on self-destructing, there is always an extraordinary trait in man of paradox, for striving for beauty and grace and
knowledge of God and the cosmos—at the very moment he is murder-
ing his fellow man in the filth of trenches, in the Holocaust of WWII.
For what do I hope? short-term goal: that man can survive himself long
enough to explore the infinite potential of himself and the world around
him. If he can last another fifty years, he might make it.

Personal goal: to survive my own bad habits.

No, the search does not equal hope. The search occurs only if there is
hope that a search is possible.

Faith, I would think, is the actual belief that what one hopes for is
attainable. A man dying of thirst in the desert may hope for water and
have no faith that he will get it. Now suppose there is a second man
who stands atop the next dune and makes a signal to him, perhaps with
semaphore, signifying 2 H's and an O. Now the first man is entitled to
faith.

Leary: Is your search for God, for sovereignty or for the search
itself?

Percy: I presume you mean the "search" for Binx Bolling, check
God.

Leary: I believe that there are two kinds of adjustments a human
being can make to reality: a comedic one; the other, tragic. What kind
of an adjustment, at base, is yours? Explain.

Percy: Check both. In writing novels, for example, I find that the comic—perhaps it is my own peculiar sense of the comic—occurs at the very heart of the human tragedy. For example, Will Barrett embarked in *The Second Coming* in a mad challenge to God, threatening God with suicide in a cave, is a comic figure. And yet we have no doubt that he is wholly serious and does intend his suicide—and is therefore tragic. The comic dimension is apparent when he develops a toothache and has to give up his nutty plan—come up to the world of men and fall into the arms of Allison, what's her name? Comic, in the old Dantean sense of the word, implying a happy outcome.

Leary: Science, as you so often point out, has failed man. But so, too, has God. How is art the solution for man who aimlessly roams the cosmos?

Percy: Explain how God has failed. Does this mean that God exists but that he might have done a better job? Or that man has screwed up and supposed, therefore, that God has failed? I didn't say art was the solution. I would agree that with a failure of religion for many people, art is often promoted as a quasi-religious vocation. I'm not sure how successfully this works, even for the most talented and committed artists and art-lover. I dealt with this interesting art-as-religion phenomenon in *Lost In The Cosmos:* for example, comparing the transcending God-likeness of Faulkner while writing *The Sound And The Fury* with the crash afterwards—drunk for a week—and the exaltation of the moviegoer after seeing a fine movie—say, *Wild Strawberries*—and then what? One hour, two hours later, what? I called this the "re-entry" problem.

Leary: You give writers a lot of bad press in your most recent work, *Lost In The Cosmos*. Why do you suppose writers are different from others and does their temperament differ significantly from other artists?

Percy: Also in *Lost In The Cosmos:* writers are in the front line of sensibility, like the canaries miners take down in the shaft to test the air. Also: writers are the "Protestants" of art, with nothing but their Scripto pencils and Blue-Horse tablets; painters the "Catholics," with concrete intermediaries, clay, paint, models, fruit, landscape, etc. This is why writers drink more and painters live longer.

Leary: What do you anticipate for the future of the sexes together: war or peace?

Percy: Don't know enough about sex or sexes. I would suppose that love/hate relationship going back at least as far as Cro-Magnon man, would sputter along pretty much the same. Each time has its own particular problems. It appears, for example, that some fem-libbers are almost as stupid about their own identity and sexuality as men have traditionally been.

Leary: For most of your life, you have chosen a life of seclusion. Why?

Percy: Because writing is murder—both joy and murder. I would agree with Flannery O'Connor that if she spends three hours in the morning writing, she has to spend the rest of the day getting over it. This doesn't leave much time for square dancing. Bourbon is better anyhow. But I am not totally secluded. I know you, don't I?

Leary: You often reject the label of "existentialist." Given the importance of naming in your philosophical system, what then are you?

Percy: God knows.

Leary: Why do you suppose so little attention has been paid to your discovery of "The Delta Factor"?

Percy: Two reasons: one, it had been discovered before—by America's greatest philosopher, C. S. Peirce, founder of Semiotics, then largely ignored by later Semoticists. This happened because the whole enterprise of modern science, including social sciences, has been mounted from the unspoken posture of a "triadic" creature studying "dyadic" phenomena. But if you recognize the Delta Factor, the posture becomes: triadic creature studying other triadic creatures—a horse of a very different color. Another reason: scientists, especially Americans, are specialized and very jealous of their own turf. They don't take kindly to amateurs trespassing.

However, business is picking up. The other day, I was quoted in a scholarly footnote in a Semiotic journal.

Leary: It's been said that Percy's plots all seem to have certain elements in common: a disturbed alienated man meets a woman, younger, worse off than he: he solves all her problems, in so doing, solves his own and they live happily ever after. Is this accurate?

Percy: A lovely concise summary. I feel you have taken care of me for all time in all textbooks of American Lit. No, really, it's true with a couple of qualifications: 1) There's something else going on besides the love story, 2) It doesn't always end happily—in fact, the only unambiguous happy ending was *The Second Coming*.

Leary: You are openly critical of joining groups. Why then, did you join the Catholic Church? (Does it not make you uncomfortable to belong to the same organization as those who worship Lawrence Welk, and so on?)

Percy: Two questions here: 1) "In view of your criticism of joining groups, why did you join the Catholic Church?" The question opens such vast areas—or should I say abysses—of misunderstanding, that I am somewhat boggled and could not begin to answer it seriously without writing a 300-page *Apologia Pro Vita Sua*. Indeed, I had supposed that all of my writings might be considered as a sort of covert answer to this question. Therefore, I will answer your question unseriously: would you like it better if I were a Methodist?

"Doesn't it make you uncomfortable to belong to the same organization as those who worship Lawrence Welk"? Organization? Group? I open my mouth, close it. What's wrong with Lawrence Welk fans? On the whole, I find them more rational and agreeable than California groupies. Would it make you more comfortable if I had joined the Sierra Club or a Transcendental Meditation group?

Leary: Freud defined "mental health" as having the ability to work and the ability to love. Are you, according to Freud, mentally healthy?

Percy: No. I am lazy and selfish—like most writers, I am quite neurotic, more so than most people. Fortunately, I live in the right time. So are most of the people I like—it takes one to know one.

Leary: Kierkegaard's remedy for the alienation of "everydayness" was "rotation." Do you agree and to what length do you pursue "rotation"?

Percy: I am not sure that he didn't say, rather, that "rotation" is a symptom of "everydayness"; or at least, a poor attempt to escape it. I rotate less and less these days. That is, see fewer movies, do less travel. On the other hand, what few rotations I do are probably worse: I enjoy watching *The Love Boat* and reading *The National Enquirer*. They are so bad they are good. That is, they are pretty good indicators of what people really want.

Leary: What were perhaps your most significant transitions philosophically?

Percy: From Tolstoy to Dostoyevsky. From Sartre to Marcel. From Plato to Aristotle. From Wolfe to Faulkner. Though, in no case did I lose admiration for the former performance. It was a matter of further discovery.

Leary: From the outside looking in, one might raise the question: you've lived a fairly privileged life: why such despair?

Percy: Who says I despair? That is to say, I would reverse Kierkegaard's aphorism—the worst despair is that despair which is unconscious of itself as despair—to: the best despair and the beginning of hope is the consciousness of despair in the very air we breathe and to look around for something better. I like to eat crawfish and drink beer. That's despair?

Leary: In your novel, *Love In the Ruins,* Dr. T. More is the inventor of an instrument which can miraculously measure the health of the human spirit. Without such a device, how might we, and why might it be important, to measure our spiritual health?

Percy: Dr. More's lapsometer was a not quite serious sci-fi device for measuring a serious condition given a not quite serious name: "Angelism Bestialism." It signifies the condition of mind-body separation which has been endemic in western civilization since the time of Descartes. It would be important to have such a condition diagnosed because then one might elect to do something about it. One psychotherapist I know recommends to some of his neurotic patients that they volunteer as aides in a cancer ward.

Leary: How much do children owe their parents and vice versa?

Percy: Don't know, beyond a certain decent respect. Love's fine, but so also is toleration. Thus, parents should recognize that most children, especially the most talented, have to rebel to become themselves. Young people should recognize their parents are not necessarily the cretins they appear to be. Each should try to put up with each other, difficult as that may be.

Leary: Do you think the distinction of Idealist versus Materialist is a meaningful philosophical one?

Percy: Not as meaningful as the issue of Realism versus Nominalism. That is, the belief that there is a real world out there which we can to a degree know (including God) versus the belief that there is nothing really knowable or scientifically lawful or meaningful but a bunch of sensory impressions which we give names to.

Leary: Is *The Incredible Hulk* really your favorite TV show?

Percy: Until it went off the air. It united two great literary traditions:

rotation (hitting the road, dropping out, adventures) and the good
monster (Beauty's beast), who is also Lancelot.

Leary: To someone contemplating suicide, what would you advise?

Percy: Go ahead and contemplate it. Then enjoy the consequences of
not doing it. (This prescription is elaborated in *Lost In the Cosmos*.)

American Writer Walker Percy: The Novelist as Searcher

Charles E. Claffey/1984

From *Boston Globe*, January 22, 1984, 26–28. Reprinted by courtesy of *The Boston Globe*.

> What is the malaise? you ask. The malaise is the pain of loss. The world is lost to you, the world and the people in it, and there remains only you and the world and you no more able to be in the world than Banquo's ghost.—Walker Percy in *The Moviegoer*

COVINGTON, La.—The door to Walker Percy's downtown office, where he does his writing, still bears the name of the previous tenant, a psychiatrist who closed up shop because, Percy explains with a smile, "I guess it didn't work out."

That Percy has never bothered to remove the psychiatrist's sign suggests the novelist's sense of humor—about himself and a society that has become so dependent on the healing powers of the 50-minute psychiatric hour.

The nameplate also serves the practical purpose of providing a pseudonymous cover: "I'd just as soon it not be known that I'm working in here," he says of his office hideaway.

Not that Percy is by any measure a reclusive man of mystery in this rural community north of New Orleans, on the other side of the 23-mile causeway across Lake Pontchartrain.

Percy has lived here since 1950, knows just about everybody in town and is regarded not as a resident celebrity but merely as an amiable man who makes his living by writing books.

On most mornings, he drives the three miles from his house to his office in a small, blue, seven-year-old pick-up truck.

Tall and slim with sparse white hair, Percy bears a resemblance to the actor Joseph Cotten, a resemblance that others have remarked on and one that he says he finds not unflattering.

He is attempting another novel, he says, one "that may or may not work out." If it develops, it will concern the further futuristic adventures of Dr. Thomas More, the besotted psychiatrist hero of his third novel, *Love in the Ruins*.

At 67, Walker Percy is an anomaly among serious American writers: He is a novelist who resists classification as strenuously as he himself inveighs against behavioral scientists who try to explain man by classifying mankind.

He is a southern writer but only by geographical circumstance. He is a physician who has never practiced medicine, a philosopher/theologian, a student of language and linguistics and an essayist who turned in middle age to novel-writing in hope of reaching a wider audience for his ruminations on the human predicament.

Although his novels—there have been five so far—are novels of ideas, he is no messianic proselytizer. Percy is an imaginative storyteller as much as a writer with a message. His books contain humor, compassion and, frequently, the bite of satire.

He is a writer "who works on the borderline of philosophy, theology and literature," wrote Dr. Robert Coles, professor of psychiatry at the Harvard Medical School in *Walker Percy: An American Search*. Coles interweaves a study of philosophy and psychiatry in the book, an interpretation of Percy and his work.

Coles said last week in a telephone interview that "part of the reason Walker functions as well as he does is that he lives in a small town like Covington.

"The reason he has such an unerring eye for American foibles is because he lives in an ordinary town in the midst of ordinary people.

"There is a side of him that's very scornful of the intellectual life," Coles notes, the kind of life lived by writers in places like "the cities of the liberal Northeast."

But then there is the other side of Walker Percy: the bookish, reflective intellectual, the man of ideas, the scientist who deplores scientific reductionism.

Percy has been called an American Christian existentialist, a categorization that he dismisses as meaningless, but his denial may be more a sign of his discomfort with pigeon-holing than an outright statement of disavowal.

In fact, it was the European existentialist tradition that helped to shape his thinking in the early 1940s: While he was a patient at a

tuberculosis sanitarium near Lake Saranac, N. Y., Percy read the works
of Dostoyevsky, Kafka, Sartre, Heidegger and Kierkegaard.

"Like most medical students (he graduated from the Columbia
College of Physicians and Surgeons), I had had a one-sided education,"
Percy said last week. "I was a professional skeptic."

During his two years of convalescence at Saranac, and later, after a
relapse, at a hospital in Wallingford, Conn., he more than compensated
for the humanistic and intellectual deficiences in his education.

Later, Percy says, he discovered the existential novelists, Camus,
Sartre and Marcel, and it was their work that eventually gave him the
idea of writing the existential novel.

His first novel, *The Moviegoer,* draws heavily on the philosophical
observations of the 19th-century Danish philosopher, Soren Kierkegaard.

Percy prefaces the novel with a quote from Kierkegaard's *The
Sickness Unto Death*: ". . . the specific character of despair is precisely
this: it is unaware of being despair."

Binx Bolling, the protagonist of *The Moviegoer,* is a 29-year-old
stockbroker, who, for most of the book, moves through life with just
such unawareness. He is, at the outset, alienated, like all the heroes of
Percy's novels. That makes him ever-vigilant for the malaise, "the
everydayness of his own life," as he struggles against boredom.

He tries to escape the malaise by endless distractions—"rotations" in
Kierkegaardian terminology—going to the movies, trips to the beach
with a succession of his secretaries in his red MG—which, he says, is
"a miserable vehicle actually, with not a single virtue save one: it is
immune to the malaise."

Percy, through Binx, talks of the "search," describing it as "what
anyone would undertake" if he were able to get beyond the daily
absorption with routine. The search begins when, for some reason, a
man "comes to, suddenly looks closely around, and notices just about
everything," the background of life we take for granted.

For Binx, the search began in 1951, when as a soldier in Korea, he
was hit, lying on the ground, his shoulder "pressed hard against the
ground." Staring at a dung beetle six inches away, he found himself
"onto something" and vowed if he got out of there he would "pursue the
search."

And so he does, at the novel's conclusion, abandoning his aimless life for medical school and marriage to the suicidal Kate. Binx has made a commitment. He and Kate will continue the search together.

All of Percy's novels end with their protagonists' undertaking the search, moving toward ending their alienation and finding meaning in life.

"One criticism of my novels is that I take the characters only to a certain point and then leave them. Maybe I give the ending a certain tilt. But I take it as far I believe a novelist can take it. A novelist can't come out with pat answers, with everything resolved, the search resolved," Percy says.

Language has long been one of his preoccupations, in particular semiotics, the science of symbols and signs in language.

In *Lost in the Cosmos: The Last Self-Help Book,* published last spring, Percy deals with semiotics in a book intended for popular consumption, trying to make the point that man, with his naming faculty, labels everything in the world, tries to understand everything but has practically no knowledge of himself.

The title of the book is intended as a jab at Carl Sagan, the Cornell physicist-astronomer, and his television series on the universe.

"I happened to pick on Carl Sagan because I was trying to establish that man is unique, and I did this by using the linguistic approach, which is very heretical doctrine."

Percy contends that man's ability to name things "runs counter to the general scientific set of mind of most psychologists, most linguists: mainly that language is different from any kind of communication between creatures.

"Man names everything out there in the universe—everything except himself, the namer."

Percy says his books sell "well enough to make a living, but I have never had what they would call a runaway best seller."

It is mainly young people who buy and read his novels, he says. "If I had to depend on my own generation, my own peers, I'd starve," he says.

"Most of the letters I get are from young people who find themselves in a predicament, like Binx in *The Movigoer.*"

Percy also told of one Greater Boston woman who called him at 2 in the morning to seek his advice. "She was suicidal. I didn't know what to tell her except that she could get some psychiatric help. She got

irritated and said I wasn't helping her at all and that anyway William
Styron had been her first choice but that she couldn't get his telephone
number." Not long after that call, Percy changed to an unlisted
telephone number.

Even though his education at the University of North Carolina and
Columbia Medical School was mainly scientific, there always existed in
him a literary side—an aspect that was fostered by his father's cousin,
William Alexander Percy.

Will Percy, who adopted Walker and his two brothers after their
parents' deaths, lived in Greenville, Miss., and wrote poetry. He also
wrote *Lanterns on the Levee,* a series of autobiographical essays covering a range of political and social issues.

At Chapel Hill as an undergraduate majoring in chemistry, Walker
Percy found time to write a couple of pieces for the *Carolina Magazine.*
He also became an avid moviegoer, there and in New York City while
he was studying medicine.

Coles interprets the moviegoer/observer aspect of Percy as "the state
of mind that prompted many to go to the movies . . . was a sense of
absurdity or futility. They may not be philosophers, but they ask
themselves those eternal and not easily answered questions which some
dwell on, writing page after page, and others shrug off as beyond their
ken."

Emotionally troubled while in medical school in the late 1930s, Percy
underwent psychoanalysis at a time when few even knew about this
psychiatric tool.

". . . Perhaps what troubled him," Coles wrote, "was not a neurosis,
but episodes of inertia or boredom or uneasiness or purposelessness."
Percy's own feeling during that period prefigured those of his fictional
Binx Bolling.

Later, Percy's philosophical explorations led him to become a convert
to the Roman Catholic Church.

Percy is an unpretentious man—a better listener than he is a talker, a
man who is always learning.

He says the writer he most admires is William Faulkner but adds that
he "came late" to the work of the Mississippi novelist. "That may be
fortunate," Percy says with a smile, quoting the late Flannery O'Connor
on Faulkner: "'When the Dixie Special comes down the tracks,

everybody gets off.' Faulkner was the Dixie Special, all right," Percy says.

Other writers he admires are John Updike and Saul Bellow and the late John Cheever and John P. Marquand.

He says of novelists that they occupy "a very low order in the ranks of knowledge. As far as a novelist offering solutions to life's predicaments, I don't think he has any business doing this."

Percy says he does not preach in his novels "because I don't know enough." But this much he knows, and this belief is an underlying philosophy of his books: "The individual always transcends every system that is created to explain him."

A Talk with Walker Percy

Elzbieta Oleksy/1984

From *Folia Literaria* 29 (Acta Universitatis Lodziensis, 1990), 153–68. A version of this interview in Polish appeared in *Literatura na Swiecie*, 5–6 (1987), 411–22. It was conducted in Covington, Louisiana on 8 May 1984.

Elzbieta Oleksy: Most interviews with you boil down to questions about existentialism. What has always intrigued me, and I don't believe you have ever spoken about it, is the presence of Pascal in your writing.

Walker Percy: Yes, it's true. People usually associate me more with Kierkegaard than they do with Pascal, but Pascal is at least as influential as Kierkegaard. Of course, Kierkegaard is much more associated with European existentialism than Pascal. I think my main debt to Pascal is, perhaps, his image of a man in a cell, a man imprisoned. What would such a man do, what should he do? Say, he has ten days to live. How should he spend his time? Well, Pascal said most men would spend that time playing cards or being depressed, but Pascal would say: "Well, I would spend my time trying to figure out how I came here, why I am here." Of course, he was comparing the prisoner's jail cell to our life. He was saying how people have a genius for diverting themselves.

E.O.: This is why I asked you about Pascal. It seems that in *The Moviegoer* you play with Pascalian concepts. You present a rather humorous version of Pascal's concepts of "diversions" and "mediocrity."

W.P.: Quite true. I combine Pascal and Kierkegaard. Kierkegaard has his playful, but also serious, notions of what he calls "rotation" and "repetition." I use that with Binx Bolling in *The Moviegoer*. Although Binx hadn't read Kierkegaard he was very much aware of "rotation" and "repetition." He did it playfully, like taking a girlfriend to a movie-house where he hadn't been for years. He would talk about this strange feeling of coming back to this same movie-house. He even remembered the seat; he made the point of sitting in the same seat. It was serious in the way that it made him think of how curious it was that fifteen years should have lapsed between the last time he was there and the present time. It made him think about the nature of time. What is time like? This time is passed and what am I doing? This is when he began, as Pascal would say, to take life seriously. That's when he began his search. Instead of taking his secretaries out he became tired, as Pascal would say, of his diversions.

E.O.: You share with Pascal, Kierkegaard, and other existentialists the mistrust of progress, the conviction of the unrelatedness of science to the human condition. Does existentialism offer any solutions as regards the human condition? In other words, is there any direct contribution to philosophy which should be described as existentialist ethics?

W.P.: Of course, you have to realize that existentialism has gotten to be a bad word. I don't know any serious philosophers who even use it any more and I don't know any serious writers who would call themselves existentialists. The word is used so loosely now that it means almost nothing. I don't use the word either. What I say in my writing, both in the fiction and non-fiction, is that the scientific method is good for understanding the world. But the scientific method cannot understand the individual human being. That is the form of existentialism. It goes back to what Kierkegaard said about Hegel. He regarded Hegel as the thinker, the scientist of his day. What he said about Hegel I would say about science. Hegel explains everything under the sun except what it is to be a man, or a woman, to be born into this world, to live, and to die. I put it differently: What people don't realize is that the scientific method has no way of uttering one word about an individual creature. Science only speaks about leaves, or stars, or people in so far as they belong to a class. In other words, science is only interested in you in so far as you are like another class of people. But science itself cannot utter one word about the individual self in so far as it is individual. It leaves a huge left-over. We almost automatically believe that science is not only our best way of knowing things but, maybe, the only way of knowing things. If a thing cannot be known scientifically, we believe it cannot be known at all. That's the general torture that we live in. Or, here, in America, anyway.

E.O.: Has existentialism offered any solutions as regards the human condition?

W.P.: Yes, it has done so. Sartre did it. However, I don't quite agree with Sartre. I'm not sure that he distinguishes between moral and immoral acts; these are not the words that he takes very seriously. In my novels, my heroes find themselves in the existential situation of being more or less alone. Most modern novels are about people who are alone. They are in the middle of a big society yet they are, to use a fashionable word, alienated; they don't feel they belong to that society, or the town, or even a family. It can also be said that they are living in a post-Christian world where the ethics of Christianity are no longer as strong as they were a hundred years ago. Napoleon was probably an exception. Christianity is not as pervasive as it once was. By the way, do you know a German writer, Romano Guardini?

E.O.: Yes?

W.P.: I use him as an epigraph to, I think, *The Last Gentleman.* He is talking about an existential predicament. He says we are living in a post-Christian world where people are alone but he also says, and this is an important thing, it's the world where there is less deception; people are alone and, yet, they are capable of forming true relationships. One lonely person finds another lonely person. From this very loneliness, this existential alienation, there is possible a true communion, which in a way is even better than it used to be, when everybody lived in the same system, everybody understood one another, say, in the nineteenth century Europe. Even in this terrible twentieth century, with these terrible wars, millions of people being killed, still, the people I write about find a certain life, and it nearly always involves someone else. What do the French call it? *Solitude à deux.* And between the two they create a new world. At the end of *The Second Coming* it takes place through the recovery of Christianity. It happens with most people, in fact. Most of us are brought up in a Christian background. In this country it's mostly nominal, it's part of the culture. Some people go to church, you know. But it's not a very important part of life.

E.O.: You've talked about alienation, a loss of faith. You've also talked about communion between two lonely persons. Would you agree that in respect to philosophical background your fiction ranges from Pascal and Kierkegaard, through Camus and Sartre, to Marcel, his concept of communion?

W.P.: And Mounier. And also the Jewish philosopher, Martin Buber. He was the one who had the "I-Thou" concept. Yes, you're right. This is what happens. It is the evolution from a nominal Christianity to a loss of Christianity, a loss of faith, isolation, alienation. Maybe first a human relationship: a man finds a woman, or something about her, or a woman finds a man or something about him. It's not like St. Anthony in a desert who goes there and finds God all alone. Except that this is what Will Barrett tries to do in *The Second Coming*. First he tries to find God alone in the cave. You see, he takes Pascal very seriously.

E.O.: Yes, he called Pascal "the only French intellectual who was not insane." But then, although Will is attracted to Pascal's idea of making a bet on God's existence, he, Will Barrett, wants to know for sure.

W.P.: I've forgotten whether he mentions Pascal. Yes, I think he does mention Pascal. But he said Pascal was not good enough. Pascal trivialized the situation. He said: "Either God exists or God doesn't. If God doesn't exist, it doesn't matter. You may just as well bet that God exists. So, what have you got to lose? If God exists you won, if God does not exist it doesn't matter anyway." That always struck me as a little silly. It strikes Will Barrett as silly. He says: "I'm not going to make a wager like that and hope that in the end I win, I am going to find out now. "And he said: "Is there any reason why I can't ask God to show Himself?" After all, that happened in the Old Testament. God showed Himself. In the New Testament, too. So he performs this really nutty experiment of going down in the cave to get an answer from God. My question to the reader and to you is: "Does he get an answer from God?"

E.O.: Yes, he does.

W.P.: What's the answer?

E.O.: A toothache, isn't it?

W.P.: Right. Here he is demanding God to manifest Himself as if he were Moses or somebody. And what does God give him? A toothache. And maybe that's the best thing God could have done. So, to get back to your earlier question, I suppose you could call it existential ethics. You start from the solitariness, then there is a search in the fashion of both, Kierkegaard and Pascal, then the human connection, the human communication and the finding of God through that human connection.

E.O.: Do you think that the shift of emphasis in contemporary American fiction from ethics toward overwhelming aesthetic issues is in any way significant concerning the future of fiction?

W.P.: I have no idea what the future of fiction is going to be. I think

ethics has also gotten to be a bad word. I'm trying to think of the last
ethical novelist, maybe somebody like Hemingway. He had a very
strange ethics. His idea of ethics was a man behaving well under stress.
What happened, though, was that for the last thirty years or so the quest
of the intellectuals, writers and readers has not been for ethics, which
they see as something imposed like ten commandments, but for authen-
ticity, self-realization. A lot of that came from the old existentialist
movement. "How to find myself, who am I," we went through twenty
years of that in this country with the rebellion of the sixties. A lot of
self-deception was involved in this movement. And the novels that
come out of it are very serious. A typical writer is Jack Kerouac. There
is no ethics involved there, it's a search for authentic experience, of
finding the right place and the right companion, so that now he can say:
"This is it, this is the real thing." By finding it he means that he has
found the right spot in California or Mexico, he has the right
companions and they're drinking the right booze or taking the right
drugs and they have great feelings. That substituted for ethics in the
American novel.

E.O.: To change the subject, your involvement and the involvement
of your family in the movement for civil rights for the blacks is well
known. What has intrigued me, however, is that the blacks frequently
appear in your fiction as butlers and housekeepers. Elgin, a graduate
from M.I.T., is at best Lancelot's confidant, not really a friend. Isn't
this a patronizing trait in your fiction?

W.P.: Maybe it is. That's the way it was. Those were the blacks that
I knew when I was growing up. I mostly write about young men and
young women who grow up in the traditional Southern environments.
Those were the kinds of blacks that we knew. It's not quite true,
though. In *Love in the Ruins,* which is a futuristic novel, there is a kind
of black revolution, Bantu rebellion. Thomas More has a few
revolutionary friends there. Willard Amadie and Victor Charles go from
being butlers, and house-boys, and waiters at the country club to active
guerrilla fighters. I guess these are the only ones. But, you know, one
writes about what one knows. I was not really in the active civil rights
movement. We have a small interracial group here, a few blacks and a
few whites, who try to do small things. Maybe some day I'll write about
that. My main interest was a traditional relationship and how that
changed. Anyhow, it's very difficult to write about civil rights move-

ment. Most of the novels written about that are not very good; they are full of passion and politics. As novels they are not too successful. I can't think of any off hand that I greatly admire. In fact, the best ones are not about politics and the movement. I'm thinking about Alice Walker's book.

E.O.: *The Color Purple?*

W.P.: That is a remarkable novel. Yet, she talks about these very black people you've mentioned: black maids, cooks, servants. The way she shows their relationships is what I call good fiction.

E.O.: You've mentioned that this may be one of your future subjects. Are you working on a novel, right now?

W.P.: Yes. I'm working tentatively on a sequel to *Love in the Ruins*. It's on what happens to Thomas More later. You see, this form, the futuristic novel, which is also satirical, gives me a chance to talk about the South and about this country in terms which are difficult to do in a straightforward novel. It gives you a lot of latitude to be satirical: about the politics, about the Republicans and the Democrats; also about medicine and about science.

E.O.: Do you consider your fiction as part of the Southern heritage? Or, is it rather that the writer, if he is any good, should transcend local limitations and relate to the American experience or human experience as such?

W.P.: That's a good question. Also, this is the question which always faces Southern writers. The Southern writer is in a unique position in American literature which is both fortunate and unfortunate. The fortunate thing is that the Southern Renascence in literature occurred rather recently, in the last fifty years, beginning with the Tennessee poets, the Nashville poets; Tate and Warren, and many others. They were good poets, and critics, too, who really established major trends in American poetry and American criticism. Then, of course, Faulkner came along about the same time. That's the first time that the South began to express itself, in fiction. I always thought it was strange because before the Civil War people in the South liked to pretend that we had a great civilization. Where was the art, where was the poetry, where was the literature? I bet you would have trouble naming a Southern writer before the Civil War. There weren't any to speak of.

E.O.: How about Poe?

W.P.: He was not very typical. But that was a good thing, this energy which suddenly found a voice, not only in their poetry, in their criticism, which was usually conservative criticism, but also in the novels which were mainly of Faulkner. But also of Robert Penn Warren, Eudora Welty, and very importantly, Flannery O'Connor. The unfortunate part of it is that Southern writing gets stereotyped in the general American view of literature. When you think of Southern writing, you think either of old romantic writing, what we call magnolia and mint juleps, or of the gothic and bizarre Southern writing, like Faulkner and O'Connor. And so, I don't like the fact that Southern writing gets pigeon-holed into these categories. For instance, I get uneasy when people call me a Southern writer because I say: "Well, you don't call, say, John Updike a Northern writer and nobody calls Saul Bellow a Midwestern writer."

E.O.: They call him a Jewish writer and this is also a category.

W.P.: True, but not as much as, say, Bernard Malamud or Philip Roth who are much more Jewish in their themes. But, of course, it's true, I am a Southern writer. I couldn't write what I write if I was born in Montana. But I noticed a real difficulty that Northern reviewers have with Southern writers. They like to categorize us into one or two pigeon-holes, and if we don't fit there they don't know what to do with us. I simply would like for Southern literature to be less parochial, so that you don't think of it as being Southern any more than you think of Updike and Cheever as being New England. But I think that's changing.

E.O.: This reminds me of what you said once about having lived a hundred miles from Faulkner and having been more influenced by Camus than Faulkner.

W.P.: That's true. I read the Russians and the French before I read Faulkner.

E.O.: You've talked about religion and the blacks. These are typically Southern themes. There is yet another Southern theme which, in your fiction, comes late. It's violence and it takes place for the first time in *Lancelot*. Do you think that writing about violence is a categoric imperative on the part of an American novelist?

W.P.: Apparently commercially yes. It is difficult to pick up a novel now that is not either very violent or explicitly sexual. But I don't think it applies to the art of the novel. Lancelot is violent for particular reasons. I chose him as a different kind of a rebel. He, too, is an outsider. He was an outsider as much as Binx Bolling, and Will Barrett, and Thomas More. But they were Pascalian. They had hope and they had embarked on various kinds of quests. The only quest that Lancelot is embarked on is, what he called: the quest of the unholy grail. He is also alienated, he is an alienated Southerner. Just like Barrett and Bolling, he does not like what he sees about American civilization. He doesn't like the vulgarization of culture, and the increase in what he sees as immorality, and the crookedness, corruption, politics. But, unlike my other protagonist, he does not undertake an interior quest. He is not interested in God. So, his solution for his alienation is a kind of fascism, or nazism. In a way, he admires the nazi; only he says: "The nazis were stupid." You know, I spent a summer with a German family, a nazi family when I was about fifteen. I saw what the early nazi movement was like. And it was very exciting. Well, here was the old Weimar republic and along comes this real elan. I'm telling you, that was a very exciting thing to see.

E.O.: You say you were fifteen at that time. Did you ever come to evaluate your initial fascination with the movement?

W.P.: Sure, well, Marcel writes about this. Marcel writes how it is very easy to condemn Hitler, Stalin, and the mass movements. He despises the mass movements all over Europe. But he says what people overlook is the excitement and the fact that mass movements answer to an emptiness in a Western soul. So, he understood it although he is the last man to approve of it. And to hear this from Marcel who was French, Jew, Catholic, existentialist, to hear him praising the excitement of nazism is extraordinary. Of course, then it turned into something which was absolutely destructive. Now, what I meant to say was that Lancelot saw the good side of nazism. He says that the trouble with the nazism of Germany was that it was stupid.

E.O.: This is quite a theory.

W.P.: I'm making up some of it. But Lancelot does say that the nazis were stupid; there was no need to persecute the Jews. It's senseless and cruel to kill six million Jews. What you do is destroy what's evil. He had this nutty idea of starting what he called the Third Revolution which was going to make America clean and wipe out all the corruption. He makes a beginning; he wipes out half of the Hollywood crew who come down there.

E.O.: It has always seemed to me that what you say in *Lancelot* is, in a way, kin to Mailer's theory of the American as hipster. You know, the new success myth based on the demonstration of courage and the purging of violent emotions; the life on the brink of death and the dream of orgy and of love. Mailer's protagonist, Stephen Rojack, is like Lancelot, a Grail Knight of a particular order, the essence of his Grail is a sexual sin. But it appears that, from what you've said, here the analogy ends.

W.P.: Well, I wanted it to be an upside-down quest for God. Lancelot says to his friend, the priest: "Don't give me any of that stuff about religion or God. The only way I could be convinced of it would be if I could find something that, I believe, is a true sin. Then I might believe in God." It's like saying: "If I can find the devil . . ."

E.O.: St. Augustine said this. The existence of God can be proved by the existence of evil.

W.P.: Right. That's exactly it. He's in the same predicament as my other protagonists, but his quest is turned upside-down, inside-out. He is searching for an absolute evil. But he is also a reformer, in a way. He wants to have the Third Revolution. He wants the best of the South to win. He is imagining himself like a Civil War soldier, a young man suntanned, standing in the gap of a mountain in Virginia. As a matter of fact, I got it from a Hollywood movie, *Cabaret,* have you seen it?

E.O.: Yes.

W.P.: *Cabaret* was about a rather degenerate Berlin society before Hitler. And, do you remember? There is a café scene. A Hitler Youth gets up and sings a song. The song goes like this: tomorrow is mine, tomorrow will be free, tomorrow is ours. Well, this is what excited Lancelot. He pictured himself as a good nazi who could accomplish a revolution without doing the atrocities of the Germans.

E.O.: You have often emphasized that people feel bad in good environments. Lancelot tells us that the only time members of his family were successful was during the time of war. Binx Bolling acquires a sense of reality after his car accident. The examples proliferate in your fiction. Do you derive your conviction from your observation of people in good environments?

W.P.: Sure. Also in bad environments. Who was it? It was a European philosopher who said: "What would man do without war?" War is men's greatest pleasure. Women have a better sense, you know, women don't believe that. Before now we had this luxury that men could go out and have war without destroying the whole world. You can't do that now. I can remember the excitement of World War II. My uncle wanted us to get in the war very badly. When the Japanese bombed Pearl Harbor was the first time I'd seen him happy for a long time. He was sick, it was shortly before he died. He was delighted that it had happened. Everybody was delighted, excited. It was much more true with the Civil War; that was the time of the greatest happiness in the South.

E.O.: One of the greatest paradoxes, isn't it?

W.P.: Sure. Of course only half of them came back and the South was destroyed. Somewhere I said people get things backwards. People are always saying: What if the Bomb falls?

E.O.: Yes, it's in "The Man on the Train: Three Existential Modes." You reverse the question.

W.P.: Yes. Suppose the Bomb does not fall. Well, my theory is that man's nature, not woman's, is such that he gets bored, and he gets excited by the prospect of violence. Why do you think there is violence on television? Because people like it. Everything is different now because even men realize that this war would be the last one. But I was always fascinated by the excitement of war. The worst thing that happened was that my two brothers went into the army. They went into most dangerous branches of the service. One brother flew a bomber, the other brother was on the Pacific, on a torpedo boat. He was on the same squadron as Jack Kennedy, he was Kennedy's friend, he saw Kennedy's boat get shot. And there I was like Castorp in *The Magic Mountain*, sitting on a mountain up in New York state. I had TB. They were the happy ones and I was the unhappy one. Then, what happened in 1964 when the Vietnam war came along, the happy ones were the ones who got out of it, who didn't go, who went to Canada. And the unhappy ones had to go. So, there's been a change.

E.O.: You have time and again expressed this paradox still differently, speaking about the blacks, who, as long as they don't live up to the standard of the affluent white people don't have their share of alienation. They're better off?

W.P.: In a way but you have a hard time convincing a black person of that. I think what Thomas More is saying in *Love in the Ruins* to one of the black revolutionaries is: "You think you've got trouble. Wait till you get what we have. Wait till you live here, in this country club." Well, it's true. That doesn't mean that there is any excuse for the oppression of the black people. Even now, in spite of the black revolution, there is discrimination against the blacks. Half of the young blacks in New Orleans are not employed. And there is serious poverty—actual hunger. It seems almost obscene to tell somebody like that who is really suffering that: "Well, we affluent, white people have our troubles, too." That doesn't make any sense. But it's true that as the black middle class arises, and there are beginning to be black middle class writers, they'll know what I'm talking about.

E.O.: Considering this very complicated contemporary scene, what is, to you, the role of a writer today?

W.P.: The role of a writer. Well, it seems to be, for me anyway, to affirm people, to affirm the reader. The general culture of the time is very scientific, one might call it "scientistic" on the one hand, and simply aesthetically oriented, on the other. This does not satisfy a certain reader. So, the reader is left in the state of confusion. The contemporary state of a young American man or woman is that he or she has more of the world's affluence than any other people on this earth and yet he is more dissatisfied, more restless. He experiences some sense of loss which he cannot understand. For him, the traditional religion does not have the answer. So the role of my kind of writer is to speak to this person about this whole area of experience that he's at or she's at. This is what you feel, this is how you feel now. My original example in "The Message in the Bottle" is that you take a commuter, the man on the train. He has everything, he succeeded. He lives in Greenwich, Connecticut. He's making a hundred thousand dollars a year, and he comes into New York every day. He's moved into a better house, to a better country club, has a very nice wife and nice kids. He is riding on this train and he wonders: what am I doing? He can open a newspaper, and he can see a column which says something about the mid-life crisis. He can read some popular advice from a popular psychologist who would say why you have your mid-life crisis. But this doesn't satisfy him. He picks up a book by an American writer, John Marquand, which is about a man like himself, a commuter on the train who has the same sense of loss. So, I say that there is a tremendous difference between a man on the train who is in a certain predicament and the same man on the same train with the same predicament who is reading a book about a man on the train. The role of a writer is very modest. It's to identify the predicament. The letters I get are from people who say: I didn't know anybody who talked like that, I know what you mean, you have described my predicament. I get letters from the businessmen (the men on the train), from young men, and from young women, and they're excited because I've named the predicament. That doesn't sound like much, that's a very modest contribution but it's very important. You see, I agree with Kierkegaard. He said: "I'm not an apostle, it's not for me to bring the good news. Even if I brought the good news, nobody would believe it." But the role of a novelist, or an artist, for that matter, is to tell the truth, and to convey a kind of knowledge which cannot be conveyed by science, or psychology, or newspapers.

E.O.: Is this edifying?

W.P.: Edifying. You've picked up all the bad words. Well, "edifying" is a perfectly good word, but it has very bad connotations in English. Well, in the largest sense, it is edifying, because it's helpful, it creates hope. At its best it's affirming, it affirms the reader in the way he or she is. It offers an openness and some hope. And that's about all a novelist can do.

Interview with Walker Percy

Linda Whitney Hobson/1984

From *Xavier Review,* 4 (Numbers 1 & 2 1984), 1–19. Reprinted by
permission of the editors of *Xavier Review* and Linda Whitney
Hobson.

For nearly ten years, now, Walker Percy has interrupted his
writing each week on Thursday for a few hours when he
invites a few friends—book-lovers all—to share conversation and lunch at Bechac's in Mandeville, Louisiana,
near his home in Covington. The group of regulars stays at
about the same number each week, but often there is a guest
or two to liven up the discussion.

On April 19, 1984, the guest was a sociobiologist, a man
given to the notion that "Science is the measure of all things."
Thus, the discussion turned on the nature of consciousness;
ways of knowing; and whether the means science provides
for studying phenomena are applicable to studying con-
sciousness/language. The sociobiologist maintained that
even though science may not presently have the technology
to prove that what we call consciousness is merely a matter of
action-reaction, eventually it will do so because nature does
not tolerate discontinuity. The proper technology will establish continuity for all matter, including man. In other words,
the material relationship between all other things in the
universe will one day be seen to describe as well the relationship between man and himself, man and objects, and man
and others.

Percy disagreed, maintaining that man—perhaps not
alone of the creatures in the universe—knows triadically, not
diadically; the objects, the sign, and man's consciousness
form a triad of knowing. That man's way of knowing is
discontinuous with other actions in the universe does not
threaten Percy.

This cool and measured paraphrase of the discussion after-
the-fact cannot adequately characterize the "liveliness" of
our table talk, but suffice it to say that when Dr. Percy and I
arrived at his home in Covington for the interview, we were
still concerned with the matter we had discussed at lunch.

Q: Percy, do you mind pursuing some of these questions about the diadic and triadic ways of knowing? And what interests me as much is the scientist's defensive response to your suggestion that the triadic model may describe man's consciousness.

Percy: His hostility is very typical, too. What I meant by triadic— and this is not my idea, by the way; it started with Charles Peirce—is that you cannot explain certain unique human phenomena and behavior by diadic theory—what psychologists call stimulus-response. No matter how refined or how complex the sequences are, you cannot explain human language or consciousness—the mind—by it. In my two books, *The Message in the Bottle* (1975) and *Lost in the Cosmos* (1983), I was trying to get at this in a very simple way. I approached it not from a theological point of view but from the point of view of trying to understand language. I was trying to make a case—starting with what I call the classic Helen Keller phenomenon—that you cannot explain what Helen Keller did during that famous scene at the well when she named the water by associating the sign w-a-t-e-r with the water being poured over her hand—and, in fact, that you cannot explain what any normal two-year-old does when he suddenly begins to name all the objects of his world—unless you take into account what Charles Peirce, who is probably America's greatest philosopher-scientist, said. Naming the objects in one's world is a triadic phenomenon. He's not saying it's anything mystical; it's not magical; it is a certain kind of reality—just as real as Pavlov's salivating dogs. But it's different. It is qualitatively different. It is not the same sort of thing. I don't care what kind of phenomena you're talking about, either: stimulus-response psychology, radiation of the sun on the earth, earthquakes, supernova, or the colli- sion of galaxies. They can all be explained by action and interaction. They can all be set up in nice models, with arrows showing A hitting B or B hitting A. This applies to chemistry, to particle physics, to stimulus-response psychology; it applies to all standard sciences. It does not apply to triadic phenomena. Now, the scientist gets his back up right away because he thinks you're saying something mystical. It's not mystical. It involves three entities: a child sees a round, red, inflated, floating object; the child hears the word "balloon"; and the child sees that the sound means the object. So, as Charles Peirce said, there have to be three things: the symbol (sign); the referent; and the third thing to put them together—a human being, such as Helen Keller or the two-year-old child. Saussure called them the *signifiant* and the *signifié*. But the third thing necessary is the self. Eccles, the neurophysiologist, calls it "mind" or "consciousness," and it is hard to qualify for scientists. A behaviorist I've been corresponding with says, "You're talking about a discontinuity, aren't you?" Science attempts to identify a continuity. You see, there's a continuity between the simplest reaction in nature, say, between hydrogen and oxygen to produce water all the way up through organic chemistry, through the one-celled organisms, through the primates, up to us. And scientists set great store by this continuity. The continuity's there. But all I'm saying is that there is a discontinuity. Something really strange happened with man—something extraordinary. Man is the only creature who has the capacity for language. Language, in a way, is the last bastion of man's uniqueness. Darwin destroyed man's claim to uniqueness by putting him in the evolutionary tree. And Galileo before him showed that man was not the center of the universe. And Freud completed the destruction by showing that man was subject to forces deep in his own mind which were beyond his control.

Q: So that both outside and inside man there is no area over which he has control?

Percy: Except for language. Language is the last holdout, the last thing which makes man unique. So you can see why there's such a controversy over language.

Q: Where does the soul fit into all this?

Percy: Well, that's a dirty word to the scientists, but not to Freud, who used the word "psyche." When you're talking to linguists or to psycholinguists or behaviorists or psychologists, it's a dirty word. What you have to do is behave with great indirection. With Socratic deception!

Q: You have to use other words that won't hold a red cape up in front of their eyes?

Percy: Yes. You say, "There is a third entity in this triad." They get suspicious, as well they might! But this is still a better way to approach it than from some vague, theological stance, which would get nowhere with them. And my theory does not depend on the belief that man is the only creature capable of triadic behavior. Maybe creatures on other planets—maybe there are creatures here—who are intelligent beings besides us. C. S. Lewis talks of such things, for example. In fact, in *Lost in the Cosmos,* I say that this argument does not depend on the fact that only man has the capacity for triadic behavior. But, despite monumental attempts with chimpanzees, with gorillas, with dolphins, it has not been proved that any other creature but man has such a capacity. In fact, the literature on animal speech is even going the other way. You know we thought that Washoe the chimp was using sign language? That he was making sentences? Well, that idea is not so popular anymore. Not since Terrace shot it down.

Q: So they believe now that some other kind of training was taking place and scientists were calling it language?

Percy: Yes. What it is is animal communication. People like Terrace, Sebeok, and others—psychologists—are saying "This is animal communication of a very high order, but it is not the same thing as human language." Human language involves sentences, assertions. You know, Washoe would say "Rock tree balloon" but they're only words. We, on the other hand, assert things, deny things, or question things. And also we have this extraordinary productivity of language. Our young children learn an infinite number of sentences, you know, without anybody trying very hard at it. This is miraculous, almost unbelievable. Scientists like the one we just had lunch with will maintain that scientists who are also Christians just try to tailor their science to their belief, and this is what makes them assert that man's language-making ability makes him unique. That may be true to a certain extent, but it's also true that scientists have their dogmas which they hold to just as fiercely. Their main dogma is that they will not tolerate discontinuity. But there's no reason why there shouldn't be discontinuity. What matters is truth.

Q: Their hostility towards discontinuity shows a certain lack of confidence, too. True science, it appears, should be based on curiosity, which by definition implies a belief in process—that you keep finding things out, not holding rigidly to any dogmatic notion such as continuity. Do you agree?

Percy: Yes. And the whole burden of my non-fiction is to suggest that man is a discontinuity. That's very offensive to scientists, let alone drag in the notion of God and all the rest. Just to suggest that man may be different is shocking to scientists. I say that man is the only alien we know about.

Q: Speaking of aliens, I heard on the radio today that an electronics firm outside of Boston, Teleplanet Services, will beam a message of 25 words or less to any area of the cosmos you choose for only $9.98. People are so eager to communicate with extraterrestrial intelligences that the company believes it will make a lot of money. Teleplanet uses a personal computer to aim its 1,000-watt transmissions at whatever goal you choose—a domestic planet or an exotic red star. What do you think of that?

Percy: That's what Carl Sagan is interested in—ETI's. He wants to find somebody out there. The interesting thing about the 25-word message is what kind of question would you ask of an ETI? That question is where Carl and I differ. Carl thinks that the question natural to ask is "What is the level of your science?" But the questions that I had my ETI's ask the earthlings, the space travelers, in *Lost in the Cosmos* were: "Are you in trouble? What sort of trouble? What order of consciousness are you? Are you C1, C2, or C3?" If you think psychologists get upset when you suggest discontinuity, you ought to see them when you suggest C1, C2, and C3 as the three levels of consciousness.

Q: So there's really more to this probing of consciousness than scientists are willing to consider?

Percy: Yes. How does this fit in with the different levels of consciousness? Suppose you have a problem on your hands. Say you're having difficulty resolving a novel. When this happens to me, the problem is on my mind more or less all the time. And solving that problem works paradoxically. If I'm sitting here concentrating on it, it escapes, but if I give up concentrating, go on to something else, or even go to sleep, the mind has its own mysterious ways of solving that problem. Somehow or another, your mind is working on the problem in ways that are better than the strictly left-brain focus.

Q: Better solutions than striving for solution?

Percy: Right. This can be absolutely maddening sometimes, too, because it means the harder you strive for solution, the farther away you are. But I had something different in mind with C1, C2, and C3. I was suggesting that the creatures the earthlings were in touch with were aware of what are generally described in theological terms: the unfallen state, the fallen state, and the redeemed state. And these are not ideas you encounter in the usual science fiction, except in *A Canticle for Leibowitz*. Prime questions I would have for any intelligent ETI would be "Which level of consciousness are you? Are you in trouble? Are you in a fallen state?" Now what do you think our friend the sociobiologist would have to say to that?

Q: I think he would disregard it entirely as the scientist might also disregard poetry. Questions like that, absent as they are of striving, of a particular rationale for solving a particular concrete problem, would seem irrelevent to him, though he'd be off the mark himself, I think. That striving kind of consciousness is not the highest one—it takes a certain kind of faith or intuition going on behind the scenes, going on almost against one's own will, to see the truth in the three levels of consciousness which you describe.

Percy: What would Carl Sagan say after waiting twenty years to address an ETI, only to have the creature ask him what level of consciousness our civilization has reached? You know, Carl's got the biggest dish in the world for receiving messages from outer space. The receiving station is down in Puerto Rico. Now, if he received a message asking about his level of consciousness, he would either say: "What are you talking about?" or he would say: "You're asking about an obsolete theology which most scientists don't even recognize." If the ETI then went on to ask, "Dr. Sagan, then tell me what has been going on in your civilization for the last one hundred years," he would have to admit that we have had two world wars, we've lost 200 million to warfare in general, and it has been the most violent century on the face of the earth. He would, of course, be describing a C2 consciousness—a fallen state—when the cause for all this is that the very people responsible for the C2 civilization have achieved a triadic breakthrough. The break-through means that you have a *choice* of being C1, C2, or C3. And they have chosen C2.

Q: And they may blow us all up before we get to C3. Love of violence seems to be at a very high level itself right now.

Percy: Of course, this gets into the question of whether there is Original Sin. In *Lost in the Cosmos,* I try to approach it linguistically instead of theologically because with language, you can actually point to things, and see what state of consciousness we are in. It makes a better argument. Sin is simply being born human. When you are born human, you are born to trouble as the sparks fly up. You have this capacity to symbolize the world. And everything is ordered for you in the form of symbols except oneself. The self is unformulable, you see, and that means you're in trouble. Arnold Gesell describes the difference between a four-year-old and a seven-year-old this way: the four-year-old is a C1 consciousness, like Helen Keller. He is in an Edenic state; he's celebrating the world. By the time he's seven, something has happened. He is "fallen." He is worried to death about his sexuality, about being naked; it's like Adam and Eve discovering their nakedness. In the book, I was trying to show the myth of The Fall in genetic terms. And it was fun trying to do it in linguistic terms. We all start off as C1's, and then something god-awful happens to us. Of course, most analysts would say it's because of your parents—they screw you up! But it's a paradox, anyway. Even if you grow up without parents, like the British schoolboys in *Lord of the Flies,* you come out of the Edenic state around seven years old, so blaming parents is a false argument.

Q: So even without parents, children come into C2 all on their own? You know, those British children nearly burned up their island in the "games" they played.

Percy: Those boys were even worse than the naval officers who were practicing "civilized war." C3 is redemption—it's the Good News.

Q: Your mentioning redemption reminds me of something you wrote in *Lost in the Cosmos.* You said, "The exile from Eden is, semiotically, the banishment of the self-conscious self from its own world of signs." The child despairs of ever being able to "name" himself, figure out the words for *himself,* the way he can do so easily for the objects in his world. The sadness that results from not being able to name the self has many negative social and personal results. Is there anything one can do to put a name to the "Nought of Self," the nothingness that each suspects is at the center of his being?

Percy: At the secular level, you can name the self through art and literature. 'Way back, I wrote an article called "The Man on the Train," in which I show the commuter, with—as the psychologists say—all his "needs" satisfied. But he is alienated as he takes the train into the city to work. He is like the people John Marquand writes about. He has a nice wife, a nice family, a nice job, but he is alienated and has something wrong with his life. "Is that all there is?" he asks. But when this man picks up a novel by Marquand and reads about another alienated commuter, a very strange redemption occurs. He recognizes himself and a social interaction takes place. He thinks, "Here is a man, J. P. Marquand, who writes about a man just like me and he understands just what I'm going through." That, in a way, is a redemption. That's what happens in almost any artistic transaction, whether we're talking about poetry or fiction or art or music. What you're doing is seeing this vulnerable self, which you can't get ahold of to save yourself, which you feel is utterly alien and alone—

Q: Empty?

Percy: —empty, yes, but all of a sudden, it connects up and somebody else is affirming you. And music affirms even the basic motions of the self; Susanne Langer said that. And fiction, of course, helps because it actually tells how the self is. That, in a way, is a secular form of redemption. Art reestablishes community, even if you're reading a book alone. If it's a great book, there is a community established between you, the writer, and the words he's using. This is a double triadic relationship, like two triangles placed base to base, with the writer and the reader the opposing points.

Q: But when the transcending experience of art is over with, when you have finished the book or poem, when the curtain comes down on the play, when the symphony is over—what do you do then to redeem or define the self? It's a terrible let-down, isn't it?

Percy: What happens is that this union of transcending selves who understand the alienation—the writer and the reader, for example—is only temporary. People have asked how long pleasure from reading a great book lasts—20 minutes? 30 minutes?

Q: At the most.

Percy: Sure. Look what happened to Faulkner. His first great novel was *The Sound and the Fury,* which he wrote in Oxford. He worked hard writing, but then he would have to go to the post office or to Reed's Drugstore. You remember what happened to him. He couldn't stand it. There's another quasi-C3 state—and it's drugs. Faulkner drank, and alcohol is a drug. A further possibility, too, for temporary redemption is making love. That provides a real, concrete, human C3 community—but again a temporary one.

Q: All these methods of transcending alienation—art, drugs, making love—are temporary. Is there no lasting human redemption, then?

Percy: Well, here you have this strange triadic creature, with his strange ups and downs, by nature transcending and depressed. And that's at best. At worst, he's just in a kind of frustrated immanence, watching T.V. all day.

Q: Surburban despair?

Percy: Of course, the only lasting C3 redemption is the Good News—the Gospel—the message in the bottle. That's one way of understanding linguistically the Good News. Of course, it can't be proven in a way the scientists find acceptable. St. Paul said that salvation comes from hearing. This is very different from what the Buddhists say; they believe that salvation comes from within, from meditation on the self. They believe that redemption doesn't involve anybody else. Of course, there's perhaps a different kind of redemption for the Buddhist in the highest states of ecstasy—of Nirvana. That's a C3 consciousness, too.

Q: But that sort of higher consciousness involves an emptying out of self, doesn't it, whereas Aquinas insists that faith is based in knowing? That was one of the points I was making at lunch—that faith involves a way of knowing.

Percy: I think the scientist knew what you were talking about; he just wasn't buying it.

Q: Does one have to have tried all the other forms of producing C3 consciousness—the secular forms we discussed earlier—before he realizes how temporary they are and before he is ready to hear the Good News?

Percy: Well, you remember that Kierkegaard said that the man who is closest to salvation and to believing the Good News is the man who is in despair and who is aware of it. The man who is farthest from salvation is the man who is in despair and who is not even aware of it—but the twentieth-century man who has all the worldly goods and all his needs satisfied, yet who has seen them turn to ashes in his mouth he could be in a state where he is open to hearing the Good News. In *The Message in the Bottle,* I used the island image to show this: a man who has acquired scientific knowledge is walking on the beach; he knows all about the island and he could be a scientist, an artist, too. He goes to concerts, takes in the good things the place has to offer. But there's something missing in his life. And all of a sudden, he becomes aware of Kierkegaard's question to Hegel: Hegel had answered all the questions which could be answered on the island—all but where did I come from? what am I doing here? and where am I going? In fact, there's a much older Anglo-Saxon image of this in Bede's story of the conversion of King Edwin. After hearing Paulinus' preachings on Christianity, an advisor to Edwin says man's life is like the swift flight of a sparrow out of the darkness, into a warm mead hall, and out a farther door into the night again. But with Christianity, the advisor thinks, something more certain is offered man than this brief interruption of the darkness. Edwin listens, agrees, and is baptized. It's a good image for the uncertainty of life on the island, too. Our scientific needs to hear the same message Paulinus gave King Edwin.

Q: O.K., now we've talked about ways out of this trouble that man feels himself to be in, trouble for which science offers no answer since it won't even allow the questions to be asked. The message in the bottle is surely an answer, but is there no other way? What about psycho-analysis as a way of mending the riven soul?

Percy: I think Freud was onto a lot of good and valuable things.

Q: What were some of those things?

Percy: In the first place, his going against the whole nineteenth-century trend of thinking that we all were progressively evolving creatures, and that it was going to work out all right. He gave a very graphic account of C2—the fallen state. God knows, there's nothing more subtle than Freud's neurotic. He said we're all neurotic. Freud's model of the human psyche is a C2 model—he said we were all in trouble. The model shows an innate conflict between the powerful superego and the id with a poor little timid ego suffering in between, trying to mediate the two, trying to survive somehow. It would be easy to translate Freud's model into a triadic model of the psyche. As the years go on, I get more sympathetic to Freud. Freud's word for psyche, by the way, is *Seele,* a far cry from the current academic model.

Q: I can see from your writing, though, that earlier you weren't very sympathetic. What caused the change?

Percy: Freud describes fallen man so well, and he's not too opti-mistic about working out of this state.

Q: Except by talking it out?

Percy: Maybe. Maybe. After years and years, maybe there'd be some understanding of self. What's going on there, of course, in the analysis is a quasi-community is set up between the doctor and the patient. That's what you get for your $100—a community. You pay someone to listen to you. It is a little commercial, but I'm much more attracted to that than I am to the Buddhist model of the individual ego—the Atman—who discovers himself by sinking into himself. There are no social dimensions. And ultimately there's nothing real out there. Freud, of course, would never have talked of God or a fallen state. But actually what he's doing is to re-create some sort of Edenic community within the analysis, between the patient and the analyst. But that gets into another kind of trouble, though.

Q: How so?

Percy: Well, the patient falls in love with the analyst—or hates him in order to mask the love or hatred of someone else. That's transference. But when it works, the analyst is able to transfer the patient's love to the outside world in a rational way. So, when psychoanalysis works, it's a kind of redemption. It's a kind of C3 consciousness that is produced, though Freud, being a good scientist, would say, "I don't know what I'm doing except dealing with the intra-physical forces." What he overlooked was the social dimension of the relationship. And what he overlooked in language was the social dimension. If you're my analyst and I tell you my dream, for example, why does it help me so much for you to see the meaning of the dream and to have me tell it to you?

Q: Well, maybe it helps because the patient can then see that he already knows what the dream means, but he didn't know that he knew it until the analyst confirmed it. So you need another person—contrary to what a Buddhist might think—to see what you know in your unconscious mind. Do you think there are any other dangers in psychoanalysis besides this uncompleted transference? What about the doctor not being able to control what is brought up from the patient's unconscious?

Percy: Sure, that's a real problem for them. I've talked to a number of them about that. I had two of them to lunch a while back and said to them, "Look, I'm writing a book about a psychiatrist who gets in trouble. What are the possibilities that a doctor would actually fall in love with a patient?" Well, it happens. After all, they're human. But that is the reason—human weakness getting in the way of science. If this happens, the patient ends up worse off than when he or she came into analysis. Of course, the doctor and patient are ethical people, none of this will come into the clinical setting except through talk. Otherwise, it's a violation, and just adds to the problems the patient came into the relationship with.

Q: Even if it's a good analysis, it sounds to me as though this is not a way to redemption for large numbers of people. The expense and the commitment of time seem to be obstacles for most people, don't you think?

Percy: Yes. And they've done studies comparing people who have been through analysis and people who haven't—large numbers of people, 5000, I think. Each group was more or less neurotic. The discouraging part of the study was that the analysis hadn't really helped the ones who had been through it. And you consider all that money—$50 to $90 an hour four times a week for a number of years!

Q: That's right. It is a lot of money. So this is not readily available to large numbers of people for any degree of healing.

Percy: No. I'm not sure I'd recommend it. But even so, over the years I've become more sympathetic to Freud because I think it is a truly humanistic discipline—he's trying to help people. On the level of triadic, individual talking to individual, you know? There's no gimmick with Freud, and no drugs to change the brain, and no electrodes. No drug like "soma" in *Brave New World* to make you feel good. Freud's analytical method is an honest, humanistic effort. Maybe it doesn't work very well, but it's a good try.

Q: I noticed recently that Carl Sagan wrote a short, authoritative article in a popular magazine on the nature of light, explaining for the public what the Impressionists knew a hundred years ago—what we see when we look at an object is not color or shape, but light. Painters paint light, not barns or seascapes or vases or flowers. The subject of the article was interesting, but what struck me more was the underlying message in his tone; the "voice" sounded like God speaking slowly and tenderly to his child-like people. And the photograph which accompanied the story had a political message, too. In the middle of smiling, racially-diverse children, there sat Carl Sagan—like Christ suffering the little children to come unto him. Roland Barthes describes the carefully chosen messages of news photos in *Music-Image-Text,* and we can infer from his argument that Carl Sagan wants to leave his reader with the subliminal notion of the scientist—himself, indeed—as God. You carry this idea a step further in *Lost in the Cosmos,* when you write: "While the scientific method may be neutral toward God, an attitude which extrapolates from the objectivity of the scientific method to an all-construing transcending objectivism cannot be neutral. There is no room in the Cosmos for an absolutely transcending mind and an absolutely transcending God. Two gods is one too many." Do scientists really regard themselves tantamount to gods, and if so, what are the implications of such a notion for genetic engineering and nuclear weaponry? Is Huxley's vision of ten, amoral, white-coated scientists ruling the world that far off the mark?

Percy: No, I don't think it is far off the mark. And the danger is not science: science is the most beautiful, the most elegant, the most satisfying discipline. As a matter of fact, science makes for more happiness as a career than just about anything else these days. I'm talking about real scientists, though—not technicians, which is what most "scientists" really are. I'm thinking of Barbara McClintock; do you know who she is?

Q: No. Tell me about her.

Percy: She got the Nobel Prize. She's an old lady in her upper '70's. She's been written up a lot. She's been working for forty years at a rather obscure laboratory in, I think, Woods Hole. Her experiments have been on Indian maize—studying the distribution of black kernels on an ear of corn—mutations. She has been trying to trace a genetic pattern, the mechanism by which the patterns of black kernels can be explained. She said that she had been working along happily for 40 or 50 years doing this. And she didn't seem to be awfully fascinated by all the attention she received as a result of the Nobel Prize. You see, she was a working scientist. "Scientism" is something else. Science becomes a religion in this case. The gentleman we were talking to this afternoon at lunch has extrapolated scientism from this lovely, elegant way of knowing. For him, instead of seeing science as one valid way of knowing, then, he elevates science to an omniscient way of approaching reality. He denies any serious reality to any other way of knowing. I think that's going to lead him into trouble. Scientism is dangerous.

Q: Well, he certainly had a fanatical gleam in his eye when he talked about "science."

Percy: Scientism is a kind of religion. Both scientism and religion have dogmas. The difference is that the former doesn't admit it.

Q: And that kind of scientism pervades technology and is perhaps the motivation behind its importance? In the technology of weapons design, for instance, is it the godly feeling of dispensation from death or punishment which leads men to build bigger and better bombs? Or is it a childish perversity which says "Now that I have this box of fireworks, I just have to set them off"? Exactly what keeps scientists from seeing the deadly paradox of creation breeding death in all these mega-weapons?

Percy: But a lot of scientists do see the paradox. I've just finished reading a book by Freeman Dyson called *Weapons and Hope*. Dyson was one of the physicists at Los Alamos with Oppenheimer. Dyson was talking about the very thing you mention. You remember earlier he made that famous statement that "Oppenheimer said we sinned when we made the Bomb, but the worst thing about it wasn't the sin but the fact that we enjoyed it so much." They were having a damn good time out there at Los Alamos. And it seemed like a legitimate program at the time, because we knew that the Germans were working on a bomb and for all we knew they were going to drop it on us first. It was a legitimate program to try and make the bomb. But it was such a perfect prototype of the position of the scientist in the modern world—it was quasi-religious. Here you have a small community of the best scientists—the best brains in the Western World: German, Scandinavian, American—in a small community removed from the rest of the country, under a kind of mystic like Oppenheimer and creating something in secret as they worked together. Now, you're talking about delusions of grandeur! All the while, they knew they were working on something with unbelievable powers of destruction. But then, you see, what happened was they had a lot of fun doing it. Dyson asked, "After the Germans quit and surrendered, why didn't we stop making the Bomb?" Well, the argument was that it would shorten the War, save thousands of American lives—but that wasn't the reason. We went on with the Bomb because we wanted to see that thing go off!

Q: That's the logical extension of Yankee ingenuity, isn't it? Benjamin Franklin writ large? The inventor as demon?

Percy: And you know, Oppenheimer used a strange Hindu reference in his writings: "I am Krishna, Destroyer of worlds." One form of Krishna is the Destroyer, pictured with six arms. Or you can talk about this in terms of Eros and Thanatos: there's a lot more Thanatos going on than Eros. That's the serious thing about it: you can understand the scientists having fun, wanting to go ahead and see if the damn thing'd work. But what really worries me is that I'm not sure but what this C2 consciousness—I talk about this in both my novels and non-fiction—doesn't love war.

Q: I remember, too, that you said that the day you saw your uncle (William Alexander Percy) happiest was Sunday afternoon, December 7, 1941. The prospect of war made him truly happy.

Percy: Of course, women have better sense than that. Do you remember Mary Chestnut's diaries? She writes about the day the Civil War broke out and says it was the happiest she had ever seen Virginians. People were beside themselves. Women know that's a lot of bull. Women don't buy that.

Q: That's probably true. I can think of a lot of things that would tempt my vanity or give me pleasure, but doing violence to anybody is certainly not one of them. Perhaps if I had to shoot the burglar to protect my own child . . . but even then, the violence is not tied to any abstraction like winning a war for God and Country.

Percy: Once the soldier gets into the trenches, too, he forgets all the abstractions that made him want to fight. But then it's too late. Of course, what we're into now is something which is getting out of control, and it's even worse. The technology has momentum of its own, and we're trying to make better weapons and they're trying to make better weapons, and there's all the misunderstanding of politics involved. There's every reason for pessimism in the world.

Q: So you think even more pessimism is justified than when *Publishers Weekly* asked you that question in a 1978 interview after *Lancelot* was published? Then you said you were "51% optimistic that the Bomb would not fall." With all the perversity you see in the human race, what do you think its chances for survival are now?

Percy: It's worse now. 49% Did you know that *one* U.S. Trident submarine has more power of destruction than there was unleashed in the entire Second World War?

Q: One? Only one? Is there any way out of this predicament?

Percy: Yes. In the novel I'm working on now, I talk about this problem. The anti-hero, Tom More, is an "impaired physician." He's done a very dumb thing. He has sold drugs to truckers, you see. So he's been out of it for two years, and like Dostoyevsky being let out of prison, when he comes back, he sees things he didn't see before. He becomes aware of this extraordinary situation that we're in. He's in a Sun-Belt place like this, you know; it could be any place in the South or Texas or California. And he sees people playing golf on their days off from working in a weapons factory, like Pantex in Amarillo. They're assembling weapons, and that type of weapon is unbelievable. Tom More is aware of the two big arguments, both of which make complete sense. On one side, Reagan calls the MX "The Peacekeeper" and argues that "We have to keep making these weapons to protect ourselves." On the other side, mostly argued by women, we hear "You all are crazy! It's never been known in the history of man that a weapon that was developed wasn't used. Sooner or later, you'll use that weapon because you want to and because you think you are bigger than they are, and you can beat 'em!" So Tom More is faced with what Kant would call an antinomy: two perfect arguments. Neither can be answered. The arguments don't engage at all—they go past each other.

Q: And what's more they're not just intellectually frustrating; the fate of the race depends on our working around the antinomy.

Percy: And also, people are not much interested in the problem. The Pentagon's interested, but people really aren't. The protestors are few among the public. Life goes on as usual, while this extraordinary, apocalyptic inferno is all around us. I seriously doubt that our children are going to live out their natural lives. The odds seem against it. People know this in one part of their minds, but in another part, they say, "I can't think about that."

Q: It's too big; you can't concentrate on it, the way it's hard to focus for very long on what happens to time when you travel the speed of light. You think about it for a few seconds. Then it's gone.

Percy: Yeah. Well, Tom More in my novel thinks about it. And he has good radar; he knows when something's wrong. He's nutty and gets in all kinds of trouble—he's an alcoholic and gets depressed. But he has great empathy for his patients, and he's picked up on the fact that something's wrong in his town. He sees that people are without their selves. There are a few people who are still themselves, but not many. He's trying to convince his fellow scientists in town that his discovery is right, and they think he's out of his mind himself. But the fact is, something is going on sure enough. There is a plot, a conspiracy, and up at Grand Gulf they're making atomic energy not from uranium but from heavy sodium. And people have lost their ability to see the real possibility of apocalypse.

Q: Let's turn to another national problem, which doesn't perhaps seem as serious by comparison with annihilation, but which still concerns many people: racism. Some ten years ago, you wrote in "Notes for a Novel About the End of the World," that ending racism was the greatest moral challenge facing America then. Do you still believe that? Have we accomplished anything since then?

Percy: I wish I could say that the churches—Catholic, Protestant, and Jewish—have had more than a little influence in affecting American opinion toward a toleration of blacks. You know, there has been tremendous progress since the 'Sixties but not because of the churches—because of the Constitutional system and recourse blacks have to the law. By gosh, it's not a small thing that there are thousands of elected black officials in the South now, where there were none when that article was written. And Jesse Jackson is third in electoral votes. That means something—that's a lot of black power. Of course, he's not going to get elected, but there's a lot of black pride involved there. There are now lots of blacks registered to vote, too. So I would like to claim more credit for the churches' leadership in ending racism and bigotry, but I don't see much difference there than in the Sixties. The South and the rest of the country are still racist. But in spite of some outbreaks of violence—in Boston, in the South, all over—most people in this country have respect for the law. They follow the law most of the time. And you know for whites there was a lot of *élan* for being part of the civil rights movement—the company, the marching—and it was mixed up with being part of the counter-culture and being anti-war and pro-environment. Those people are middle-aged now, making good money, and other people haven't taken their place.

Q: Flannery O'Connor wrote in one of her letters that "The unedu-cated Southern Negro is not the clown he is made out to be. He's a man of very elaborate manners and great formality which he uses superbly for his own protection and to insure his own privacy." To critics who may see some paternalism in O'Connor's remarks, Sally Fitzgerald, O'Connor's editor, writes, "There is a great deal of respect in this characterization but, sentimental about no one else, she was equally unsentimental about blacks as individuals." Could you comment on the need for unsentimentality in race relations as an antidote to condescen-sion or what used to be called paternalism?

Percy: A character in one of my books—Will Barrett in *The Last Gentleman*—was unsentimental in that way. I agree that it's important. When Will came back home, he was looking at this family and the servants in the house, you know, and he thought things like, "I must be the only white man in the South who doesn't think he knows everything there is to know about the Negro." Will, who was also nutty but had a good eye and sharp radar, watched the blacks. And the blacks knew it, too. He would hang around the kitchen more than he did with white folks. He was very much aware of the extraordinary social skills of blacks and the way they behaved—the way they were watching him watching them. They were afraid of Will because he was the only white man who was actually seeing them. They thought he was spooky. For a white man, he was. They could con any other white man, you see, but not Will, so that made him different. That's how they protected themselves, by being able to make whites believe any old thing. But Will's radar let him know what both sides were doing.

Q: Jay Tolson, in the spring '84 issue of the *Wilson Quarterly,* has written an essay-review of *The Percys of Mississippi.* Tolson brings up again the old argument about whether or not you are really a Southern writer. Here's his side of it: " . . . [D]espite his denials of being a 'typical' Southern writer, Percy delves brilliantly into the subject of the hold of the past on the individual. One's own history, for better and for worse, constitutes a large part of one's individuality. A person who cannot come to terms with what he came from will never amount to much, at least not in Percy's fictional worlds." It's undeniable that one must come to terms with his past, but what about being a "Southern" novelist by dint of that reconciliation? Are you or aren't you?

Percy: Of course I'm a Southern novelist; I couldn't be anything else. But the reason I protest the term is that it categorizes you the way other novelists are not categorized. You don't think of Saul Bellow as a Chicago novelist, do you? You don't think of John Cheever as a New England novelist. But when you say "Southern novelist," it puts you into a certain category in the American mind—magnolias, gothic horrors, or bizarre folks like Flannery O'Connor's, and it's hard for a writer to break out of that mold. That's why I object to the phrase. "Southern novelist" is a different phrase from "Northern novelist." "Northern novelist" doesn't mean much of anything, actually.

Q: So you see yourself, then, as a novelist who is a Southerner writing about life in America but using the South as a setting?

Percy: Yeah. In the first place, it's bad for business. Once you get known as a "Southern novelist," you have a hell of a time selling books! When was the last best-seller that was a Southern novel?

Q: "Southern novelist" is a terrible stigma, then?

Percy: It's a cultural strait-jacket. Even booksellers and publishers of Southern writers are guilty of saying, "Why, this boy's almost as good as Faulkner. Let's encourage him." It's like being a Southern boy in

New York—you can never break loose from it. Actually things are already better. If I meet somebody who has happened to have read my novels, they don't now say they like them—or dislike them—because they're "Southern." But I still get compared unfavorably with my Uncle Will, who had the "real" Southern point of view—mostly, fortunately, by old blue-haired ladies.

Difficult Times

Jan Nordby Gretlund/1985

Unpublished, 29 January 1985. Reprinted with the gracious permission of Jan Nordby Gretlund.

This interview was conducted with Walker Percy in his home in Covington, Louisiana. Also present was Ann Ebrecht, the literary critic, who went to school with one of Percy's daughters.

Gretlund: Why did you start your university education at Chapel Hill?

Percy: That was my uncle's idea [William Alexander Percy], he chose Chapel Hill for me. He wanted me to attend a school of the solid Anglo-Saxon yeomanry, and his beloved Sewanee did not qualify, it seems. He also thought Chapel Hill was still small enough to have a relationship—as a school—with the community there. This was in the mid-30s.

Gretlund: Why did you choose to study medicine?

Percy: Everybody in my family had been lawyers, it was a tradition in the family to be going into law. And I knew damn well I didn't want to do that. I had no use for it at all.

Traditionally, the only professions left were law, medicine, the military, and the priesthood. It was that way for a long time. I ruled out three immediately, so that left medicine. No, I guess it was more than that. I was interested in science, I was good in science in high school, and I liked biology and pre-med. I liked the science of medicine.

Gretlund: And there was no doubt in your mind that it was medicine you wanted to study?

Percy: No, there probably wasn't, because I immediately went into pre-med when I got to Chapel Hill. I already knew before I came. In a way it was a mistake—I say "in a way"—who knows?

In those days you took as many courses as you could in science, thinking that was going to help you when you went to medical school. So I took up a major in chemistry, a minor in physics, and I think I took

maybe three courses in English. I took *one* English elective! I took
freshman English, which everybody had to take, and one course in
Shakespeare by a very good teacher at Chapel Hill named Taylor. That
was all the English I had. I also took a minor in German.

Gretlund: Did you learn enough German to speak the language?

Percy: No, no you didn't learn language like that. You learned to
conjugate and decline. I learned enough so that I could read German.
I remember reading Thomas Mann's *Buddenbrooks*. And I remember
taking a trip to Germany with my German professor after my freshman
year, in 1934. We stayed with a family, at a friend of our German
professor at Chapel Hill, they lived in Bonn. The father was in the
S.A. and the son in the *Hitlerjugend*. That was in the early period of
Nazism. What I was thinking of was the spirit of the *Hitlerjugend* at
the time, which hád not got into anti-Semitism and was full of brilliant
German nationalism. We saw the good part of it, we didn't see the bad
part of it.

Gretlund: In your novels we can read that our desperate trouble did
not stop with the Nazis. A lot is still hopelessly wrong with the world.
But you write and publish, which implies a hope that the world will be
affected by your jeremiads.

Percy: After all, Jeremiah was not in despair, even though a jeremiad
is supposed to be a desperate evocation of doom and gloom. But if he
had been in despair, he would not have bothered. I mean, despair *is* loss
of hope, and he was saying all this in order to say: "Look, you have to
turn to the Lord, to save yourselves from the mess you're in!" What else
can you do?

Gretlund: Couldn't you voice your warnings in short stories, rather
than in long novels?

Percy: Never, never. Never would it cross my mind to write a short
story!

Gretlund: Wouldn't it be a challenge to write a good short story?

Percy: No, not at all. People don't read short stories. And you're too
limited. It is like writing a sonnet, you have to figure out how everything works. In a novel you are free. I fall free in a novel, so I can
follow where it goes.

Gretlund: With the possible exception of *The Second Coming,* your
novels are pessimistic about our future.

Percy: I like to write about people who live in the shadow of
catastrophe, people who are living in the eye of the hurricane. And

when you think of it, when you take things seriously, if you are a writer
and feel some obligation to write about the situation you are in, you
can't help but compare your situation now with that before WW II, and
even right after. The world was a fairly safe place, even if the Germans
had killed millions of people, even if the Russians had killed millions. It
wasn't so bad, things were going to look better. Surely, this was the end
of the last war of all. We didn't have the capacity to destroy ourselves.

Now the situation is so incredibly bad you can't even think about it!
Nobody can think about it! Which is an interesting situation to be in. It
is the first time in the history of the world that we are actually sitting
here with the power to destroy ourselves, with two fingers on the
trigger, depending on whether some jerk in Moscow or Washington is
going to do it. And nobody can think about it.

The mystery to me is that you are sitting over there in Europe acting
cheerful. You have the SS 20s trained right on you, and you got the
American Pershings sitting in your back-yard. And everything is great?
But it may be the reason why people in Europe know how to appreciate
life more than the people of South Dakota. The people of South Dakota
are all depressed. They are not about to be killed by anybody.

Gretlund: Although it is a rejection, your 1956 essay on Southern
Stoicism has a positive tone. Is Stoicism of any help to us in the present
situation?

Percy: It *is* very positive. What I was trying to say was that Stoicism
is the main Southern ethos, which is not ordinarily recognized in a
certain class. According to Flannery O'Connor it is Protestant Christianity which is the main spiritual source, fundamental Christianity, which
mainly informs the South. She is right about that, about what *she* saw
among the South Georgia people. But I was talking about the planter
class, my uncle, his friends, and his ancestors, and the way they were
brought up.

In the South before the Civil War, and even after it, there were little
private academies all over, with professors of Greek. Everybody took
Greek and Latin. And they called their cities Corinth, Ithaca, and
Demopolis. All well educated young Southern gentlemen knew their
Cicero and their Horace, their Virgil, and their Seneca, as well as their
Marcus Aurelius.

Gretlund: Were you saying in your essay that there is something
wrong with the Southern tradition of Stoicism?

Percy: No. I was just trying to bring out the fact that everybody knows all about Fundamentalist Christianity informing the South, and that people don't usually know how strong the Greco-Roman Stoic tradition was among the educated classes.

Gretlund: Why do you reject Southern Stoicism in your novels?

Percy: I don't! I don't!

Gretlund: *"I dont. I dont! I dont hate it! I dont hate it!"*

Percy: That was Quentin Compson. I didn't say that. No, it is altogether admirable—when I think of my two brothers, who are admirable fellows. They do great community work in the tradition of our uncle. How can I argue with that tradition.—Ann [Ebrecht] talked about the different cultural aspects of Catholicism, and I guess my main cultural character would be the idea of the good English Christian knight: Sir Thomas More, who is a righteous man, a good man, who'll fight. He is a warrior. And the Knights of the Round Table, e.g. Lancelot, I always liked him because he got into so much trouble. He was an adulterer, a violent man, and yet he was one of the two knights who saw the Grail! I always thought that was a strange part of the legend. I don't see Christianity and Stoicism as antithetical.

Gretlund: So you don't have to reject Stoicism to be a good Catholic.

Percy: No!

Gretlund: You said once in an interview that "the infinite mystery is also an infinite delight." How can a mystery be a delight?

Percy: I don't know what that means! What is "an infinite mystery"?

Gretlund: God, His ways, your Faith!

Percy: So it bothers you that the solution to the search turns out to be a mystery? All right, Faith consists of two or three mysteries: the Incarnation is a mystery, the Trinity is a mystery, and the real Presence in the Eucharist is a mystery. But that is the end of the search, that is the end of the quest, you don't go beyond that. Either you believe that, or you don't.

Gretlund: Is the novel you are working on [*The Thanatos Syndrome*] an expression of your Faith?

Percy: Yes. It is set a little further along than *Love in the Ruins*. I'm about half way through. I'm having a tough time with it, but I've been working on it pretty well. It is not as optimistic as *The Second Coming*. I got a letter yesterday from a girl in Griffin, Georgia. She's a reporter on a local paper, twenty-three years old, she said she liked all of my

novels, and she really wrote knowledgeably about the connection
between Kiekegaard's philosophy and the actual situations in the novels.
She understood it perfectly, but she couldn't understand *why* it was
necessary at the end of my novels a man had to fall in love and get
married: boy meets girl, and sure enough boy falls in love and marries
girl. She said, "Is that necessary? Do you have to get married?" I hadn't
thought about it, I guess they did mostly get married. It seems that the
nearest approximation, humanly speaking, of happiness is human love.
You would like for your characters to get out of the fix they are in and
achieve some kind of happiness. The best way to do it, the easiest way
to do it, is to fall in love. A man falls in love with a woman or vice
versa. If both happen at the same time that's pretty good. But Tom
More is not doing too well in his marriage right now. His wife is not
very happy with him. They have fallen on difficult times.

A Novelist Views the Novel

John R. Kemp/1985

From *Mississippi: A View of the Magnolia State*, 3 (May-June 1985), 95, 97, 101–102. Reprinted by permission of *Mississippi Magazine* and John R. Kemp.

Walker Percy, novelist and Socrates with a Southern accent, is hailed by Mississippians as one of their preeminent writers. The former Greenville resident periodically ventures forth from his wooded and secluded homesite in Covington, Louisiana, to reflect upon morality, the theological and metaphysical meanings of mankind, the current state of world events, or Johnny Carson's latest guest star. Not even Percy's chosen medium—the novel—is safe from his biting critique.

Most novels on the market today are shallow and lack spiritual substance, Percy says, a strong statement considering the blockbuster success of many recent novels.

But according to Percy, America is in the throes of a declining literacy accompanied by a rise in "philistinism" that is preoccupied with the "skillfully marketed packaged product for the consumption of the mass man"—the top ten television shows, NFL broadcasts, and a few big commercial novels.

"The fact is that novels these days, even so-called literary novels, are not very good," Percy says. "In fact, with one or two exceptions, they are terrible."

American novelists, even those with established reputations, "once full of energy and the good vinegar of protest of the 1960s," are now repeating themselves or writing about the private reveries of Marilyn Monroe and Grand Ole Opry stars, he says.

Percy sees an envying of Alexander Solzhenitsyn's sufferings buried deep in the American novelist's soul. "There, imprisoned in the Gulag, is the indomitable novelist writing his novel in secret and on toilet paper and here is the American novelist, free, uncensored, with word processor and plenty of paper, and stuck on dead center, stalled out, paralyzed by freedom."

The American protest novelist takes on the establishment, attacks middle-class values, and nobody cares. There is no knock on the door by the FBI. He watches presidential news conferences waiting to be denounced, but nobody denounces him. In fact, Percy claims, nobody pays much attention to him. The novelist then suffers the greatest of all indignities: his book becomes a commercial success, Hollywood buys it, and the poor protest writer becomes a rich protest writer.

"He is like the wretched man in Dostoyevsky's *Notes from Underground* who swore to get even with his enemy by walking directly toward him on the sidewalk and forcing him to yield and who at the last second yields himself, without the other even noticing."

Percy contends that American novelists are taken seriously only when they write about the human condition. "It is both the curse and blessing of American novelists that no one has taken them seriously since Harriet Beecher Stowe."

It is a curse, he says, because the American writer feels he occupies a marginal place in society. He seems irrelevant to the main concerns of society. It also is a blessing because the American novelist, "dispensed against his will from effective ideological partisanship, has to come across on a bigger scale, in spite of his ideology."

If the novel on a national level is in poor shape, Percy says the Southern novel, once endowed with a sense of time, place, and history, is in worse shape.

Young fiction writers, with a few exceptions, are in a state of creative emptiness. According to Percy, the great "Southern Literary Renascence" is over and the "Great Southern Literary Depression" has set in.

"There are any number of literary conferences held each year which celebrate the Southern Literary Renascence," Percy says. These reflect upon works of such Southern writers as William Faulkner, Robert Penn Warren, Eudora Welty, and Flannery O'Connor. "But what nobody likes to talk about is the fact there are few, if any, writers under forty who could be called renascent." While concluding that young Southern writers have not had much to say lately, Percy makes two exceptions to this observation: Padgett Powell's *Edisto* and James Wilcox's *Southern Baptist*. "They are two young Southern novelists of great potentiality."

Percy may sound like the late caustic wit and critic H.L. Mencken who once characterized the South as "the Sahara of the Bozart"—a vast wasteland devoid of cultural significance. Perhaps the South today is not

Mencken's scorched wasteland, but as Percy sees it, the oasis of
Southern letters is growing more and more arid.

Percy labels the new Southern type of novel as the Tennessee-Texas
school of the "picaresque adventures of country-music types, . . . good
ol' boys whose profoundest thoughts were about bad crops and bad
preachers—a far cry from the Nashville poets of the 1920s." Their
literary quality, he says, falls just short of *Smokey and the Bandit*. The
new Southern cultural heroes include such media-made stars as Burt
Reynolds, Kenny Rogers, and Hershel Walker. When the late Bear
Bryant won his 315th football game, Southern senators sponsored a vote
of acclamation, Percy notes, adding that he does not recall a similar
vote when William Faulkner won the Nobel Prize or Eudora Welty won
the Gold Medal for American literature.

Southern women novelists do not escape Percy's criticism. He says
they are moving into a new genre. While their Northern sisters write
feminists' accounts of the alienation of Teaneck housewives or
depression and suicide among Radcliffe grads, an increasing number of
Southern women novelists are writing what Percy calls "the Southern
belle confessional novels or *What Really Went on at Sweet Briar?*"

He also sees a reversal of social roles taking place among female
novelists in the South. Women writers in the past, like George Eliot and
George Sand, were known for their unconventional sexual behavior "but
nevertheless wrote the standard fictive prose acceptable to polite
society." Female Southern writers today, Percy says, "talk nice and
write dirty."

Percy also questions why Southern writers, like Catholic writers,
don't fare better in the book-buying marketplace. He said that it could
be that many Americans simply don't like Southerners or Catholics. But
these same Americans presumably don't like Jews either, he continues.
However, Jewish novelists such as Saul Bellow, Bernard Malamud, and
Philip Roth do well, and readers don't hold regionalism against John
Cheever or John Updike when they write about the Northeastern upper
middle class.

Americans' proclivity for labeling has much to do with the problem,
Percy says. Books labeled Southern or Catholic or Southern Catholic
convey "exotic and recognizable properties" that give book-buyers the
impression they already know what the books are about before they read
them.

But Southerners themselves are not totally blameless for these precon-
ceptions. Southern writers can easily fall to the temptation and past successes of "playing the old game of amazing and tantalizing Yankees."
Percy suspects even Faulkner of consciously "writing Southern" because
it was expected of him—"in much the same way that a Southerner
might find himself talking more Southern on Fifth Avenue than we
would dream of talking on Peachtree Street."

The so-called Southern novel also became a victim of its own
success. Southern writers are in a quandary about what to do now that
the old defeated and exotic South has become a victorious and prosperous Sunbelt. How can a Southern writer recapture his rural roots as
he sits in a high-rise in Houston or Atlanta? Chances are he has never
seen a sharecropper's cabin or a cracker except when he was driving
through Georgia on his way to Fort Lauderdale.

Percy's search for meanings to the great mysteries of life comes
through clearly in his own writings. In his first novel, *The Moviegoer*
(1961), for which he won the National Book Award that same year,
young Binx Bolling, enveloped by the aristocratic attitudes of his Old
South family, searched for his own identity. In *Love in the Ruins* (1971),
a satirical comment on the social upheaval of the 1960s, Percy described
the disintegration of American society with tribal battles between races,
cultures, and countercultures. In *The Second Coming* (1980), Will
Barrett is involved in an almost self-destroying search for theological
answers, which he eventually finds.

Percy's self-described Judeo-Christian quest for meanings may have
its roots in his personal life. Orphaned at an early age, Percy and his
two brothers went to live with a cousin, "Uncle Will" Percy (William
Alexander Percy), a planter and poet in the Mississippi Delta town of
Greenville. Percy went on to study at the University of North Carolina
at Chapel Hill and then went into medicine at Columbia University.
While interning, he contracted tuberculosis. During his recovery, he
read a book by the existentialist Gabriel Marcel which apparently had a
profound impact on his life.

His most recent work, characteristically entitled *Lost in the Cosmos*
and subtitled "The Last Great Self-Help Book," is an answer of sorts to
Carl Sagan's best-seller, *Cosmos*.

Percy sees a common strain between the Southern novel of a generation ago and the Jewish novel "which, though apparently past its prime,

is the liveliest of current American literary phenomena." They both deal with the tragedy and comedy of people embarked on a pilgrimage for good and ill.

However, the Jewish experience in the South has not found a voice among fiction writers, he says. "The Southern WASP, Catholic, and humanist traditions have found voices. The Southern woman novelist is, of course, preeminent. There are distinguished black voices. But the Southern Jewish voice, with few exceptions, is yet to be heard."

The next Southern literary revival, Percy predicts, will be led by a Jewish mother: "a shrewd self-possessed woman with a sharp eye and a cunning retentive mind who sees the small follies and triumphs and tragedies around her."

Percy says Southern writers are still heir to a unique literary legacy. They can see the American scene from the inside and outside. The Sunbelt Southerner is more American than ever, yet "he is still Southern whether he likes it or not, which is to say he can still see the American proposition from a tragic historical perspective." The Southerner knows to the marrow of his bones that things "can come to grief and probably will." And, Percy adds, "He is also more likely to know that man is tragically flawed and is born to trouble as the sparks fly up."

Percy claims that the Southern writer has a natural mission to probe, challenge, attack, and satirize. "Satire attacks one thing in order to affirm another," he says. "It assaults the fake and the phony in the name of truth. It ridicules the inhuman in order to affirm the human. Satire is always launched in the mode of hope."

But Percy refuses to knell the doom of Southern letters. "Writers turn up in the unlikeliest places," he said, calling to mind the "outrageous, funny, yet eminently serious" writings of Pulitzer Prize winners Beth Henley of Mississippi, author of *Crimes of the Heart,* and the late John Kennedy Toole of New Orleans, author of *A Confederacy of Dunces.*

Percy still holds a finger-crossing optimism about the future of the Southern novel. "The possibilities of the Southern novel are unlimited," he says, "unlimited both in its ability to recreate the South and to shape American literature."

Walker Percy on the Church, Abortion, Faith, and Nuclear War

Charlotte Hays/1986

From *National Catholic Register,* 62 (January 1986), 1, 7, 9. Reprinted by permission of the editor at *National Catholic Register.*

On the State of the Church, 5 January 1986

Register: A number of Catholic writers, including yourself, seem to believe that we are, or soon will be, living in a post-Christian age. Yet Catholics must believe that the Church will endure through all time. How do you square the two beliefs?

Percy: By "Christian," in that context, obviously I was talking about Christendom, or a culture informed by Christianity. I think that it would be fair to say that the Western world has been Christian, in the sense of Christendom, from the fifth to the 19th or early 20th century. I'm talking about what Kierkegaard called Christendom. There is a distinction between Christendom, which after all is a cultural artifact informed in a way by Christianity, and Christianity or the Catholic Church. You can have multifarious forms of Christendom, some of them bad and some of them good. I can conceive of a period before Christendom, the beginnings of the Church before Constantine when the Church became established and actually informed the Roman Empire and Europe as European Christendom. I can as easily envision an end to Christendom, which, of course, is now.

But I meant by post-Christian, to answer your question, a time when there is really no Christian consensus as there was even in the 19th century. In this century we call it pluralism. Maybe in the 19th century you could speak of America being Christian. I'm not too sure you could call it Christian now. Maybe the majority of the people are, nominally. But clearly there has occurred a decline and fading of belief. I do not presume to call such a historical change bad or good.

Register: What do you see happening to the Catholic Church in this post-Christian future?

113

Percy: That's a big question. Well, it's having a hard time. "She," I should say, right? Clearly not "he." From one extreme it looks as if the Church is coming apart at the seams with the rise of all sorts of dissent and heterodoxy and radical feminism and so on. Of course, if one is Catholic, one believes that the Church will prevail. That's part of Catholic belief. But we are obviously in a time of serious troubles.

Register: Are we really in a period of serious trouble for the Church, or does it just seem that way to *us* because we live in this period? After all, the Church has survived times of trouble for 2,000 years.

Percy: I'm not an expert on these matters, certainly not a student of Church history. I'm just thinking of my own first-hand experience, comparing the Church 35 years ago during and after World War II with the Church now. And it's not all bad. Vatican II was a valuable event. But there were disturbing consequences. As you say, the Church has been in trouble for 2,000 years. I'm not as worried as some people. Now and then I read the Catholic press. It seems even more confused than the secular media. Is that bad? Not necessarily. This is a pilgrim Church. We are not very smart.

I live in a backwater of Louisiana. I'm sure there's a vocal minority that is anti-papal, anti-Magisterium, or opposed to this or that belief or this or that doctrine. I remember first moving to New Orleans some 35 years ago. A common sight was seeing nuns all over the place. The other day my grandson was reading a school book about nuns and he said, "What's a nun?" I showed him a picture of a nun in an old book. The comfortable Church of the mid-century is no longer with us. Maybe, in a way, it's just as well.

Register: Why do you think that it's now no longer an attractive thing to be a nun?

Percy: I didn't say it wasn't. But maybe the question should be turned around. I was always amazed that anyone would have the courage to do it in the first place. After all, it is an extraordinary sacrifice to ask of someone. All one gives is one's life. As a non-Catholic, I was floored by nuns and priests. Were they crazy?

I can remember after World War II there was a tremendous increase in vocations. I remember a Trappist monastery, where I met Thomas Merton. It was setting up branches like Big Macs all over the place. The seminaries were bulging at the seams. Maybe wartime is a time of coming up against the reality of death and trial and crisis and that had

something to do with it. But, of course, the answers to the question are
both familiar and mysterious. The answers surely have to do with 30
years of peace, affluence, 30 years of rising prosperity and 30 years of
consumerism. Who wants to give up all the good things of American
life? Not me. As I say, I'm astonished when people go into religious
life. The hero in my book is the parish priest.

Register: But what do you think happened to religious life? Some
nuns have made such a complete turnaround and become angry and
bitter about religious life. Could it be simply that the women's orders
were asked to re-evaluate the charism of their communities at a time
when radical feminism was ascendant and they were affected by it?

Percy: I don't know. Something extraordinary did happen. Again,
one hates to make broad statements about what happened to women
Religious—and men too, of course—because it didn't happen to all.
I'm not even sure it happened to the majority. Maybe it's a very vocal
minority.

What happened? Well, again I think maybe it was an over-reaction.
Maybe—dare I suggest it?—it was a lack of maturity in American
women, American Catholic women. I am thinking of the stereotypical
American nun of 40 years ago. I remember the nuns in Greenville,
Miss. They were right out of Central Casting. They were the nuns with
the downcast eyes and great humility and "Father says." They were almost caricatures of the virtues of humility, submission, and obedience.

Now, 30 or 40 years later, it's almost as if everything is turned upside
down. Now you have the same nuns—some of whom I know—and
they've turned into radical feminists who even put secular feminists to
shame. From the Flying Nun to Bella Abzug in one generation. We
have more than our share of viragos and barracudas.

This will irritate no end of people, but it occurs to me that it might be
a question of maturity. I will be happy when the American Catholic
Church grows up. After all, we're still only two generations past an
immigrant Church. We're just a few years past Mother Cabrini and the
Italians, the Irish, and Germans and so on. And, without denigrating the
virtues of feminism, which I certainly defend as a proper cause, we're
seeing radical, even bizarre, manifestations of it.

When I think of the great saints of the Church and the best women
now, in and out of the Church, I think of women who are sufficiently
mature and certain of their own identities that they don't feel obliged to

go in for radical feminism. The great women of the Church didn't worry about competing with men. They probably knew they were superior.

It may be that some of the women who are most vocal—whom I won't name—some of the signers of the notorious advertisement in the New York Times and the Sister who shook her finger at the Holy Father—I sometimes wonder if there aren't more psychological than theological reasons for their protest. It seems obvious to me that they are sexists, but not in the way *they* mean sexist. What I mean is the dislike of men. The way they talk about the Holy Father is nothing less than termagant hatred. I can see that nun shaking her finger at John Paul II. Poor fellow. It's more than doctrine and politics.

It's almost saying, "Only if I stand up against you and tell you off am I a woman in my own right."

Take another nun, Mother Teresa. I don't think that it's even crossed her mind that she is being persecuted by a male, monarchical Church or the Holy Father. She has better things to do.

It's a question of maturity, of being more concerned with service, love of God, love of your fellow man, love of the wretched of the earth.

Register: Is this turnaround among Religious simply because some were caricatures of virtues like submission and obedience and now all these pent-up things are coming out?

Percy: Well, what else? Of course, some people will blame Vatican II. But I don't think there's anything wrong with Vatican II. I'm not a student of Vatican II, but at the same time I don't remember reading in any of the institutes or publications anything I disagreed with. I do remember the openness of John XXIII, his ideas, what he wanted to achieve for the Church, what he *did* achieve. That was all to the good. People often forget that John emphasized all through the council that these things are necessary for the life and health of the Church. But don't forget that he insisted on preserving "the sacred deposit of faith," as he called it.

I know many old-style Catholics who were scandalized by the Church's giving up Latin. I know Catholics who think that all the trouble started when Latin was dropped. But that's not part of the sacred deposit of the faith. Some very intellectual, high falutin' Catholics talk about the trivialization of the liturgy. Well, that's probably true too. You hear about people like Auberon Waugh [Evelyn Waugh's son] who was so disgusted by the vulgarization of the liturgy following Vatican II that he left the Catholic Church for the Anglican Church. Then he came back because the Anglican liturgy was even worse.

Beautiful liturgy is all very well. We have a Benedictine abbey here that's very high on liturgy, and that's wonderful. I'm all for it. I love to go out and hear plainsong at Vespers. But that's not integral to the unity and integrity of the faith.

Register: Why have so many people gotten hung up on all of that sort of thing?

Percy: Well, I think it's a question of polarization. On one side, you have radical feminists and nutty, heterodox priests who, I sometimes think, want to chuck the whole thing, people like Fathers Schillebeeckx and Kung, who I'm not sure are Christians, from what I read by them. They are questioning not only practice but doctrine. And on the other extreme are the right-wingers—one sees quite a few down here—who think you have to cling to every accidental of the faith as it was 50 years ago.

Surely it's a sign of insecurity when people are scandalized just because Latin is dropped and women distribute communion and a choir plays guitars.

Register: Is it a question of a lack of faith?

Percy: I don't know. But I was just about to say that one hears these bad things about the Church falling apart, and they are all probably true, but one goes to Mass here or in New Orleans and there are seven Masses a day and the people are still there. They aren't the ones you read about in the Catholic journals—in *Commonweal* and *America*. They are just ordinary, Catholic people and they are still there.

Register: Some of my conservative friends contend that the followers of Archbishop Marcel Lefebvre somehow aren't as bad as the dissenters on the left. But isn't it a case of six of one, half a dozen of the other?

Percy: I can see what they mean in that at least the Lefebvrites aren't throwing out doctrine, aren't questioning the sacred deposit of faith. But they are questioning someting extremely important, namely the Magisterium. So maybe it *is* six of one, half a dozen of the other. I don't know many Lefebvrites. You don't read much about them because, with a few exceptions, the national Catholic press is pretty far to the left.

Register: But would you agree that the Lefebvrites are just as bad as the left-wingers who want to throw things out?

Percy: Maybe not quite as bad when you consider heterodox priests and heretical theologians—is there such a thing as heresy anymore? I'm not sure what, if any, doctrines [Church] liberals would retain, except apparently a vague congregationalist idea of the people of God, which seems to be a sort of low-grade Unitarianism.

Register: What do you think of the Religious who signed the pro-choice advertisement that appeared in the *New York Times* in 1984?

Percy: I think they are wrong. They say they want to dialogue. They want to dialogue about abortion. There's nothing to dialogue about. You don't dialogue with murder.

Register: Who are some of the theologians you like?

Percy: I'm not much of a theologian. I'm a novelist, a pretty low-grade profession. I guess I'm pretty old-fashioned. The last theologian I read was John of St. Thomas, who was a 17th century commentator on Aquinas. He's just been translated in a wonderful new book by the University of California Press. He's been revived as an early founder of the very popular discipline of semiotics.

Recent theologians who've meant the most to me are Maritain, Guardini and some of Rahner. But I'm not really competent in theology.

Register: In your novel *Love in the Ruins,* a schismatic group of Catholics celebrate something called Property Rights Sunday. Can you tell us what you had in mind with this holiday?

Percy: That was written during the time of the troubles here: the civil rights movement and the right-wing reaction. There was a lot of polarization in the community between segregationists and a few liberals, and between blacks and whites. The Church was similarly divided between Catholic liberals and Catholic conservatives, who somehow felt that segregation was part of orthodoxy. The hierarchy was in favor of civil rights.

What I did was to imagine a future when the Church had split. There was a tri-partite schism. On the left there were Dutch Catholics—even then the Dutch were the most heterodox—who were being led by some married and divorced priests and nuns who were petitioning for the right to remarry. It was a caricature of the Dutch Church then, not now. Now it doesn't seem to be a caricature.

That was one schism. Another was the Cicero Catholics. I think that I picked that name because there were racist, anti-black, anti-Jewish demonstrations in Cicero, Ill. Very conservative, local ethnic Catholics

were protesting against any kind of move to integrate their neighborhoods and churches.

The Cicero Catholics had split to the right, so they were the ones who
celebrated Property Rights Sunday. In other words the sacredness of
private property as opposed to the "communist" trends of the federal
government. They sang the national anthem at the elevation of the host
during Mass. It was a patriotic Mass.

There remained a saving remnant of old Roman Catholics.

Register: Do you think there's going to be a schism in the Church?

Percy: It may well happen. I was joking 10 years ago when I wrote
that book, but I think it may well happen. Already there's a fashionable
trend of Pope-bashing and Rome-hating by comfortable professor-
theologians who make a very good living going around, giving lectures
and reviling the Church.

Register: It seems that some Catholics are flirting with Rev. Jerry
Falwell and other fundamentalists. What do you think of this?

Percy: Well, as a Jesuit friend of mine said, it's very easy to make
fun of Jerry Falwell and some of the fundamentalist preachers, but with
that many followers, they must be doing something right. I'm aware of
fundamentalists on the tube, and I'm amazed at the phenomenon. Down
here Jimmy Swaggart is the big attraction. It's easy to find fault. The
fact that money-raising takes up so much time, for example. There's a
question of good faith. When one hears "Send me money right away
because of the starving children in Ethiopia," one wonders how much of
the money actually goes there.

But what appeals to people is the emphasis, however sincere or
insincere, on traditional values. There is a commonality between fundamentalists and Catholics. After all, if Kung and Schillebeeckx don't
believe in the Resurrection and Falwell and Robertson do, where does
the commonality lie? What's regrettable are the excesses and the
money-grubbing.

On Abortion, Faith, and Nuclear War, 12 January 1986

Register: I sense from your writing that you might be becoming a bit
more politically conservative. Is this the case?

Percy: I voted for Reagan. I might not again. To be specific, I was
strong for John Kennedy and Harry Truman. But, when I consider

somebody like Walter Mondale or Ted Kennedy, neither one has had a new idea in 25 years. I don't think liberal Democrats have had a new idea since Roosevelt. The Democrats, and I'm one of them, seem to have become a mish-mash of minorities and pressure groups without any overriding political faith.

But I have not become more conservative about race, or the treatment of the disadvantaged, minorities or the Third World. So I don't find myself at home with the New Right. I find it difficult to categorize myself. I could even vote for [Gov. Mario] Cuomo if he were more intellectually honest.

Register: Did Geraldine Ferraro's stand on abortion affect your vote?

Percy: I thought she was a big pain. A real phony. She tried to have it both ways. I prefer an honest abortionist. And I strenuously object to the idea that, well, I'm personally opposed, but I will not do anything about it publicly or politically. That's like saying, "I'm against murder but I won't do anything to pass a law prosecuting murderers." Not that I think that Republicans are paragons of statesmanship. But 60 percent of the people voted for Reagan and they have pretty good instincts.

Register: What do you think of Cuomo? Is he the model of the next generation of Catholic politicians?

Percy: I think he's extremely gifted. But, here again, he waffled on abortion. Like Ferraro, he's got to have it both ways. But I must say he's the hope of the Democrats. He's very attractive. I'm interested in how he's going to turn out. He might even turn out to be honest.

Register: Is abortion a litmus test for our age, revealing how one feels about the ultimate sanctity of human life?

Percy: It is, with this reservation: I know a great many people who make it a litmus test—and I'm talking about political conservatives. (Strangely enough, you hear more talk about abortion from conservative fundamentalists than Catholics.) I have reservations, though, when people make that a litmus test but have absolutely no interest in preserving the sanctity of life in such areas as the prevention of war, capital punishment and helping women—the young, poor women—who get pregnant. I notice that a lot of people who are extremely opposed to abortion don't want to do anything to preserve life in other areas. I'm proud that the Catholic Church is on the side of life and not death—in all areas.

One of the things that runs through all of my novels is that we live in the century of death. If the 20th century is characterized by anything, it's death. More people have been killed by other people in this century than in all other centuries put together. In fact, my next novel is called *The Thanatos Syndrome.* So I'm very proud that the Church comes down on the side of life against death. I don't think you can be selective.

Yet abortion, on the present mass scale, is something new under the sun and something extremely unpleasant. You're killing innocent people. But I agree with Cardinal Joseph Bernardin, who speaks of "the seamless garment"—meaning you're prolife whenever life is threatened, not just in the case of abortion.

Register: Why do you think that the intellectual establishment of our era is so anti-Christian?

Percy: It's worse than that! They aren't interested. I think that everybody—intellectuals and scientists—have their own bailiwicks of power and influence and narrow specialized confines of knowledge. I am scandalized by the fact that in my own profession—medicine— American doctors have the dubious distinction of being the first generation of doctors in 6,000 years to accept abortion with hardly a murmur. Abortion has been something absolutely disallowed by the medical profession in the entire Western world since the oath of Hippocrates. We're talking 2,500 years ago. That's on the Greek side. For 6,000 years before that in the Jewish tradition. Yet we in the last two generations—judges and doctors—have not only made it legal but have done it willingly. There's been no outcry, not one letter of protest in the august *New England Journal of Medicine.* I can offhand think of only one doctor—a Jewish doctor—who keeps saying this is wrong.

Register: Do you think there will be a nuclear war?

Percy: Well, the logic of history is not encouraging. Man has never developed a weapon he has not used. If somebody had said 40 years ago, this is the way the world is going to be: two superpowers will have the ability to destroy not only each other but the world, nobody would have believed it. The reality is too horrible to think about. All it proves is that human beings can get used to anything. So we don't think about it. We're used to living on the brink. To answer your question, nobody really knows. I just feel dreadfully sorry for our children. And I wonder if they are going to live out their life spans.

Register: *The Tablet,* an English Catholic periodical, ran a contest recently in which people were asked to write an essay on the topic, can a novelist be a saint? Piers Paul Read, who posed the question, said no. What do you think?

Percy: That does sound like one of Piers Paul Read's questions. I don't know offhand of any novelists who are saints. I suppose theoretically it's not impossible for a novelist to be a saint. But usually the best things that happen in novels have to do with the exploration of this or that evil and the tension between good and evil. Whereas a saint presumably would be more interested in turning his back on evil. When I think of the rawest case, it would be St. Anthony in the desert being pursued by all manner of devils and demons. He did a good job of withstanding the temptations and getting rid of them. But I don't think he would have made a good novelist. I can only think of one Catholic novelist who might qualify.

Register: Who?

Percy: Flannery O'Connor. She was certainly heroic. Who knows about sanctity? When I consider what she did—that from the first time she published her first word, she knew that she was dying—I can only think in terms of heroism, if not sanctity. I certainly wouldn't do it. She had a writing lifespan of about 10 years, during which time she knew she had a fatal progressive disease. And yet she pursued her vocation with absolute fidelity.

Register: Is it hard to be a Catholic and a novelist?

Percy: I was at a literary gathering the other day to celebrate the founders of the *Southern Review*. And we were talking about Allen Tate and Caroline Gordon. And a couple of writers said to me, "You know, they both became Catholics and quit writing good books." The thesis being that you can be a good Catholic but it ruins you for writing. Well, of course, I don't agree. After all, Dante was a pretty good poet. Cervantes was not a bad novelist. Can you imagine Graham Greene as a Baptist or a comfortable humanist like Walter Cronkhite?

I guess I'd go back to Flannery O'Connor. She was a militant Catholic. She said, "Everything I do or write is informed by my belief." We talked about it. We said that being Catholic is an advantage. The conventional wisdom is that if you're Catholic you're in trouble as a creative writer because you're subject to constraints. You can't say such and such.

But critics overlook the essential thing. Christianity and the Catholic faith by definition are congenial to the vocation of a novelist, because the novel has to do with narration, and narration has to do with a person born to trouble as the sparks fly up. That sounds familiar, doesn't it? Christianity and the novel are both predicamental. A novel is always about somebody in trouble or incomplete or unfulfilled and their flawed journey through life. The whole thrust of Catholic belief is that man is *homo viator*. Man is real and man is in trouble. In theological terms, man is fallen. His life is a journey.

There aren't many good novels by Buddhists because—number one—they don't believe that life is "real" or that man is "fallen," or that God is to be sought. God is within and the world is not real. So why bother to write a bunch of adventures about an unreal world peopled by unreal beings? For me the Catholic faith is an asset to a novelist rather than a hindrance. As for the Church constraining a novelist these days, can one imagine such a thing?

Register: What do you think of Mary Gordon [author of *Final Payments*]?

Percy: I've only read one of her novels. She's a very good writer. My reservation is that she falls into a certain genre, what I call the Northeast Catholic novel, written by Catholics or ex-Catholics who can't find anything to write about except the miseries of their Catholic girlhood or Catholic boyhood, how rotten the priests were or how oppressive and stifling the nuns were. Well, that's OK. You can write about that for one or two novels. But you've got to go beyond that. Sometimes I think I was lucky not to have had a Catholic boyhood.

Register: How did you feel about the Extraordinary Synod in Rome? Are you optimistic?

Percy: Yes, I'm optimistic because I think it was necessary. The Church is in serious danger—serious temporal danger. And the danger is not so much from communism, not so much from [Poland's Wojciech] Jaruzelski or [Nicaragua's Daniel] Ortega—although that danger is clear and present. But the worst danger is within. The worst danger is from the heterodox, if not worse, theologians, politicized priests and deranged nuns who, being highly educated and well-read and having much influence in Western intellectual circles, are attacking the foundation of the Catholic faith. They on the one side and the radical feminists on the other: Between the two they're a formidable team of termites. I prefer communists and atheists—as long as they're outside, not inside, the Church.

Register: But what about the Soviet Union? Catholics used to pray for the conversion of Russia. Is it an "evil empire"?

Percy: Sure. In the obvious sense of being committed by Lenin to the idea that two societies, one Christian and one atheistic, can't co-exist. But condemnations of the Soviet Union are always tempered by the terrible corruption of the Western world. I can imagine the kings of Judah, just like Reagan hurling down imprecations on Babylon—the evil empire then—on Nebuchadnezzar, while at the same time a few prophets in the desert were talking about what is wrong with Judah, what is wrong with *us,* and how we might even deserve the assault of Nebuchadnezzar. If we lose to the Marxist-Leninists, it will be for the same reason Judah lost to the Babylonians—and it doesn't take a prophet to see that.

Register: What's wrong with the Christian West?

Percy: I don't feel like answering that, because the answer is familiar to everyone. Let's just say that it stinks, but it is not hopeless, whereas Marxism-Leninism not only stinks but is also hopeless. Anyhow, I'm only a novelist, not a prophet. I chronicle the world as I see it.

Register: What do you think of liberation theology?

Percy: I'm more afraid of liberation theologians like [Leonardo] Boff and radical feminists like [Rosemary] Reuther than I am of Nicaraguan revolutionaries.

Register: Why are you concerned about liberation theology?

Percy: It is a perversion of Christianity. They are saying that the only way to correct an evil—and God knows there are evils down there—the only way to correct it is by violence, violent revolution. And toward that end they justify not only killing but also joining Marxist-Leninist revolutions. Liberation theology is a perversion of Christianity masquerading as Christianity and therefore more seductive than a bloody fascist or Soviet communist coming at you.

Register: And yet so many intellectuals seem to be attracted to liberation theology.

Percy: I keep coming back to Mother Teresa. I wish she could be cloned about 10,000 times. That would be a solution to our problems. It's simple to say that the Gospel is about love, not hatred, and that the Gospel is about embracing, not killing. I'm a member of the Pope's party. I don't have any use for the criminal rich in Central America, who have been exploiting the Indians for 300 years. But I also don't believe in priests and nuns picking up guns and joining revolutions. They could be much more radical by doing what Mother Teresa does.

Register: What do you think of John Paul II?

Percy: I got a letter from a nun who's compiling a book. It was going to be a collection of articles from assorted people, and the question was what would you do if you were the Pope. She said she would give me 10,000 words. But I said, "Well, I can say what I'd do in a half page. I admire this Pope, and my ambition would be to be half as good as he is." And I said, "You're welcome to publish this as my contribution, no charge."

Register: Why do you like this Pope so much?

Percy: I like John Paul II because he's not Italian. That's one reason. I've nothing against the Italians but it was important for the universal Church to break out of the Italian mold. He's an intellectual, an athlete, a skier, and a phenomenologist. Most importantly, he's a whole man, a *mensch*. Who ever heard of a phenomenologist becoming Pope?

I just like everything about him. I am dismayed by the violence and antipathy toward him in some elements of the Western Church. What comes to mind is the rotten reception he received in Holland. The Pope stands for orthodoxy without oppression. Of course, the other side says he stands for oppression and a medieval papacy. But they, his enemies, stand for heterodoxy or worse. It grieves me to see the Church split this way.

Register: And what do you think about Cardinal Joseph Ratzinger?

Percy: I haven't read the famous interview yet. I've only read about him. But since he's being reviled by so many people whom I have no use for, I may send off to get the interview and see what he said. I like what he wants the synod to be—to rescue the Church not from Vatican II but from the excesses which followed Vatican II. Considering some of his enemies, I suspect he's probably on the right track

Register: One thing about the Catholic right that bothers a lot of people is the meanspiritedness of some of its members. What do you think about this?

Percy: The Lord never promised the Church that everybody was going to be a saint. He only issued the invitation. He didn't do too well with His own Twelve Apostles. One of them was a traitor. Peter himself was a turncoat. They were a pretty sorry lot, to tell you the truth. So I don't have to feel too bad about being mean and lazy.

Register: What about your own religious upbringing?

Percy: I was brought up by a good agnostic and scientist. I went to medical school with two Catholic students. They'd get up and go to Mass, and hang one of those garish Catholic calendars on the wall. That struck me as outrageous. I was offended by Catholicism. The offense is part of the clue, of course, part of the secret. I began to wonder, how dare any Church make this outrageous claim, that it's unique in time? I think that what offends is the singularity of it, the singularity of the Judeo-Christian claim. The first offense is Jewish. The Jewish claim is equally outrageous.

Register: Why did you become a Catholic?

Percy: That's a long story. I don't have the time to tell you. It had to do with being in science and thinking that science had the answers and then seeing that it did not. It's a gift from God, I'd as soon leave it at that. God has peculiar ways. I don't know why he chooses certain people to give the gift of faith to. I was the last person you'd have thought. I've always been a smart aleck and sarcastic. When I was in college I was known as an iconoclast. My whole bent is toward black humor and satire. Why I should be stuck with the Catholic faith I don't know. It is not convenient.

Register: You've said that the South isn't really a Christian society, and yet Flannery O'Connor has described it as intrinsically Christian. I think she might have used the term "Christ-haunted." Which is it—is the South Christian or secular?

Percy: It consists of two opposing strains. One is a Protestant, fundamentalist strain. And the other is the setting I was brought up in, which was a kind of upper-class, post-Christian, Southern society. My Uncle Will, who raised me, actually owed more to the Roman stoic tradition than he did to the Christian tradition. My uncle's hero was not this or that Christian saint but Marcus Aurelius, the great Roman emperor. After all, the South used to be full of little Greek academies.

I can remember the kind of talk and advice you heard. You behaved like a gentleman, the Southern honor code, chivalry, grace doing right, treating women with respect. If somebody insults you, then fight. Aren't these the Roman stoic virtues? There's very little said about turning the other cheek. It was a kind of tough, Roman, chivalric code which was much more military than Christian. There is something to be said for it.

An Interview with Walker Percy

Patrick H. Samway, S. J./1986

From *America: The National Catholic Weekly*, 154 (February 15, 1986), 121–23. Reprinted by permission of *America* and Patrick H. Samway, S. J.

Walker Percy, distinguished novelist and man of letters, was selected by the editorial board of the Catholic Book Club to receive the St. Edmund Campion, S.J., Medallion "for long and eminent service in the cause of Christian letters." The presentation took place on Sunday, Feb. 2, 1986, in the Danna Center of Loyola University, New Orleans, La.

The Campion Award was established in 1955 by Harold C. Gardiner, S.J., then editorial chairman of the Catholic Book Club and literary editor of *AMERICA*. Jacques Maritain was chosen in May 1955 as the first recipient of the award. Since then, recipients have included the following: Helen Constance White (1956), Paul Horgan (1957), James Brodrick, S.J. (1958), Sister M. Madeleva, C.S.C. (1959), Frank Sheed and Maisie Ward (1960), John LaFarge, S.J. (1961), Harold C. Gardiner, S.J. (1962), T.S. Eliot (1963), Barbara Ward (1964), Msgr. John Tracy Ellis (1965), John Courtney Murray, S.J. (1966), Phyllis McGinley (1967), George N. Shuster (1968), G.B. Harrison (1970), Walter and Jean Kerr (1971), Karl Rahner, S.J. (1974), John Delaney (1976), and Raymond E. Brown, S.S. (1984).

The award is named after St. Edmund Campion, S.J., who was put to death on the gibbet of Tyburn, London, in 1581 because he would not deny his faith or his priesthood. He was canonized in 1970. Campion stirred English hearts before his tragic death by his daring missionary efforts and the extraordinary power of his pen. Evelyn Waugh said of him that Tyburn's gallows cut short a career that might have been one of the glories of English literature. Campion left Oxford to prepare for the priesthood at Douai, France, and later returned to England to serve the Catholic community during a period of religious persecution under Queen Elizabeth. Campion's "Brag" in defense of his faith has become a classic and moving example of a man of faith, chivalry and unusual literary talent; this award pays tribute to those same qualities in the modern authors.

The 22nd recipient of the award is Walker Percy, born on May 28, 1916, in Birmingham, Ala., the eldest son of Leroy Pratt and Martha Phinizy Percy. After his father's death, young Walker, at age 13, moved with his family to Athens, Ga. After the death of his mother two years later, the three Percy brothers were adopted by William Alexander Percy of Greenville, Miss., a lawyer, poet and author of the famous *Lanterns on the Levee* (1941). Walker Percy graduated from high school in Greenville and then entered the University of North Carolina at Chapel Hill, from which he graduated in 1937 with honors in chemistry. In 1941, he received his M.D. degree from the College of Physicians and Surgeons of Columbia University, N.Y. During the fall of 1941, Dr. Percy worked as an intern at Bellevue Hospital in New York City and shortly afterward he contracted pulmonary tuberculosis. From 1942 to 1944, he went through a period of recuperation at the Trudeau Sanitarium in the Adirondacks.

Once having made the decision not to continue with his medical practice, Dr. Percy devoted himself even more to a study of the existential writers, including Kierkegaard, Jaspers, Heidegger, Marcel, Camus and Sartre. On Nov. 7, 1946, he married Mary Townsend, and they subsequently moved to Covington, La., where they still live. Both Dr. and Mrs. Percy are converts to Roman Catholicism and have two married daughters, who also live in Covington.

Dr. Percy's first novel, *The Moviegoer* (1961), won the National Book Award. His second novel, *The Last Gentlemen* (1966), likewise was well received and nominated for the National Book Award. His subsequent three novels have all met with high acclaim: *Love in the Ruins* (1971), *Lancelot* (1977) and *The Second Coming* (1980). In addition, Dr. Percy has written a collection of essays on language, symbol and communication entitled *The Message in the Bottle* (1975), and what he has termed the last of the self-help books, entitled *Lost in the Cosmos* (1983).

Your novels, at least according to your critics, have blended a philosophical perspective with religious belief. I am sure the readers of AMERICA *would be interested in learning how you see this process taking place in your works.*

The question is legitimate but somewhat depressing. There is nothing wrong with the adjectives "philosophical" and "religious," but when you apply them to a novel, it is enough to make the novelist turn pale. Worse still, the reader, if she should visit a bookstore and see a section labeled "philosophical and religious novels," will probably head straight for cookbooks and Sidney Sheldon and Judy Blume, and I wouldn't blame her. (I say "she" because it is usually a she, not a he, who buys a book.)

Well, anyhow, I didn't set out to blend a philosophical perspective with religious belief. I suppose I would agree with Flannery O'Connor, who said that she was a Catholic and that her faith informed her and the way she saw the world, and that she could not help but write accordingly. What she meant, I think, was that a good novelist does not sit down and say, "Well, let's see, since I am a Catholic and a Thomist, or since I am a Jew and a Freudian, let me figure out how I can write a novel that will blend the two." Only a very doctrinaire novelist—I think of some Marxist novels—would do such a thing. All that one can be sure of about such a novel is that it will be bad. The only "Catholic" novel of this sort that comes to mind—I'm sure there are others—is Cardinal Spellman's *The Foundling*. Cardinal Spellman may have been an excellent churchman, but. . . .

In my writings there is, in fact a rather direct connection between philosophy and religion—in a very special sense. It stems, I suppose, from a good deal of reading and my conviction, based on what is loosely called "existentialism," that an individual man or woman cannot be encompassed by scientific theories, that after the last word is spoken by science, man remains a wayfarer. Of course, once man is so defined, he becomes *pari passu* a religious creature. So it was inevitable, I guess, that my main characters should behave accordingly in my novels—religiously, not necessarily in the institutional sense, but in the sense of searching, however unconsciously, for God.

Incidentally, I don't think it is an accident that the Catholic writer finds the novel a natural form of expression. The Catholic view of man as incarnate spirit, of the world as sacramental, of man's situation in the world as predicamental, is made to order for the novelist. He or she writes about real, incarnate beings, who are in real trouble and who transact with other such beings and with things in the world that mirror in themselves, however dimly, something beyond themselves. That is to

say, the novelist is almost by definition Judeo-Christian—Catholic or
Jewish or Methodist, or ex-Catholic, ex-Jewish or ex-Methodist. How
many Buddhist or ex-Buddhist novelists do you know?

*You and your wife converted to Catholicism approximately 20 years
before Vatican II. Do you see the changes that have taken place in the
church in the last 20 years as having an effect on your work? If so, in
what ways?*

The changes you speak of have not, I think, affected the main
energies and the thrust of my work. Since I am by nature a satirist, I
find some of the postconciliar changes irresistible. By changes, I am not
speaking of any change in faith and doctrine, which, as I see it, has not
in fact occurred as a consequence of Vatican II, but rather certain
excesses of behavior both on the left and the right. I have not been able
to resist some of the more bizarre manifestations of radical feminism,
for example, and some of the radically conservative reactions. In a
futuristic novel I wrote a few years ago, I envisioned a tripartite schism
in which the "Dutch Catholic Church" split off to the left. In this
church, nuns and priests petition not for the right to marry but to remarry
after divorce. To the right were the "Cicero Catholics," who, in protest
against a socially activist clergy, made a point of celebrating Property
Rights Sunday and singing the "Star-Spangled Banner" at the elevation.
There remained the Roman Catholic Church, a somewhat beleaguered
remnant. At the time, I was not entirely serious and was enjoying
myself. I am enjoying less now. A novelist is out of his league in the
prophetic business. If any of this does in fact come to pass, the only part
I don't feel bad about is that the Catholic Church should find itself
beleaguered, a saving remnant. This is probably no more or less than it
should be. It befits Her and She's good at it.

A number of your works, Love in the Ruins *and* Lost in the Cosmos
*for example, seem distinctly apocalyptic. Would you discuss your
interest in the apocalypse?*

It's hard for a novelist not to be concerned with the apocalypse these
days, isn't it? I mean when you consider the fact that the only reason we
are not all dead at this very moment is that the Soviets, for whatever
reason, did not choose to press the button 30 minutes ago; this is a
matter of some interest. There is no historical precedent. So, if by
"apocalypse" you mean the Last Days, the novelist has reasonable
grounds for exploring this territory. It is also good novelistic practice.

Characters behave more interestingly both before the ultimate catastrophe and after. The prospect gets one's attention. It removes the ennui of ordinary Wednesday afternoons. If the Bomb is going to fall any minute, all things become possible, even love. A novelist is always interested in boy-meets-girl, but not the great novelist, not even Shakespeare, could contrive to have boy meeting girl and falling in love on the regular 5:30 PM. commuter train to Hackensack. But if the Bomb is going to vaporize New Jersey any minute and the boy knows how to get the girl to Delaware in time—we're suddenly in the realm of the old master Hitchcock, if not the Bard.

Accordingly, I also like to explore the somewhat ominous reasons why people may secretly relish the Bomb. For some people in my novels, there is something worse than the prospect of the Bomb falling. It is the prospect of the Bomb not falling.

Apocalypse is also useful for exploring the Time After, the adventures of the few survivors who have to resume life and love in the ruins. This technique not only makes for ordinary good adventure but for interesting theological experiments. What is good and what is bad about wiping out the whole crazy edifice of Western civilization? What realities, good and bad, does a survivor confront who finds himself alone in a rest stop off I-80 in Utah?

Of course I am speaking only of novelistic practice and not as a serious chiliast—unlike some evangelists, such as Jimmy Swaggart, who actually believe the Last Days are at hand. Maybe they are, but as I recall, the Lord said something about us not worrying about setting the date.

In the last few years, what authors have impressed you?

I am ashamed to say that no names spring immediately to mind. There are a couple of dozen very promising young writers, perhaps more than half women, but I hesitate to name two or three for fear of not mentioning another two or three just as good—including half-a-dozen real comers in the South, after quite a dry spell.

What rather comes to mind is the opposite, the large number of nonauthors and nonbooks that people are buying and reading by the millions. One has only to look at the best-seller lists. Numbers one and two for months have been nonbooks by an auto executive and a test pilot, not "written" exactly, but "told" to a writer. An honorable exception on the lists is Garrison Keillor's *Lake Wobegon Days*.

To come back to your question: I have to say that I keep rereading some of my favorite contemporaries, for example, Bellow, Updike, Cheever, and Malamud and such like. Perhaps this is a consequence of aging.

Since World War II, have you perceived a direction in American literature? Or directions? Where do you see your novels and essays fitting in?

Well, there is one new sort of novelist who has appeared in the last few decades. He or she is usually connected to a university and is quite conscious of recent directions in literary criticism, semiotics, epistemology and such, and makes quite conscious decisions in writing fiction accordingly. Though not widely read, such a novelist plans fictional strategies in a kind of loose alliance with trends in what is called "structuralism" and "deconstructionism." There is also the American equivalent of the French *nouveau roman,* which deliberately eschews such usual equipment of the novelist as plot, characterization, *mise en scène.* Some of these experiments are interesting. The novelist's rule is pragmatic: If it works, don't knock it. My reservation has rather to do with a certain malevolence in some of these authors—I can think of half-a-dozen, whom I will not name because we scribblers have a hard enough time without picking on each other—plus a deliberate antiepistemological stance that shoots down the entire novelistic enterprise, an enterprise which, one would suppose, entails an author with an intention, a work to convey what he intends, a reader to receive it and, to a degree, grasp it. Some critics, and a few novelists, say that this communication of meaning cannot and does not occur. If this is the case, one cannot help wondering on what grounds these writers undertake to write books, accept lecture fees, take jobs as writers-in-residence.

In your last novel, The Second Coming, *Will Barrett goes through a rather complex process of conversion as he opens himself up to the love that he literally falls into. Do you see Will's life as a paradigm of the Christian experience? And what plans do you have for the protagonist in your next novel,* The Thanatos Syndrome?

I had not thought of Will's experience as a paradigm of the Christian experience, but only as something that might happen between a middle-aged Southerner of a certain sort and a young psychotic woman, each with all the assets and burdens of being Southern and psychotic, plus a dash of grace.

All I can say now about my next book, *The Thanatos Syndrome,* a sequel to *Love in the Ruins,* is that Dr. Thomas More has got himself in a great deal of trouble, that something is about to happen that is a lot worse than the physical meltdown in *The China Syndrome* and that I'm by no means sure how he's going to get out of it.

The Art of Fiction XCVII: Walker Percy

Zoltán Abádi-Nagy/1986

Orphaned at a young age, Walker Percy was raised by his adoptive father, the poet and memoirist William Alexander Percy. He studied chemistry and mathematics at the University of North Carolina at Chapel Hill, and went on to medical school at Columbia University. His studies there were halted, however, when he contracted tuberculosis. Though he has never abandoned his interest in the sciences in general, and psychiatry in particular, during his long convalescence he came to realize, he says, that the individual "will be left out of even the most rigorous scientific formulation."

As one of America's foremost novelists, Percy likens his role to that of "the canary the coal miners used to take down into the shaft with them, to test the air." His books—*The Moviegoer* (1961), *The Last Gentleman* (1966), *Love in the Ruins* (1971), *The Message in the Bottle* (1975), *Lancelot* (1977), *The Second Coming* (1980), *Lost in the Cosmos* (1983), and, most recently, *The Thanatos Syndrome* (1987)—reflect that sense of prophetic mission. They are propelled by a sharply defined moral vision which reflects a rare diversity of influences—the work of the existentialists, particularly Kierkegaard and Marcel; the novels of Camus, Sartre, Dostoyevsky, Faulkner, and others; his background in the sciences; and, later in life, his conversion to Catholicism.

This interview was conducted by mail, from May to October 1986, at an enormous geographical distance; but the interviewer does cherish the memory of a personal meeting. It was on May 4, 1973, a warm Louisiana evening, at Percy's home in Covington, a small town at the northern end of the causeway running across Lake Pontchartrain (New Orleans is at the southern end). The house is in a wooded area by the bayou, along the Bogue Falaya River. Percy is a tall, slender, handsome

man, with a distinguished and thoughtful mien. His manner that day
was unassuming, gracious, and gentle. Since then, his graying hair may
have become grayer; but judging from our correspondence, he is still the
same warm, helpful, generous, and patient person, as the very existence
of this interview, carried out under such difficult circumstances, will
testify.

Interviewer: How did you spend your seventieth birthday?

Percy: An ordinary day. I went with my wife and some friends to a
neighborhood restaurant in New Orleans. I think I had crawfish. What
distinguishes Louisianians is that they suck the heads.

Interviewer: You and your wife recently celebrated your fortieth
anniversary. Is it easy, do you imagine, to be married to a writer?

Walker Percy: Mine has been a happy marriage—thanks mainly to
my wife. Who would want to live with a novelist? A man underfoot in
the house all day? A man, moreover, subject to solitary funks and
strange elations. If I were a woman, I'd prefer a traveling salesman.
There is no secret, or rather the secrets are buried in platitudes. That is
to say, it has something to do with love, commitment, and family. As to
the institution, it is something like Churchill's description of democracy:
vicissitudinous yes, but look at the alternatives.

Interviewer: What are the decisive moments, turning points that you
regard as the milestones of those seven decades?

Percy: What comes to mind is something like this: one, losing both
parents in my early teens and being adopted by my uncle, a poet, and
being exposed to the full force of a remarkable literary imagination;
two, contracting a non-fatal case of tuberculosis while serving as an
intern in Bellevue Hospital in New York, an event which did not so
much change my life as give me leave to change it; three, getting married; four, becoming a Catholic.

Interviewer: If you had the chance, would you decide to be reborn or
to flee back into William Blake's "vales of Har"?

Percy: No vales of Har, thank you. No rebirth either, but I wouldn't
mind a visit in the year 2050—a short visit, not more than half an
hour—say, to a park bench at the southeast corner of Central Park in
New York, with a portable radio. Just to have a look around, just to see
whether we made it and if so, in what style. One could tell in half an
hour. By "we" of course, I do not mean just Americans, but the species.
Homo sapiens sapiens.

Interviewer: Once you said that if you were starting over, you might like to make films. Would there be other decisions that would be different?

Percy: I might study linguistics—not in the current academic meanings of the word, but with a fresh eye, like Newton watching the falling apple: How come? What's going on here?

Interviewer: Apropos of your fascination with film, most of it finds its way into your novels on the thematic level, especially in *The Moviegoer* and *Lancelot*. Does it happen that film or television influences you in less noticeable ways as well, such as cinematic structuring of material and so on?

Percy: I can only answer in the most general way: that what television and movies give the writer is a new community and a new set of referents. Since nearly everyone watches television a certain number of hours a day (whether they admit it or not), certain turns of plot are ready-made for satirical use, namely the Western shoot-out, one man calling another out, a mythical dance of honor. In my last novel I described one character as looking something like Blake Carrington. Now you may not know who Blake Carrington is—though sooner or later most Hungarians will. A hundred million Americans do know.*

Interviewer: Could you tell me how you feel about your inspiring beliefs, how faithful you have remained to them?

Percy: If you mean, am I still a Catholic, the answer is yes. The main difference after thirty-five years is that my belief is less self-conscious, less ideological, less polemical. My ideal is Thomas More, an English Catholic—a peculiar breed nowadays—who wore his faith with grace, merriment, and a certain wryness. Incidentally, I reincarnated him again in my new novel and I'm sorry to say he has fallen upon hard times; he is a far cry from the saint, drinks too much, and watches reruns of *M*A*S*H* on TV.

Interviewer: As for philosophy and religion, do you still regard yourself as a philosophical Catholic existentialist?

Percy: Philosophical? Existentialist? Religion? Pretty heavy. These are perfectly good words—except perhaps "existentialist"—but over the years they have acquired barnacle-like connotative excrescences. Uttering them induces a certain dreariness and heaviness in the neck

*He is John Forsythe's character in the television series *Dynasty*.

muscles. As for "existentialist," I'm not sure it presently has a sufficiently clear referent to be of use. Even "existentialists" forswear the
term. It fell into disuse some years ago when certain novelists began
saying things like: I beat up my wife in an existential moment—
meaning a sudden, irrational impulse.

Interviewer: Is it possible to define your Catholic existentialism in a
few sentences?

Percy: I suppose I would prefer to describe it as a certain view of
man, an anthropology, if you like; of man as wayfarer, in a rather
conscious contrast to prevailing views of man as organism, as encul-
tured creature, as consumer, Marxist, as subject to such and such a
scientific or psychological understanding—all of which he is, but not
entirely. It is the "not entirely" I'm interested in—like the man
Kierkegaard described who read Hegel, understood himself and the
universe perfectly by noon but then had the problem of living out the
rest of the day. It, my "anthropology," has been expressed better in an
earlier, more traditional language—e.g., scriptural: man born to trouble
as the sparks fly up; Gabriel Marcel's *Homo viator*.

Interviewer: You converted to Catholicism in the 1940s. What was
the motive behind the decision?

Percy: There are several ways to answer the question. One is theological. The technical theological term is grace, the gratuitous unmerited
gift from God. Another answer is less theological: what else is there?
Did you expect me to become a Methodist? A Buddhist? A Marxist? A
comfortable avuncular humanist like Walter Cronkhite? An exhibitionist
like Allen Ginsberg? A proper literary-philosophical-existentialist answer is that the occasion was the reading of Kierkegaard's extraordinary
essay: "On the Difference Between a Genius and an Apostle." Like the
readings that mean most to you, what it did was to confirm something I
suspected but that it took Sören Kierkegaard to put into words: that what
the greatest geniuses in science, literature, art, philosophy utter are
sentences which convey truths *sub specie aeternitatis,* that is to say,
sentences which can be confirmed by appropriate methods and by
anyone, anywhere, any time. But only the apostle can utter sentences
which can be accepted on the authority of the apostle, that is, his
credentials, sobriety, trustworthiness as a newsbearer. These sentences
convey not knowledge *sub specie aeternitatis* but news.

Interviewer: I noticed that you rarely refer to other converted novelists like Graham Greene and Evelyn Waugh when discussing your ideas. Or if you do, it is rarely, if ever, in this context.

Percy: Maybe it's because novelists don't talk much about each other. Maybe this is because novelists secrete a certain B.O. which only other novelists detect, like certain buzzards who emit a repellent pheromone detectable only by other buzzards, which is to say that only a novelist can know how neurotic, devious, underhanded a novelist can be. Actually I have the greatest admiration for both writers, not necessarily for their religion, but for their consummate craft.

Interviewer: Can we discuss the "losangelized" and re-Christianized New South? Is there anything new in the way the South is developing in the 1980s or in the way you read the South or your own relation to it?

Percy: The odd thing I've noticed is that while of course the South is more and more indistinguishable from the rest of the country (Atlanta, for example, which has become one of the three or four megalopolises of the U.S., is in fact, I'm told by blacks, their favorite American city) the fact is that as Faulkner said fifty years ago, as soon as you cross the Mason-Dixon Line, you still know it. This, after fifty years of listening to the same radio and watching millions of hours of *Barnaby Jones*. I don't know whether it's the heat or a certain lingering civility but people will slow down on interstates to let you get in traffic. Strangers speak in post offices, hold doors for each other without being thought queer or running a con game or making a sexual advance. I could have killed the last cab driver I had in New York. Ask Eudora Welty, she was in the same cab.

Interviewer: Have your views concerning being a writer in the South undergone a change during the past decades? Is being a writer in the South in 1987 the same as it was when you started to write?

Percy: Southern writers—that's the question everybody asks. I still don't know the answer. All I know is that there is still something about living in the South which turns one inward, makes one secretive, sly and scheming, makes one capable of a degree of malice, humor and outrageousness. At any rate, despite the losangelization of the South there are right here, in the New Orleans area, perhaps half a dozen very promising young writers—which is more than can be said of Los Angeles. It comes, not from the famous storytelling gregariousness one hears about, but from the shy, sly young woman, say, who watches, listens, gets a fill of it and slips off to do a number on it. And it comes, not from having arrived at last in the Great American Mainstream along with the likes of Emerson and Sandburg, but from being close enough to have a good look at one's fellow Americans, fellow Southerners, yet keep a certain wary distance, enough to nourish a secret, subversive conviction: I can do a number on those guys—and on me—and it will be good for all of us.

Interviewer: Apropos of Southern writing, does regionalism still apply?

Percy: Sure, in the better sense of the word, in the sense that Chekhov and Flaubert and Mark Twain are regionalists—not in the sense that Joel Chandler Harris and Bret Harte were regionalists.

Interviewer: You studied science at Chapel Hill and became a medical doctor at Columbia. In your recently published essay "The Diagnostic Novel" you suggest that serious art is "just as cognitive" as science is and "the serious novelist is quite as much concerned with discovering reality as a serious physicist." Art explores reality in a way which "cannot be done any other way." What are some of the ways that are specific to artistic as opposed to scientific exploration of reality?

Percy: The most commonplace example of the cognitive dimension in fiction is the reader's recognition—sometimes the shock of recognition—the "verification" of a sector of reality which he had known but not known that he had known. I think of letters I get from readers which may refer to a certain scene and say, in effect, yes! that's the way it is! For example, Binx in *The Moviegoer* describes one moviegoing experience, going to see *Panic in the Streets,* a film shot in New Orleans, going to a movie theater in the very neighborhood where the same scenes in the movie were filmed. Binx tells his girlfriend Kate about his reasons for enjoying the film—that it, the film, "certifies" the reality of the neighborhood in a peculiar sense in which the direct experience of the neighborhood, living in the neighborhood, does not. I have heard from many readers about this and other such scenes—as have other novelists, I'm sure—saying they *know* exactly what Binx is talking about. I think it is reasonable to call such a transaction cognitive, sciencing. This sort of sciencing is closely related to the cognitive dimension of psychoanalysis. The patient, let's say, relates a dream. Such and such happened. The analyst suggests that perhaps the dream "means" such and such. It sometimes happens that the patient—perhaps after a pause, a frown, a shaking of head—will suddenly "see" it. Yes, by God! Which is to say: in sciencing, there are forms of verification other than pointer-readings.

Interviewer: As for your view that it is a mistake to draw a moral and be edifying in art—is Lancelot's naive-fascistoid idea of the Third Revolution illustrative of this?

Percy: I was speaking of the everyday use of the words "moral" and "edifying"—which is to say, preachy—in the sense that, say, Ayn Rand's novels are preachy, have a message, but may in the deepest sense of the words be immoral. So is Lancelot's "Third Revolution" in the deepest sense immoral and, I hope, is so taken by the reader. To tell the truth, I don't see how any serious fiction-writer or poet can fail to be moral and edifying in the technical non-connotative sense of these words, since he or she cannot fail to be informed by his own deep sense of the way things should be or should not be, by a sense of pathology and hence a sense of health. If a writer writes from a sense of outrage—and most serious writers do—isn't he by definition a moral writer?

Interviewer: The influence of Dostoyevsky, Camus, Sartre, and other novelists upon you has often been discussed. Is there any literary influence that joined the rest recently?

Percy: Chekhov reread—in a little reading group we have here in Covington. His stories "In the Ravine" and "Ward Six" are simply breathtaking. Also recently, the German novelist Peter Handke whose latest, *The Weight of the World,* is somehow exhilarating in the spontaneity of its free-form diary entries. The accurate depiction of despair can be exhilarating, a cognitive emotion.

Interviewer: What is your attitude towards the reader?

Percy: I hold out for some sort of contractual relationship between novelist and reader, however flawed, misapprehended or fragmentary. Perhaps the contract is ultimately narratological, perhaps not. But something keeps—or fails to keep—the reader reading the next sentence. Even the "antinovel" presupposes some sort of contractual venture at the very moment the "antinovelist" is attacking narrativity. Such a venture implies that the writer is up to something, going abroad like Don Quixote—if only to attack windmills—and that the reader is with him. Otherwise why would the latter bother? The antinovelist is like a Protestant. His protests might be valid, but where would he be without the Catholic Church? I have no objection to "anti-story" novels. What I object to is any excursion by the author which violates the novelistic contract between writer and reader which I take to be an intersubjective transaction entailing the transmission of a set of symbols, a text. The writer violates the contract when he trashes the reader by pornography or scatological political assaults, e.g., depicting President Nixon in a novel buggering Ethel Rosenberg in Times Square, or LBJ plotting the assassination of JFK. Take pornography, a difficult, slippery case. It is not necessary to get into a discussion of First Amendment rights—for all I know it has them. And for all I know, pornography has its uses. All I suggest is that pornography and literature stimulate different organs. If we can agree that a literary text is a set of signals transmitted from sender to receiver in a certain code, pornography is a different set of signals and a different code.

Interviewer: Can it be said that in your case the primary business of literature and art is cognitive whereas with John Gardner it is "to be morally judgmental"? It is clear that you and Gardner are not talking about the same thing.

Percy: I expect there is an overlap between Gardner's "moral fiction" and my "diagnostic novel." But Gardner makes me nervous with his moralizing. When he talks about literature "establishing models of human actions," he seems to be using literature to influence what people do. I think he is confusing two different orders of reality. Aquinas and the Schoolmen were probably right: art is making, morality is doing. Art is a virtue of the practical intellect, which is to say making something. This is not to say that art, fiction, is not moral in the most radical sense—if it is made right. But if you write a novel with the goal of trying to make somebody do right, you're writing a tract—which may be an admirable enterprise but it is not literature. Dostoyevsky's *Notes from Underground* is in my opinion a work of art, but it would probably not pass Gardner's moral test. Come to think of it, I think my reflexes are medical rather than moral. This comes, I guess, from having been a pathologist. Now I am perfectly willing to believe Flannery O'Connor when she said, and she wasn't kidding, that the modern world is a territory largely occupied by the devil. No one doubts the malevolence abroad in the world. But the world is also deranged. What interests me as a novelist is not the malevolence of man—so what else is new?—but his looniness. The looniness, that is to say, of the "normal" denizen of the Western world who, I think it fair to say, doesn't know who he is, what he believes, or what he is doing. This unprecedented state of affairs is, I suggest, the domain of the "diagnostic" novelist.

Interviewer: Are there any trends or authors in contemporary American innovative fiction that you regard with sympathy?

Percy: Yes, there are quite a few younger writers whom I will not name but whom I would characterize as innovative "minimalist" writers who have been influenced by Donald Barthelme without succumbing to him, which is easy to do, or as young Southern writers who have been influenced by Faulkner and Welty without succumbing to them, which is also easy to do.

Interviewer: If I were asked whose work I feel to be closest to yours—the whole terrain of contemporary American fiction considered—I would choose Saul Bellow.

Percy: Why?

Interviewer: Because of the philosophical bent, because both of you are satirical moralists, because Bellow's is also a quest informed by an awareness that man *can* do something about alienation, and because philosophical abstraction and concrete social commentary are equally balanced.

Percy: I take that kindly. I admire Barth, Pynchon, Heller, Vonnegut—you could also throw in Updike, Cheever and Malamud—but perhaps Bellow most of all. He bears the same relationship to the streets of Chicago and upper Broadway—has inserted himself into them—the way I have in the Gentilly district of New Orleans or a country town in West Feliciana Parish in Louisiana.

Interviewer: What exactly moves you to write? An idea? An image? A character? A landscape? A memory? Something that happened to you or to someone else? You have said about *The Moviegoer* that you "liked the idea of putting a young man down in a faceless suburb."

Percy: The spark might have come from Sartre's Roquentin in *Nausea* sitting in that library watching the Self-Taught Man or sitting in that cafe watching the waiter. Why not have a younger, less perverse Roquentin, a Southerner of a certain sort, and put him down in a movie house in Gentilly, a middle-class district of New Orleans, not unlike Sartre's Bouville.

Interviewer: If every writer writes from his own predicament, could you give a few hints as to how *The Moviegoer* illustrates this point?

Percy: After the war, not doing medicine, writing and publishing articles in psychiatric, philosophical, and political journals, I was living in New Orleans and going to the movies. You can't make a living writing articles for *The Journal of Philosophy and Phenomenological Research.* The thought crossed my mind: why not do what French philosophers often do and Americans almost never—novelize philosophy, incarnate ideas in a person and a place, which latter is after all a noble Southern tradition in fiction.

Interviewer: Did you model any characters on your brothers, wife, children, grandchildren?

Percy: Not in any way anyone would recognize.

Interviewer: In connection with *Message in the Bottle,* a collection of essays that had been published over two-and-a-half decades, what attracted you to linguistics and semiotics, to the theories of language, meaning, signs, and symbols?

Percy: That's a big question, too big to answer in more than a couple of sentences. It has to do with the first piece of writing I ever got published. I was sitting around Saranac Lake getting over a light case of tuberculosis. There was nothing to do but read. I got hold of Susanne Langer's *Philosophy in a New Key* in which she focuses on man's unique symbol-mongering behavior. This was an eye-opener to me, a good physician-scientist brought up in the respectable behaviorist tradition of U.N.C. and Columbia. I was so excited, I wrote a review and sent it to *Thought* quarterly. It was accepted! I was paid by twenty-five reprints. That was enough. What was important was seeing my scribble in *print!*

Interviewer: Can you recollect what was involved in your getting started with *The Last Gentleman?*

Percy: I wanted to create someone not quite as flat as Binx in *The Moviegoer,* more disturbed, more passionate, more in love and, above all, *on the move.* He is in pilgrimage without quite knowing it—doing a Kierkegaardian repetition, that is, going back to his past to find himself, then from home and self to the *West* following the summons of a queer sort of apostle, mad doctor Sutter. "Going West" is U.S. colloquial for dying.

Interviewer: *Love in the Ruins?*

Percy: *Love in the Ruins* was a picnic, with everything in it but the kitchen sink. It was written during the Time of Troubles in the sixties, with all manner of polarization in the country, black vs. white, North

vs. South, hippie vs. square, liberal vs. conservative, McCarthyism vs.
commies, etc.—the whole seasoned with a Southern flavor and
featuring sci-fi, futurism and Dr. More, a whimsical descendent of the
saint. After the solemnities of *The Moviegoer* and *The Last Gentleman,*
why not enjoy myself? I did. Now I have seen fit to resurrect Dr. More
in the novel I just finished, *The Thanatos Syndrome.* He is in trouble as
usual and I am enjoying it.

Interviewer: *Lancelot?*

Percy: *Lancelot* might have come from an upside-down theological
notion, not about God but about sin, more specfically the falling into
disrepute of the word "sin." So it seemed entirely fitting that Lancelot,
a proper Southern gent raised in a long tradition of knightly virtues,
chiefly by way of Walter Scott, the most widely read novelist in the
South for a hundred years, should have undertaken his own sort of quest
for his own peculiar Grail, i.e., sin, which quest is after all a sort of
search for God. Lancelot wouldn't be caught dead looking for God but
he is endlessly intrigued by the search for evil. Is there such a thing—
malevolence over and beyond psychological and sociological categories? The miscarriage of his search issues, quite logically I think, in his
own peculiar brand of fascism, which is far more attractive and
seductive, I think, than Huey Long's.

Interviewer: Let me ask about *The Second Coming,* too, since
although it developed into a sequel to *The Last Gentleman,* originally it
was not conceived as a sequel.

Percy: *The Second Coming* was a sure-enough love story—a genre I
would ordinarily steer clear of. What made it possible was the, to me,
appealing notion of the encounter of Allie and Will, like the crossing of
two lines on a graph, one going up, the other down: the man who has
"succeeded" in life, made it, has the best of worlds, and yet falls down
in sand traps on the golf course, gazes at clouds, and is haunted by
memory, is in fact in despair; the girl, a total "failure," a schizophrenic
who has flunked life, as she puts it, yet who despite all sees the world
afresh and full of hope. It was the paradox of it that interested me. What
happens when he meets her? What is the effect on his ghostlike
consciousness of her strange, yet prescient, schizophrenic speech?

Interviewer: Nonfiction. *Lost in the Cosmos?*

Percy: *Lost in the Cosmos* was a sly, perhaps even devious, attempt
to approach a semiotic of the self. Circumspection was necessary here,
because semioticists have no use for the self, and votaries of the self—

poets, humanists, novel-readers etc.—have no use for semiotics. It was a quite ambitious attempt actually, not necessarily successful, to derive the self, a very nebulous entity indeed, through semiotics, specifically the emergence of self as a consequence of the child's entry into the symbol-mongering world of men—and even more specifically, through the acquisition of language. What was underhanded about the book was the insertion of a forty-page "primer of semiotics" in the middle of the book with a note of reassurance to the reader that he could skip it if he wanted to. Of course I was hoping he, or more likely she, would be sufficiently intrigued to take the dare and read it, since it is of course the keystone of the book. Having derived the self semiotically, then the fun came from deriving the various options of the self semiotically—the various "re-entries" of the self from the orbits most people find themselves in. Such options are ordinarily regarded as the territory of the novelist, the queer things his characters do. The fun was like the fun of Mendeleyev who devised his periodic table of elements and then looked to see if all the elements were there. Technically speaking, it was a modest attempt to give the "existentialia" of Heidegger some semiotic grounding—this, of course, in the ancient tradition of Anglo-Saxon empiricism administering therapy to the European tendency to neurotic introspection. It was also fun to administer a dose of semiotics to Phil Donahue and Carl Sagan, splendid fellows both, but who's perfect?

Interviewer: Which of your novels do you expect to weather time best and why?

Percy: I've no idea.

Interviewer: Would you rewrite any of your works from any aspect at any point if you could?

Percy: No, I hardly think about them. Sometimes in the middle of the night, however, something will occur to me which I would use in a revision. For example, in the chapter called "Metaphor as Mistake" in *The Message in the Bottle* I wish I had used this example. In Charity Hospital in New Orleans, which serves mainly poor blacks, the surgical condition, fibroids of the uterus, an accurate if somewhat prosaic definition, is known to many patients more creatively as "fireballs of the Eucharist."

Interviewer: Is it correct to say that your *oeuvre* forms an organic whole and that there is a consistent logic that takes you from one work to the next as you explore reality step by step?

Percy: Yes, I hope so—though the organic quality, if there is any, occurred more by happenstance than by design. The "fruits of the search" are here—to the extent they are allowed in the modest enterprise of the novel. That is to say, the novelist has no business setting up as the Answer Man. Or, as Binx says in the epilogue of *The Moviegoer*: "As for my search, I have not the inclination to say much on the subject. For one thing, I have not the authority, as the great Danish philosopher declared, to speak of such matters . . ." But the novelist is entitled to a degree of artifice and cunning, as Joyce said; or the "indirect method," as Kierkegaard said; or the comic-bizarre for shock therapy, as Flannery O'Connor did. For example, a hint of the resolution of Binx's search is given in a single four-word sentence on page 240.* The reader should know by now that Binx, for all his faults, never bullshits especially not with children. In *Lancelot* the resolution of the conflict between Lancelot and Percival is given by a single word, the last word in the book. Which holds out hope for Lancelot.

Interviewer: Hope in what sense? Isn't he beyond reach for Percival anyway?

Percy: No, Lancelot is not beyond the reach of Percival and accordingly Lancelot is not beyond hope. The entire novel is Lancelot's spiel to Percival. Percival does not *in the novel* reply in kind. At the end Lancelot asks him if he has anything to say. Percival merely says, "yes." Lancelot, presumably, will listen. It is precisely my perception of the esthetic limitations of the novel-form that this is all Percival can say. But the novelist is allowed to nourish the secret hope that the reader may remember that in the legend it was only Percival and Lancelot, of all the knights, who saw the Grail.

Interviewer: I guess *Lancelot* was meant as your bicentenary novel. But the two radical points of view, Lancelot's "pagan Greco-Roman Nazi and so on tradition" and Percival's orthodox Christianity, are unacceptable for most people, as you once explained. So, another guess, what you could teach America in *Lancelot* was what was wrong, and what you could work out in *The Second Coming* was what you could *recommend* to the nation.

Percy: If you say so, though I had nothing so grand in mind as "recommending to the nation." I never lose sight of the lowly vocation of the novelist. He is mainly out to give pleasure to a reader—one would hope, esthetic pleasure. He operates in the esthetic sphere, not

---

*"He'll be like you."

the religious or even the ethical. That is to say, he is in the business, like all other artists, of making, not doing, certainly not lecturing to the nation. He hopes to make well and so sell what he makes.

Interviewer: Isn't it safe to say, though, that *Lancelot* and *The Second Coming* are twin novels in the sense that while Lance embarks on a quest to meet the devil, Barrett's quest is to meet God? The latter's physical journey downwards seems to be an ironic counterpoint to his yearning, which is upward. Barrett's route leads him—through his fall into the greenhouse—to a different reality: perhaps the correction of direction you recommend to the South and to America. Is this stretching things too far?

Percy: Yes indeed. Will Barrett falls out of the cave into Allie's arms, i.e., out of his nutty gnostic quest into sacramental reality. I liked the idea of falling out of a cave. I permitted myself a veiled optimism here, that one can in fact fall out of a cave, i.e., despair and depression, when aware of themselves as such, can be closest to life. From cave to greenhouse, courtesy of Sören Kierkegaard and Dr. Jung. Same reservation, however, about "a message to the South." The South is by and large in no mood for messages from Walker Percy, being, for one thing, too busy watching *Dallas, Love Boat* and the NFL on the tube. Or Jimmy Swaggart.

Interviewer: Do the times have anything to do with your reaching this breakthrough to eros, affirmation and celebration in 1980 and not before? In other words, could *The Second Coming* have been written in the fifties or sixties? Or was your own age and life experience needed to reach this stage?

Percy: Yes, no, yes. Also artistic development. Also luck—as I said before. You're sitting at your typewriter, nine in the morning, a bad time, or four in the afternoon, a worse time. Sunk as usual. In the cave. What's going to happen to these poor people? They're on their own. I'll be damned if I'm going to impose a solution on them, a chic unhappy existential ending or an upbeat Fannie Hurst ending. What does this poor guy do? He falls out of the cave, what else?

Interviewer: Can we look at much of what goes on in innovative fiction, when it is not self-indulgent and cynical, in light of what you call "defamiliarization" in *Lost in the Cosmos*? That is, the artist tries to "wrench signifier out of context and exhibit it in all its queerness and splendor"?

Percy: Absolutely, but I would apply the principle even more broadly, indeed to much that is beautiful in poetry. Take Shakespeare's lovely lines: "Daffodils that come before the swallow dares/And take the winds of March with beauty." Surely the wrenching out of context and hence defamiliarization of such ordinary words as *daffodils, swallow, dare, March,* and even the curious use of *take,* has something to do with the beauty. Obviously Empson's theory of ambiguity in poetry is closely akin.

Interviewer: It is clear that once we are dealing with a "post-religious technological society," transcendence is possible for the self by science or art but not by religion. Where does this leave the heroes of your novels with their metaphysical yearnings—Binx, Barrett, More, Lance?

Percy: I would have to question your premise, i.e., the death of religion. The word itself, *religion,* is all but moribund, true, smelling of dust and wax—though of course in its denotative sense it is accurate enough. I have referred to the age as "post-Christian" but it does not follow from this that there are not Christians or that they are wrong. Possibly the age is wrong. Catholics—who are the only Christians I can speak for—still believe that God entered history as a man, founded a church and will come again. This is not the best of times for the Catholic Church, but it has seen and survived worse. I see the religious "transcendence" you speak of as curiously paradoxical. Thus it is only by a movement, "transcendence," toward God that these characters, Binx *et al.,* become themselves, not abstracted like scientists but fully incarnate beings in the world. Kierkegaard put it more succinctly: the self only becomes itself when it becomes itself transparently before God.

Interviewer: The second half of the question still applies: is it possible to describe Binx and the others in terms of your semiotic typology of the self?

Percy: I would think in terms of the semiotic typology of self described in *The Message in the Bottle.* The semiotic receptor or "self" described here is perceived as being—unlike the "responding organism" of Skinner or Morris or Ogden-and-Richards—attuned to the reception of *sentences,* asserted subject-predicate pairings, namings, etc. There is adumbrated here a classification of sentences—not grammatically but existentially, that is, how the semiotic self construes the sentences in relation to his "world" (*Welt* not *Umwelt*), the latter itself a semiotic construction. Thus:

I. Sentences conveying "island news": there is fresh water in the next cove; the price of eggs is fifty cents a dozen; Nicaragua has invaded El Salvador; my head hurts; etc.

II. Sentences conveying truths *sub specie aeternitatis* (i.e., valid on any island anywhere): 2 plus 2 equals 4; $E = MC^2$ (mathematical sentences); to thine own self be true, etc. (poetic sentences); wolves are carnivorous (scientific sentences, true of all known wolves anywhere).

III. Sentences announcing news from across the seas: the French fleet is on its way to Saint Helena to rescue you (a sentence of possible significance to Napoleon). Or: A certain event occurred in history, in the Middle East some two thousand years ago, which is of utmost importance to every living human. Presumably it was just some such sentence, however indirectly, obscurely, distortedly uttered, which might have been uttered or was about to be uttered to Binx Bolling, Will Barrett, at the end of these novels—by such unlikely souls as Sutter. Notice too that it is only this last sort of sentence, the good news from across the seas, which requires the credential of the newsbearer. Or, as Kierkegaard phrased the sentence: Only I, an apostle (that is, messenger), have the authority to bring you this piece of news. It is true and I make you eternally responsible for whether or not you believe it. Certainly it is not the business of the novelist to utter sentences of Class III, but only a certain sort of Class II sentence. Also, *mutatis mutandis,* it is Dr. Thomas More who, in *The Thanatos Syndrome,* hears the Class III sentence as a non-sentence, devalued, ossified, not so much nonsense as part merely of a religious decor, like the whiff of incense or a plastic Jesus on the dashboard, or a bumper sticker common here in Louisiana: Jesus Saves.

Interviewer: Is it possible that the idea central to your semiotic theory of the self—namely, that the self has no sign of itself—has something to do with Jung's idea in his *Modern Man in Search of a Soul* where he speaks about the difficulty man has expressing the inexpressible in his language?

Percy: Actually I would suppose that my notions about the "semiotic origins" of the self are more closely related, at least in my own mind, to the existentialist philosophers, Heidegger and Marcel and Jaspers, and to the existentialist school of psychiatrists. Some years ago I published a paper which sought to do precisely that: derive many of the so-called "existentialia"—anxiety, notion of a "world"—from this very structure of man's peculiar triadic relation to his environment: interpreter-symbol-referent.

Interviewer: The Jungian idea in *The Thanatos Syndrome* is mentioned in the book—that anxiety and depression might be trying to tell the patient something he does not understand. Doesn't this contradict the "semiotic-predicament-of-the-self" theory in *Cosmos,* i.e., its unspeakableness in a world of signs?

Percy: I don't think so. The concept of an unsignified self stranded in a world of solid signs (trees, apples, Alabama, Ralphs, Zoltáns) is very useful in thinking about the various psychiatric ways patients "fall" into inauthenticity, the way frantic selves grope for any mask at hand to disguise their nakedness. Sartre's various descriptions of bad faith in role-playing are marvelous phenomenological renderings of this quest of the self for some, any, kind of habiliment. This being the case, perhaps the patient's "symptoms"—anxiety, depression, and whatnot—may be read as a sort of warning or summons of the self to itself, of the "authentic" self to the "fallen" or inauthentic self. Heidegger speaks of the "fall" of the self into the "world." I am thinking of the first character you encounter in *The Thanatos Syndrome* through the eyes of Dr. More: the woman who lives at the country club and thinks she has everything and yet is in the middle of a panic attack. She is also the last person you encounter in the book—after being "relieved" of her symptoms by the strange goings-on in the book. So here she is at the end confronting her anxiety. She is about to listen to herself tell herself something. The last sentence in the novel is: She opens her mouth to speak. Jung, of course, would have understood this patient as this or that element of the self speaking to itself, perhaps anima-self to animus-self. Perhaps he is right, but I find it more congenial and less occult to speak in terms of observables and semiotic elements. Perhaps it is the Anglo-Saxon empiricist in me.

Interviewer: One way to sum up *The Thanatos Syndrome*—without giving away the plot—is to call it an ecological novel. What made you turn to the ecological theme?

Percy: I wasn't particularly aware of the ecological theme. It is true that the Louisiana of the novel is an ecological mess—as indeed it is now—but this I took to be significant only in so far as it shows the peculiar indifference of the strange new breed of Louisianians in the novel. After all, chimp-like creatures do not generally form environ-mental-protection-societies.

Interviewer: Novels like Cheever's *Oh! What a Paradise It Seems,* Gardner's *Mickelsson's Ghosts* and Don DeLillo's *White Noise* are about the contamination of the environment. Were you influenced by those novels or by any others with similar topics?

Percy: Not really. If you want to locate a contemporary influence, it would be something like a cross between Bellow and Vonnegut—aiming at Bellow's depth in his central characters and Vonnegut's out-rageousness and satirical use of sci-fi.

Interviewer: Did you make up the "pre-frontal cortical deficit," the Tauber test and other things, the way you invented Hausmann's Syn-drome for inappropriate longing in *The Second Coming*?

Percy: No, they're not made up. There is just enough present-day evidence to make my "syndrome" plausible, or at least credible. One advantage of futuristic novel-writing is that it relieves one of restriction to the current state of the art of brain function. Another way of saying this is that, fortunately, the present knowledge of cortical function is so primitive that it gives the novelist considerable *carte blanche.*

Interviewer: What about in *The Thanatos Syndrome*—is the pharma-cological effect of Na^{24} on the cortex known?

Percy: Not that I know of, but perhaps some shrink will write me, as one did about Hausmann's Syndrome, and report that, sure enough, administration of Na^{24} to patients in the Veteran's Hospital in Seattle has been shown to reduce anxiety and improve sexual performance both in quantity and quality and variety (for example, presenting rearward).

Interviewer: What led you to the idea of cortex manipulation?

Percy: Well of course the cortex is the neurological seat of the pri-mate's, and man's, "higher functions." But I was particularly intrigued by the work of neurologists like John Eccles who locate the "self" in the language areas of the cortex—which squares very well with the semiotic origins of the self in the origins of language—as that which gives names, utters sentences. It seems, despite the most intensive training, chimps do neither.

Interviewer: The idea of man regressing to a pre-lingual stage must be a satiric device to get at what you experience in human communicative behavior today?

Percy: Well, I might have had at the edge of my mind some literary critics, philosophers and semioticians, who seem hell-bent on denying the very qualities of language and literature which have been held in such high esteem in the past: namely, that it is possible to know something about the world, that the world actually exists, that one person can actually say or write about the world and that other people can understand him. That, in a word, communication is possible. Some poets and critics outdo me in regression. I was content to regress some characters to a rather endearing pongid-primate level. But one poet I read about claimed that the poet's truest self could only be arrived at if he regressed himself clear back to the inorganic level, namely, a stone.

Interviewer: When at the end of the book you hint that earlier poets wrote two-word sentences, uttered howls or routinely exposed themselves during their readings, I thought you meant the counterculture.

Percy: I was thinking of Ginsberg and company—and some of his imitators who can be found in our genteel Southern universities. I do not imply that Ginsberg had been intoxicated by Na^{24}, but only that such poets might suffer cortical deficits of a more obscure sort. The fact that American writers-in-residence and poets-in-residence often behave worse than football players does not necessarily imply that they are more stoned than the latter. There is more than one way to assault the cortex.

Interviewer: You have said literature can be a living social force, that the segregationists could feel the impact of a satirical line about Valley Forge Academy in *Love in the Ruins*. Do you expect *The Thanatos Syndrome* to be effective in that way?

Percy: I would hope that it would have some small influence in the great debate on the sanctity of life in the face of technology. For one thing, I would hope to raise the level of the debate above the crude polemics of the current pro-abortion/pro-life wrangle. When people and issues get completely polarized, somebody needs to take a step back, take a deep breath, take a new look.

Interviewer: Aren't there more immediate ways besides writing satirical fiction? Have you ever been engaged in political activity?

Percy: Only in a small way in the sixties. For a while I had the honor of being labeled a nigger-lover and a bleeding heart. One small bomb threat from the Klan and one interesting night in the attic with my family and a shotgun, feeling both pleased and ridiculous and beset with ambiguities—for I knew some of the Klan people and they are not bad fellows, no worse probably than bleeding-heart liberals.

Interviewer: Is there any concrete issue that engages your attention most in connection with what is going on in America at the moment?

Percy: Probably the fear of seeing America, with all its great strength and beauty and freedom—"Now in these dread latter days of the old violent beloved U.S.A.," and so on—gradually subside into decay through default and be defeated, not by the Communist movement, demonstrably a bankrupt system, but from within by weariness, boredom, cynicism, greed, and in the end helplessness before its great problems. Probably the greatest is the rise of a black underclass. Maybe Faulkner was right. Slavery was America's Original Sin and the one thing that can defeat us. I trust not.

Interviewer: In connection with what is going on in the world?

Percy: Ditto: the West losing by spiritual acedia. A Judaic view is not inappropriate here: Communism may be God's punishment for the sins of the West. Dostoyevsky thought so.

Interviewer: You have often spoken about the postpartum depression you are in when you finish a novel. To put the question in Lost-in-the-Cosmos terms: now that you have finished another novel, which re-entry option is open to you?

Percy: Thanks for taking re-entries seriously. Probably re-entry (3)—travel (geographical—I'm going to Maine where I've never been). Plus re-entry (2), anaesthesia—a slight dose of bourbon.

Interviewer: In 1981 you spoke about a novel you were writing about two amnesiacs traveling on a Greyhound bus. You also said that you had been at that novel for two years. *Thanatos* is obviously not that novel. Did you give up on that one?

Percy: I can't remember.

Interviewer: Do you have any plans for future works?

Percy: It is in my mind to write a short work on semiotics showing how the current discipline has been screwed up by followers of Charles Peirce and de Saussure, the founders of modern semiotics. The extraordinary insight of Peirce into the *triadic* nature of meaning for humans and of de Saussure into the nature of the sign—as a union of the signifier and the signified—has been largely perverted by the current European tradition of structuralism and deconstruction and the American version of "dyadic" psychology, that is, various versions of behaviorism, so-called "cognitive" psychology, artificial intelligence, and so on. It would be nice if someone pursued Peirce's and de Saussure's breakthroughs. On the other hand, I may not have the time or the energy.

Interviewe: Are there hopes that you would like the eighth decade of your life to fulfill?

Percy: I was thinking of getting a word processor.

Interviewer: The minimum a seventy-year-old man deserves is a birthday present. Since the person in question happens to be a writer, and since he has shown in a self-interview that he is the best man to answer the questions, the birthday present is that he can *ask* the last question.

Percy: Question: Since you are a satirical novelist and since the main source of the satirist's energy is anger about something amiss or wrong about the world, what is the main target of your anger in *The Thanatos Syndrome*?

Answer: It is the widespread and ongoing devaluation of human life in the western world—under various sentimental disguises: "quality of life," "pointless suffering," "termination of life without meaning," etc. I trace it to a certain mind-set in the biological and social sciences which is extraordinarily influential among educated folk—so much so that it has almost achieved the status of a quasi-religious orthodoxy. If I had to give it a name, it would be something like: The Holy Office of the Secular Inquisition. It is not to be confused with "secular humanism" because, for one thing, it is anti-human. Although it drapes itself in the mantle of the scientific method and free scientific inquiry, it is neither free nor scientific. Indeed it relies on certain hidden dogma where dogma has no place. I can think of two holy commandments which the Secular Inquisition lays down for all scientists and believers. The first: In your investigations and theories, Thou shalt not find anything unique about the human animal even if the evidence points to such uniqueness. Example: Despite heroic attempts to teach sign language to other animals, the evidence is that even the cleverest chimpanzee has never spontaneously named a single object or uttered a single sentence. Yet dogma requires that, despite traditional belief in the soul or the mind, and the work of more recent workers like Peirce and Langer in man's unique symbolizing capacity, *Homo sapiens sapiens* be declared to be not qualitatively different from other animals. Another dogma: Thou shalt not suggest that there is a unique and fatal flaw in *Homo sapiens sapiens* or indeed any perverse trait that cannot be laid to the influence of Western civilization. Examples: (1) An entire generation came under the influence of Margaret Mead's *Coming of Age in Samoa* and its message: that the Samoans were an innocent, happy and Edenic people until they were corrupted by missionaries and technology. That this turned out not to be true, that indeed the Samoans appear to have been at least as neurotic as New Yorkers, has not changed the myth or the mind-set. (2) The gentle Tasaday people of the Philippines, an isolated Stone Age tribe, were also described as innocents, peace-loving and benevolent. When asked to describe evil, they replied: "We cannot think of anything that is not good." That the Tasaday story has turned out to be like an *erratum* corrected in a footnote and as inconsequential. (3) The eminent Mayans are still perceived as not only the builders of a high culture, practitioners of the arts and sciences, but a gentle folk—this despite the fact that recent deciphering of Mayan hieroglyphs have disclosed the Mayans to have been a cruel, warlike people capable of tortures even more vicious than the Aztecs. Scholars, after ignoring the findings, have admitted that the "new image" of the Mayans is perhaps "less romantic" than we had supposed. Conclusion: It is easy to criticize the absurdities of fundamentalist beliefs like "scientific creationism"—that the world and its creatures were created six thousand years ago. But it is also necessary to criticize other dogmas parading as science and the bad faith of some scientists who have their own dogmatic agendas to promote under the guise of "free scientific inquiry." Scientific inquiry should in fact be free. The warning: If it is not, if it is subject to this or that ideology, then do not be surprised if the history of the Weimar doctors is repeated. Weimar leads to Auschwitz. The nihilism of some scientists in the name of ideology or sentimentality and the consequent devaluation of individual human life leads straight to the gas chamber.

Interview on *Worldnet*

Claude Richard, Simone Vauthier, Jean Rouberol,
and Regis Durand/1986

The Moviegoer and the *Agrégation d'anglais*: Walker Percy discusses his novel for French University students.

From a television conversation, moderated in Washington, D.C., by Judlyne Lilly, and in Paris, France, by Claude Richard, conducted via satellite with Dr. Percy in a New Orleans studio on 3 December 3 1986. Produced as *Worldnet Program 295/Euronet 170,* the program was made by the United States Information Agency for use by European and worldwide audiences. The transcription and editing have been done by Victor A. Kramer. A tape of the program was first made in Denmark, and has been provided for this book through the courtesy of Jan Gretlund. Permission has been granted by the United States Information Agency to use this material.

Lilly: Good afternoon and welcome to WORLDNET. Joining us today in Paris in conjunction with this year's *Agrégation d'anglais* is a French panel of distinguished professors of American Studies and literature. The *Agrégation* is France's major qualifying examination for French teachers of English and American Studies. Each year the *Agrégation* selects a series of specific topics to be covered in the year's examinations. These may be literature, history, social science, geography, or other topics. Only recently has the role of American thinking and American arts and literature been reflected in this examination. This year one of the topics is the work of the important American author Walker Percy. Mr. Percy is a novelist who incorporates philosophical and religious themes in his writing. He sees our modern world in a state of moral confusion; the values of the past no longer hold. His novels include *The Moviegoer,* for which he won the 1962 National Book Award for fiction. His other novels include: *The Last Gentleman, Love in the Ruins, Lancelot,* and *The Second Coming.* Mr. Percy is considered a philosophical novelist, particularly concerned with the problem of being. Firmly grounded in social observation, his rendering of characters and scenes is strikingly fresh, vivid, and bitingly satirical. Mr. Percy is joining us today from New Orleans. Mr. Percy, welcome to WORLDNET.

Percy: Thank you. I'm glad to be here.

Lilly: I'd like to go to the *Agrégation d'anglais* panel in Paris for your first question. Please remember to identify yourself for our guest.

Claude Richard: Welcome to WORLDNET Mr. Percy. Mr. Percy, allow me first to introduce the members of the panel: Professor Simone Vauthier, who teaches American Literature at the University of Strasbourg; Professor Regis Durand, who teaches American Literature at the University of Lille; Professor Jean Rouberol, who teaches American Literature at the University of Paris Four, and my name is Professor Claude Richard, and I teach at the University of Montpeiller. Mr. Percy, you are a famous American novelist and essayist, the author of six widely read novels and two very provocative collections of essays. You have been chosen by a national panel to be on the reading list for the *Agrégation d'anglais,* the highest degree for future teachers of English and American Literature. On the list with you are such writers as Shakespeare, John Donne, Oliver Goldsmith, Alfred Lord Tennyson, and Dashiell Hammett. To be on the reading list for the *Agrégation* is, in France, like ultimate recognition. The particular novel the students are supposed to work on is *The Moviegoer,* which accounts for the fact that after some more general questions, we shall concentrate on that novel, your first, originally published in 1961 and now a classic. My first question will deal with your background. You live and work in the South. You write in the South and about the South. Do you consider yourself as a Southern writer, and, if so, what features of your work do you regard as peculiarly Southern?

Percy: Well, thank you. May I first say a word to the *Agrégation d'anglais*? I want to thank you for inviting me to speak with you. It is indeed an honor, and I want to thank Professors Vauthier, whom I know, Richard, Rouberol, and Durand. It is indeed an honor to speak with such distinguished professors. And to the candidates of the *Agrégation*—I understand that you have been required to read *The Moviegoer,* so in a sense I feel I have a captive audience. I remember being a student and having to read books, and therefore not being too fond of the books, but I hope it hasn't been too much of an ordeal for you to read *The Moviegoer*. I would also like to say that one particular pleasure of speaking to you is being able to express my debt to French literature and to some particular French writers, whom we can speak about later, perhaps.

To answer your question about being a Southern writer: Yes, of course, I'm a Southern writer. I was born and raised in the South here, and I always lived here, except for going to school in New York. Yes, I'm a Southern writer in the sense that I depend on my Southern background for the decor, the setting, a sense of place, which any novelist must have. But I must tell you straight off, I may not be a typical example of a Southern writer. To tell you the truth, even though I lived only a few miles from William Faulkner and he used to play tennis with my uncle, I owe less to Faulkner, and Southern writers, and indeed American writers, than to certain French writers. To be specific, Jean-Paul Sartre, Albert Camus, Gabriel Marcel, and to go back-a-ways, Blaise Pascal. So, let me admit my Southern background, but also pay my debt to these French writers, among others.

Durand: Good afternoon Mr. Percy.

Percy: Good afternoon.

Durand: *The Moviegoer* was published 25 years ago in a place and time which now seem to us very different indeed. Very far away, indeed, from our world. This year the novel is being read by several thousand young French students. I want to ask you what your reaction was to this encounter with a public so different from the one you originally had in mind. Or, to put it another way, what do you think *The Moviegoer* can communicate to a young European audience?

Percy: Well, I'm not sure what it can communicate. However, I have noticed that among my American peers, it's a source of great pleasure to me that most of the letters I get, most of the reaction I get from readers, even to *The Moviegoer*, which was published 25 years ago, are not from my contemporaries but from young people, people [who are] in college or graduate school. I would like to think that it speaks, in some sense, to the younger generation. How, I can't say, except that I would hope like any good novel it simply, I like to say, names sectors of experience. And if a novel is good, what it does is it describes, points out, talks about certain states of consciousness, certain predicaments, which are recognized by the reader. Perhaps young men like Binx Bolling, the protagonist of this novel is not unlike . . . I would like to

think he is not unlike a young American of the same age in New
Orleans, or New York, and perhaps a young French student in Paris or
Marseilles. At least, that's my hope.

Rouberol: Good afternoon, Mr. Percy. Do you feel that your novel is
informed by a system of values and if so, what values? In other words,
in spite of what Binx says in the "Epilogue," would you claim that *The
Moviegoer* is not, somehow, an edifying novel?

Percy: As Binx himself says in the last chapter, he doesn't feel much
inclined to speak of such matters as edification. You know, the vocation
of a novelist is a rather humble vocation. As the great philosopher
Kierkegaard said, he doesn't have the authority to be edifying. His
vocation has to do with narrative, entertainment, perhaps verification or
certification of experience. If it turns out to be edifying, well that may
be a byproduct or maybe a certain trick to which this author is not going
to own up to.

Vauthier: Good afternoon, Mr. Percy. My question is somehow
related to the question of Professor Rouberol. I would like you to tell us
what do you now see as your role as a Catholic novelist, and are the
problems you face as a Catholic novelist today different from what they
were 25 years ago?

Percy: Is this Simone Vauthier? Am I speaking with Simone
Vauthier?

Vauthier: Yes, yes. This is a very different meeting from our last
meeting in the bus station at Covington.

Percy: I remember that. It's very nice to talk to you. I wish I could
see you. I can only say that like Flannery O'Connor, I'm a Catholic
novelist in the sense that the Catholic faith, which is the Judeo-Christian
background, informs me as a writer. In that sense, what I write is a
consequence of the way I'm informed. It has not to do so much with an
explicit faith, or transmitting an explicit faith in my writings as it has to
do with what I would call an anthropology. Anthropology not in the
American sense of an ethnology, but more in the European sense of a
view of man, of a theory of man—man as more than organism, as more
than consumer, man as Gabriel Marcel describes him, *Homo Viator,*
Man the Wayfarer, Man the Pilgrim, Man in transit, on a journey. So
I like to think that in that sense I'm a—quote—Catholic novelist. You
know it's the very nature of language and of the times we live in, which
is a Post-Christian era. The novelist has difficulty with language in

speaking of such things as faith and religion. The words are overused, worn out, worn thin, so he'd better be wary about how he uses them. As James Joyce would say, he proceeds with a certain indirection, guile, maybe even a modicum of deceit.

Richard: I'm going to ask the next question. Mr. Percy, I would like to ask you a question about your main character, Binx Bolling. Binx, the moviegoer who does not go to the movies, may be regarded as a modern hero, insofar as what I call somewhere his exile, his renunciation, his negative quest, his nominalism, could be described as a form of wisdom. Would you agree with this vision of Binx, and would you care to comment upon his peculiar wisdom?

Percy: Well, Binx is a moviegoer, but only in a peculiar sense. He doesn't go to movies as most people go to the movies—as a source of entertainment or diversion. He's playing a certain game. He doesn't know it, he's not conscious of it, but he's doing what Kierkegaard would call exercises in repetition and rotation so that this is all part of his search. Binx makes much of the fact that he has undertaken a search. He speaks of two different kinds of search. One is what he calls his vertical search, namely . . . he's spent a good deal of time reading what he calls the most profound scientific works, Einstein's theory, or H.G. Wells' study of history, *The Universe as I See It, The Structure of the Atom* by Schroedinger, and books like that. As I recall, he describes a scene where he was in a motel room in Birmingham, Alabama, and he'd just finished a book, *The Universe as I See It,* or some book like that, and to his satisfaction the book explained the nature of the universe, the nature of the cosmos, the nature of the electron, Einstein's theory, but as he said when he finished the book, the world was explained, the cosmos was explained, but there he was with himself as a kind of leftover, having to draw one breath and then the next. So, he sees himself as having explained the world, but sees himself as a leftover from it. In a sense, he's a victim of your great philosopher Réne Descartes, to whom I attribute many of the troubles of the modern world, if it doesn't offend you to say so. When Descartes divided reality between the *res cogitans* and the *res extensa,* the thinking consciousness and the physical world, it led to many of Binx's troubles, to be specific. So there is Binx as a leftover from all the theories about the universe.

So then he undertakes what he calls his horizontal search; that is to say, he goes out into the world. He leaves his motel room, he leaves his aunt's house in New Orleans, he moves out into Gentilly, which is a pleasant middle-class suburb of New Orleans, and there undertakes a rather peculiar search which he calls horizontal, meaning that he is out in the world, he's put his books down. He goes out with his secretaries, he goes to movies, and he looks for signs. One sign to his way of thinking are Jews. He has Jewish friends, and he thinks that when he sees a Jew that this person cannot be subsumed by the theories of the books that he has read. So to him, in his own peculiar way, the Jews are a sign. And the moviegoing is an exercise in what Kierkegaard would call repetition and rotation. He does peculiar exercises like going to see an old John Wayne movie which he's seen ten years ago, and which he goes to see again. He goes to the same movie theater, he sits in the same seat where he made a mark with his thumbnail ten years ago. This is his peculiar way of trying to understand the nature of time. He's thinking what has happened to this seat? This seat has been here persisting in time for ten years. John Wayne was in his movie. The movie was *Red River,* incidentally, one of John Wayne's best, and here he is again, John Wayne doing the same thing up on the screen, and here's my girlfriend sitting next to me, and here I am, and here's a lapse of ten years. So, that's Binx's peculiar way of exploring reality, in this case time.

Durand: Mr. Percy, this is a question which has to do with happiness, and I've been urged to ask it by my students. I do it very willingly because I think it's an interesting problem. The formulation, however, is entirely my own. In his essay *On the Myth of Sisyphus* Albert Camus says at one point that we ought to think of Sisyphus as being happy. Are we to think of Binx Bolling as [being] happy? Or is he, on the contrary, a stranger in a strange land, completely isolated in his own world, and what in fact is the nature of his secret or inner desires of his quest, if you like?

Percy: Well, I think Binx is not unhappy. But I think that he would be horrified if it were proposed to him that he was trying to be happy. What he's doing is looking for something. The "happiness" is a concomitant byproduct of the search itself. I think he would laugh at the idea, and he would take a dim view of his fellow Americans' quest for happiness. He's certainly happier living in Gentilly, which is a kind of desert. He's a stock and bond broker, and he does very well, but he reads his book in between phone calls and customers, the book *Arabia*

Deserta, and it's probably not an accident that he enjoys the descriptions of the travels of this man in Arabia. He himself, Binx Bolling, is in kind of a desert in Gentilly. I will leave you to draw your own conclusions about the place of the pilgrim in the desert.

Rouberol: You once said that you were concerned, as a novelist, with the dislocation of man in the modern world. Do you feel that this dislocation refers to the treatment of space in your novels? Would you care to comment upon the general question of this dislocation of structures in the book?

Percy: The dislocation of space is real. He, Binx, has been dislocated from his previous residence, but the dislocation of space is a symbol, or an objective correlative, of his real dislocation. And his real dislocation has to do with a dislocation from the ordinary modes of existence in America: existence as a consumer, as a recipient of all the goods and services of technology, so that even his moviegoing is done with a kind of objective view of what's going on as he does it. Also he's dislocated or in exile from his own traditions. I placed him very consciously as a certain consciousness placed between two traditions in the South. One is from his father's side, his aunt's family, which I can only describe in terms of Graeco-Roman Stoicism, a very strong, ethical, stoic tradition which owes less to Christianity than it does to the Emperor Marcus Aurelius and the Stoic philosophers. His aunt typifies this tradition. One doesn't hear about it very much because one thinks of the South as being a strongly Protestant section of the country, but actually in the upper class, Anglo-Saxon Southerners, and particularly in the military caste, this Stoic tradition was at least as strong as the Christian tradition. The other tradition is his mother's family, which is middle-class, bourgeois, New Orleans Catholics. Binx, at the beginning of the book, is deracinated, alienated from both traditions. He's left his aunt's house. He doesn't think that her view of the world helps him in his search. His mother's family, his brothers and sisters there, their Catholicism he finds irrelevant to what he's trying to do. So you know, it's a curious thing that this book is often misread, particularly by my Southern contemporaries. I suppose the favorite scene which my contemporaries in the South always quote to me, which they identify with me, thinking that I wrote the scene as one sympathetic to it, is the scene toward the end of the book when Aunt Emily scolds Binx for what she sees as his misbehavior. And she reminds him of the high ideals of his tradition, of correct behavior, of the sense of the honor code and rectitude. She speaks of how men in our family have behaved with a sense of honor, a sense of gentleness, and sweetness, and gaiety towards women. And she speaks with contempt of what she calls the American common man. When I say common, I mean common as hell. So I need to be congratulated for that denunciation by Aunt Emily of her errant nephew Binx Bolling. Whereas in fact he's not buying that at all, although you see in the end he does accept the sort of responsibility that Kierkegaard calls the ethical stage of existence—he marries Kate and he becomes a responsible citizen. And at the same time, in the beginning he defects from his mother's Catholic tradition, and in the end perhaps there's a reconciliation with that. So again, I'm thinking of your question: in this novel, as in all of my novels, I balance the question very delicately between the hero or the protagonist of most of my novels who is in some sense or other, more or less dislocated, alienated, deracinated— like most heroes of modern fiction. But the question I pose to the reader is: who is abnormal? He? She? Who is dislocated? The consumers? The businessmen? The professional men? The happy scientists who are busy with their various works? Maybe the philosophical progenitor is Pascal, who said to be born, to live, is to be dislocated. So the question is posed as to whether dislocation is perhaps the proper state of Binx Bolling and man or woman.

Vauthier: Mr. Percy, could we return to the question of time, and could you address the general problem of time in *The Moviegoer*?

Percy: Time? Well, at the end of the Mardi Gras season, the last scene and the last day of *The Moviegoer* is Ash Wednesday, so there's a certain relevance here of the time of the action. The celebration of Mardi Gras is in New Orleans the biggest festival of the year with six weeks of parades and six weeks of parties. It ends with Ash Wednesday which is generally more or less ignored by most people who take part in Mardi Gras. So it's understated but it's nevertheless important. I think one of the last scenes in *The Moviegoer* is Binx waiting to meet Kate and he walks past a church and I don't think Binx himself is even aware that it's Ash Wednesday. He notices a man, a black man, coming out of a church. Binx, as you know, is in his own way very observant. He has what he calls good radar. He's very much attuned to people. As he says, he likes to see the way people fit themselves into the world. And he sees a man whom he doesn't know come down the steps of the church. He sees something on his forehead, and he describes his forehead as having a sienna color, and he sees a smudge on his forehead. As I recall, Binx remembers that it's Ash Wednesday when he sees the smudge of ashes on the man's forehead. And Binx has a certain recollection, a certain thought, about what the significance of Ash Wednesday is. He speaks just in passing in a couple of sentences about the dim, dazzling effects of grace, which is the question he poses for himself. Of course the other mention of time has to do with Binx's investigation of time, which I have already mentioned, which he, in his little games of moviegoing, likes to explore time by repetition by going to the same movie or movie house in which he thinks. As he says, he can sense time, he can taste time. He says with the accidents of the events in time removed, as he says it is like eating peanut brittle with the peanuts removed. So those are the two explorations of time that come to mind in *The Moviegoer*.

Vauthier: This is not really a follow-up, but an American critic recently asserted that today the movies and the thought referred to in *The Moviegoer* has no value, as he said. And I was curious to test such an idea with my students. I found out that they disagreed completely. In fact, we all agreed that the cinema functions in your novels as most of the literary allusions and quotations do. That is to say they function as a strategy of communication and as a mark of cultural intertextuality. I wonder if you had any other responses similar to that of your American critic and whether you would care to comment on your views of moviegoing in *The Moviegoer*?

Percy: I can just say that people I hear from do seem to understand the strategy of moviegoing as I use it and as Binx uses it in the novel. I remember, for example, one particular episode of moviegoing: when he goes to the movies with Kate. Before he went to the movies with a succession of his secretaries—Linda, Sharon, Stephanie—who didn't care much for the movies; they were as willing to go as not, but they would rather have been taken to the Blue Room of the Roosevelt Hotel to go dancing. That would be much more to their liking. They didn't think much of Binx taking them, without a car, getting on a bus to go out to the sticks, the suburbs, to see a movie. But it's important that when he goes with Kate, who after all is the one person who understands him, he makes a point of going to see a movie, a very good movie incidentally, *Panic in the Streets,* which was filmed in New Orleans with Richard Widmark, an excellent actor. The movie was being shown in a movie house on Tchoupitoulas Street, which was in

the very neighborhood where the movie was filmed. So Binx is sitting
there enjoying himself, enjoying the fact that he's in the movie house in
the area, in the very neighborhood, where the movie was filmed. Kate is
watching the movie, but she is on to him, she is watching him, and she
says I know what you're doing. And he says what. She says the reason
you're enjoying it, and the reason I'm enjoying it, is that it represents
certification, doesn't it. And he says yes. You see, the peculiar reality
of movies is that it certifies the place. That is why even though movies
are the ultimate unreality, Americans seem to accept them as even more
real than their real lives or their real neighborhoods. So what could be
more real than to be in the very neighborhood [where a movie was
filmed]. Living in an ordinary neighborhood, as Binx says, one is
uncertified, one sees the same people, one goes about one's business,
sees people who are alive maybe more dead than alive, sees the same
buildings, and everything falls victim to what Heidegger would call
alltäglichkeit, everydayness. And yet when this very same ordinary
scene is represented in the movies it all of a sudden becomes alive, it
becomes certified so that Binx and Kate are experiencing the phenomenon of certification. So she understands it, and when they walk out
of the moviehouse, you see, in his own peculiar way of thinking, which
is always peculiar, always aberrant, but which I trust has a certain grain
of truth to it and I think so, to answer your question, because I hear
from people who say about his moviegoing experiences as with his other
experiences, I know what you mean, I know exactly what you mean.
So, this one example of Binx's theory of certification. . . . Of course,
the same thing happens at the beginning of the book when he is leaving
Gentilly on his way to his aunt's house and he hears that Bill Holden is
making a movie in the French Quarter. And he doesn't want to meet
Bill Holden; by lucky chance he does see him and falls in behind him.
What Binx wants to see is the reaction of other people to Bill Holden.
And he's interested in this extraordinary phenomenon—and I am too—
the aura of reality around movie stars, who are perhaps the most unreal
of all people, in truth. But as he says, an aura of reality seems to
surround Holden as he walks down the street. People notice him, and
like to talk to him, and Binx, the Cartesian *res cogitans,* is there
watching Bill Holden, and trying to figure out why this is, what is the
purpose, what's the reason for this phenomenon. I hope that goes partly
to your question.

Durand: Mr. Percy, in your essay "Notes for a Novel about the End of the World," you observe that, I quote, "what the novelist sees, or rather senses, is a certain quality of the post-modern consciousness as he finds it and as he incarnates it in his own characters." In what ways are *The Moviegoer* and the character of Binx Bolling characteristic of this new breed of consciousness and of fiction, and how would you qualify this statement today after post-modernism has been so much talked about in recent years?

Percy: Well, that's a very large question. To address that would be to talk about nothing less than the subject matter of the whole post-modern novel. That is what the novelist is writing about both in this country and in Europe. I don't know quite how to address that except to say that it is a quality of consciousness which has to do with a divorce, a separation, of the individual consciousness not only from the physical world but even from other consciousnesses. Again, I am irresistibly drawn back to René Descartes, who I think might have started most of the difficulty. What I write about, not only Binx Bolling, is the adventures, the various options, that are open to an isolated consciousness, how he goes about relating, or trying to relate, trying to break out of the coccoon of solipsism. As a matter of fact, I suppose my novels can be read as an exploration of the various options which are open, or which are at least attempted, by the isolated post-modern consciousness.

And most American novelists are up to the same thing.

My particular orientation goes back to some writings and studies I did in the philosophy of language, and in semiotics. As a matter of fact, the reason I started writing novels was because I had written and published a dozen or so articles on the nature of language, particularly I was trying to derive this very consciousness we are speaking of in a linguistic manner by semiotic theory. And I got into something which has been variously called triadic theory based on the philosophy of the American philosopher Charles Peirce, de Saussure, Cassirer, in which I was trying to derive the self semiotically and then, later, to try to actually define the various options open to the self in trying to re-enter the "world," which had come into being as the result of his entrance into the world of language. So having written these articles which a few people read, which I was not making a living at, again, I must confess my debt to the French tradition, which is much more French than it is American, of a academic or a philosopher having certain philosophical ideas, in this case semiotics, and then translating them into a dramatic, narrative, or novelistic form. This is what Americans seldom do and what the French do often with people like Claudel, Sartre, Mauriac, who began as philosophers and ended as novelists. So I've found it very congenial to try to express these ideas in novelistic form, and that is no accident because like Sartre my ideas have very much to do with the concrete predicament of a self, a consciousness, placed down in a world. So, again, let me say that even though I am a Catholic, and Sartre was an atheist and a Marxist, and Camus was certainly not a Christian, [yet] I found myself much more congenial with the style and the method of people like Jean-Paul Sartre and Albert Camus. The very opening of their novels, Camus beginning his novel by saying "My mother died today, or maybe it was yesterday." and Sartre beginning his diary by saying "He's going to the library." and he says "I noticed today that my hand looks strange." That stylistic approach to novel writing was much more congenial to me than say the traditional Southern novel, even Faulkner, as great as he is, and is much as he is admired in France, that approach meant much more to me than Faulkner or say to the traditional Catholic novelist in France, Mauriac, Claudel. That may be a paradox, but that's the way it is.

Rouberol: You have already spoken of the end of the novel or certain aspects of it. Would you care to comment, more specifically, on the "Epilogue" which some people seem to have had some trouble with it?

Percy: Well there again I can only say as Binx says in the "Epilogue" I don't have an inclination to talk about this. I will only refer your reader and members of the, or candidates of your *Agrégation* to the last three pages of *The Moviegoer*, particularly to Binx's conversation with his brothers and sisters. In the same way, I suppose that Dostoyevsky, if you ask a question about the end of the meaning of *The Brothers Karamazov*, he might well say, well, read the last two pages, read what Alyosha, the young monk, says to the young brothers and sisters of Kolia who has just died. If you read that, it will probably tell you, it will probably clarify the questions about the Epilogue.

Richard: Mr. Percy, before asking you the last question, I want to thank you most warmly for this wonderful interview. I won't have time to come back. I thank you most warmly for an interview which is going to be extremely useful to all our students, to say nothing of the panel, naturally.

My last question, which is probably going to be final, will have to do

with language. I would like to ask you a question about the formal
qualities of *The Moviegoer*. In this novel there is a very characteristic
treatment of language, a specific tone of detached irony, or allusiveness,
and even, to me, playfulness, as well as a very original, perhaps
symbolical, use of objects like cars, for instance. Would you care to
comment upon your attitude about language as a semantic vehicle?

Percy: It's a good question. I very consciously, in almost all of my
novels, I deal with the pathology of language. There is usually some
character or some person who has difficulty speaking, or perhaps has
some pathology in his speech or her speech—cannot speak at all,
perhaps one character can only tap messages through a wall. This has to
do with the fact, which I've written about and studied elsewhere in the
philosophy of language and semiotics, of the phenomenon of the
exhaustion of language, the wearing out of language. The Russian
Formalist Victor Shklovsky speaks of the over familiarization of words
so that words become, instead of transmitting meaning, a kind of
simulacrum, a covering, a disguise of meaning. So that it is a task of the
poet, and the artist, to break through the simulacrum in order to, as
Shklovsky says, to defamiliarize, to render strange words and symbols
so that they then convey. So, when I have people speaking strangely,
the idea is that in spite of the strangeness, in spite of the dislocations in
syntax, or the inappropriateness of the use of the words, the intention is
that the words nevertheless convey meaning whereas the ordinary words
do not. For instance, the ordinary words of the Creed: "I believe in
God, the Father Almighty . . . " and so forth, this gets rattled off, and
Binx has been hearing this, and the words become a simulacrum. And
the trick of the novelist, the task of the artist, is always to somehow
renew language, make it fresh, make it strange, if you like,
pathological, if you like, anything in order to transmit meaning, and to
renew the process of communication.

Lilly: This concludes today's discussion. I'd like to thank our
distinguished panel in Paris and Mr. Walker Percy for being with us.
I'm Judlyne Lilly for WORLDNET.

Moralist of the South

Malcolm Jones/1987

From *The New York Times Magazine,* March 22, 1987, 42, 44, 46.
Reprinted by permission of The New York Times © 1987 by The
New York Times Company.

While the guide for the house tour drones through the history of Greenwood Plantation, 100 miles up the Mississippi from New Orleans, the
novelist Walker Percy and his wife, Mary Bernice, stand in a back
parlor over a small table and study an odd and troubling list. They have
found the list on the table amid photographs of the century-old Doric
columns rising from the rubble left when fire destroyed the house in
1960, blueprints quilted together from evidence in old photos, and news
clippings of the years of meticulous restoration by the present owner.
There is also a book advertising one of the television productions, "The
North and South," filmed at Greenwood. Percy grins sardonically as he
learns that some of the outbuildings, including the mausoleum and its
surrounding cemetery, were built by visitors from Hollywood.

The list in Percy's hands is something altogether different. It is an
inventory of the plantation property, drawn up in 1862. In addition to
linens and silver and furniture, it includes each of the plantation's 553
slaves: "Man Levi aged 21 of BLK color, valued and appraised at the
sum of one thousand dollars." Percy and his wife study the list in
silence.

The table's odd collage, joining screwball humor and indelible
tragedy, could with no trouble have come from one of Percy's half-
dozen novels. He has, in fact, used a few of Greenwood's features in
his new book, *The Thanatos Syndrome,* due next month from Farrar,
Straus and Giroux. In this novel, as in the others, he creates a South in
which illusion is always undermining everyday reality, and the past is
always barging in on the present.

In West Feliciana Parish, where Percy has come on this warm, gray
January day, towns are small and scarce. Plantations abound. Plantation tours are a mainstay of the local economy, which is otherwise
depressed. Feliciana depends on its past.

169

Starting the meandering three-hour drive home to Covington, near
New Orleans, Percy stares out at the landscape. Even in winter, Louisiana is green, the pale green of a dollar bill that's gone through the wash.
Nothing stirs. After a moment, he wonders aloud what it is like to live
so far away from people, and he says that he would not want that much
solitude himself.

For a few miles, the Percys tease each other about what they've seen.
Married for 40 years, Walker and Mary Bernice (called Bunt) get on
with a practiced, absent-minded risibility. Each looks after the other
with unobtrusive fondness. She is the more gregarious, he the more
habitually deferential, and though he is unvaryingly polite, there is
something remote about him. He would rather ask questions than
answer them, even though he is an opinionated man.

Suddenly he laughs, thinking of Greenwood. "The whole thing's like
a movie set," he says, and pauses, and then goes on, in a voice that
sounds bewildered and awed and a little angry. "I'll tell you one thing
that wasn't phony: the list of those slaves. That thing gets to you."

With the publication of *The Moviegoer,* his first novel, in 1961, when
he was 45 years old, Percy claimed a position, never relinquished, as
not only a major Southern novelist, but as one of the unique voices in
American fiction. More than any, his six novels are responsible for
taking the focus of Southern letters off the front porch of the country
store and putting it on the golf course and in the subdivisions that
characterize the modern South. In Percy's South, historical monuments
and Hollywood fakery coexist cheerfully: Sunbelt newcomers pull on
riding boots and take to drawling; the descendants of Civil War generals
move to the suburbs and make fortunes converting slave quarters to
$400,000 condos.

At rock bottom—and there is a rock bottom in Percy's world—things
are finally not funny. He is one of our severest moralists, and one of our
most philosophical novelists. "I was more influenced by the so-called
French existentialists than I was by William Faulkner next door," he
says. His lawyers and doctors are not deaf to the imperatives of the past,
but they are very much citizens of modern, homogenized America, all
searching for an answer to the question Percy himself once posed in an
essay: "Why does man feel so sad in the twentieth century?"

Robert Giroux, his longtime book editor, thinks that although Percy
is a "Southern writer" to the extent that as a stylist he can keep company

with Faulkner and Eudora Welty and Flannery O'Connor, "he's unlike any other Southern writer. He's a loner. He has a very original cast of mind."

The critic Cleanth Brooks has called Percy "our most acute commentator on the social life of the South—particularly of the South during the last quarter of a century."

The Thanatos Syndrome is vintage Percy in several ways. It is, loosely, a sequel to *Love in the Ruins,* his most broadly satirical novel, and it borrows that novel's hero, Dr. Thomas More, the somewhat seedy, slightly disreputable psychiatrist. Once again, there are odd goings-on, and once again Dr. More is the first to discover the trouble and do something about it.

At the same time, there are significant differences. *The Thanatos Syndrome* is less fantastic, more focused than its predecessor; there is more of the smell of the world in it. Its most immediately startling aspect is its plot. It is a thriller, a complicated mystery full of scenes of antic, adroitly rendered action set against a Mississippi River plantation background.

Giroux is pleased that prepublication reviews have praised the new book's accessibility. "Not that I don't think all his books are accessible," he says, "but because advance reviewers feel he's going to have a larger audience, and I do, too, because it's such a whopping good narrative." The publishing company is strongly behind the book, having scheduled a first printing of 75,000 books (25,000 more than his last novel, *The Second Coming,* in 1980), the largest ever for a Percy novel and far better than that accorded most books of serious fiction; it is also a dual main selection of the Book-of-the-Month Club.

The skeletal linearity of the new novel's plot gives it a visceral force only indirectly present in Percy's previous work—wry, elliptical novels of alienation and spiritual quest. *The Thanatos Syndrome* slices deep with its uncompromising critique of the ethical, even religious pitfalls inherent in social engineering generally and euthanasia in particular.

And yet, this is Percy's most optimistic work. It not only holds out some hope, it gives it an address: the little unassuming office of Dr. More, where one man, having abandoned the dream of saving the world that he entertained in *Love in the Ruins,* works patiently to heal others. Percy plainly places great faith in the unspectacular, but not unheroic, efforts of individuals to help one another.

His face is proud and heavy-featured, creased and somewhat weath-
ered. His eyes are deep-set and bright and quick. He favors khakis and
corduroys, cardigans, leather lace-ups or running shoes, and in wet
weather he tugs on a shapeless green canvas hat. At 70, he is spare and
nimble and often restless. Habitually, he stand at an angle, his weight
on one foot, hands in pockets or clasped behind his back, his head
ducked and tucked into his shoulder.

He is a Southerner from a fine old Mississippi family. His great-uncle
was a United States Senator. His first cousin once removed was the poet
and essayist William Alexander Percy, author of the autobiographical
memoir *Lanterns on the Levee*. Percy's father was a Birmingham
lawyer, and Percy grew up beside the No. 6 hole of the golf course of
the new country club. When Walker Percy was 13, his father committed
suicide. Three years later, his mother died in an automobile accident.
By then, Walker and his two younger brothers had gone to live with
Will Percy.

In an introduction to a recent edition of *Lanterns on the Levee*, Percy
calls "Uncle Will" the most extraordinary man he ever met. "He was the
fabled relative, the one you liked to speculate about," Percy wrote. "His
father was a United States Senator and he had been a decorated infantry
officer in World War I. Besides that, he was a poet. The fact that he
was also a lawyer and a planter did not cut much ice—after all, the
South was full of lawyer-planters. But how many people did you know
who were war heroes and wrote books of poetry?"

Will Percy's Greenville, Miss., home was one of the region's best-
known cultural hubs, "a kind of standard stopover for people who were
studying the South," Percy recalls. One man came for the weekend to
talk to Will Percy about writing a book and stayed for a year to write it.
"That was the kind of house it was," Percy says. "There was Dave
Cohn, up in one of the wings of that old house, writing *God Shakes
Creation,* his memoir about the Delta."

One visitor who made a deep impression on Percy was the psychiatrist Harry Stack Sullivan: "He was notable because he didn't take
things too seriously. He got a three-week's grant to study the race
problem in Mississippi. He spent the whole time in Uncle Will's back
pantry, a wonderful place, and sitting back there and mixing vodka
martinis. First time I'd ever heard of a vodka martini. He had sense
enough to know that this was an absurd project, but he also had sense

enough to know to talk to Uncle Will's servants. He'd sit back there in
the pantry and talk to the cook, the houseman, and listen to them and
see what was going on."

Sullivan figures in *The Thanatos Syndrome,* and Thomas More
attributes his optimistic philosophy of psychiatry to something Sullivan
tells his residents: "You take the last patient we saw. . . . A loser by all
counts. . . . If I were he, I'd be depressed, too. Right? Wrong. You're
thinking the most we can do for him is make him feel a little better, give
him a pill or two. . . . Here's the peculiar thing and I'll never understand why this is so: *Each patient this side of psychosis, and even some
psychotics, has the means of obtaining what he needs, she needs, with a
little help from you.*"

Percy went to undergraduate school at the University of North
Carolina and then on to medical school at Columbia University. He
aimed to be a psychiatrist himself. It never crossed his mind to be a
writer. Fifty years ago in the South "it was like it used to be 100 years
earlier," he says. There were four career choices for a respectable
gentleman: law, medicine, the military or the clergy. "And I sure as hell
wasn't thinking about the military or the clergy. Most people in my
family had been lawyers, I didn't want to do that. Medicine was left as
the obvious last resort."

He interned at Bellevue, but he never practiced. In 1942, he contracted pulmonary tuberculosis. He spent three years recuperating in
sanitariums in New York, Connecticut and New Mexico. He spent most
of that time in Saranac Lake, N.Y., flat on his back, reading voraciously,
mostly fiction and philosophy, especially the 19th-century Russian
novelists, the French existentialists and Soren Kierkegaard. He calls
tuberculosis "the best disease I ever had. If I hadn't had it, I might be a
second-rate shrink practicing in Birmingham, at best."

When he finished his convalescence, at a dude ranch in New Mexico,
he went back to the South: "It's funny, but as beautiful as Santa Fe is,
after six months of Santa Fe, you miss the green of the Deep South."
There, in short order, he married, converted to Catholicism and, thanks
to an inheritance, took up a life of contemplation and writing, first
essays on a variety of philosophical topics, then fiction.

He is reluctant to talk much about his conversion, except to say that
it came as a result of his three years of reading and thinking while
recuperating from "what could have been a fatal disease," and that he is

indebted to Kierkegaard, whose critique of Hegelianism articulated Percy's own doubts about the scientific method; it explained, he says, "everything under the sun but what it is like to be born as an individual, to live and die."

He did not turn his back entirely on his scientific and medical training. The elegance of scientific thought still excites him, and the diagnostic method has proved oddly valuable to his writing. It's all a matter, he says, of starting with the assumption that something is wrong, whether it be the culture or the country or the neighbors.

"For some time now," the new novel begins, "I have noticed that something strange is occurring in our region." Dr. Thomas More, previously the hero of *Love in the Ruins,* is fresh out of jail for selling amphetamines to truckers. A man of dubious record and dubious faith but a good man, he has come home to Feliciana to pick up the pieces of his modest psychiatric practice. He quickly notices that his former patients—even his wife—have a whole new set of problems. Instead of the old neuroses and psychoses, they are somehow vacant, more sexually uninhibited. Investigating further, More begins to uncover evidence of a conspiracy to chemically alter the behavior of the people of Feliciana. Enlisting the help of his cousin, Lucy Lipscomb, he starts fighting back.

"I like the idea of a novel starting out in a normal, everyday way and then a little something going wrong," Percy says. His voice is a light Southern tenor, as mild as his manner, and he speaks quickly, though haltingly, and he often ends a sentence with a question mark, as though he were thinking out loud: "Somebody gets onto something. What's going on?" He decided to write a conspiracy thriller as a way out of "writing yet another novel of a young man or woman in quest of herself or himself."

All of the heroes in Percy's novels are upper-middle-class Southern-ers. Two are lawyers, one is a doctor, one sells stocks and bonds. None wants for any material thing, and yet all are radically alienated from society. Percy thinks of them as Quentin Compson grown up. William Faulkner's sensitive Southern youth off at Harvard "had this whole Southern thing on his back—the old tradition, the Sartorises, everybody, his sister and Southern sexuality and decayed aristocracy. Although there are Southerners who are not as desperate or as depressed or as suicidal as Quentin Compson, I know plenty of them who are just as dislocated."

Ultimately, he sees the problem from a religious perspective. The dislocation is not peculiar to the South or even to this age; it is a part of being human. The "something wrong with people" is original sin. "The fall of man sure enough took place, no matter what the psychologists say."

Percy despises the notion that he might be writing tracts dressed up as stories, and he cringes at the label "religious novelist": "If I saw a bookshelf in a bookstore that said 'religious novelists,' I'd steer clear of it." Acknowledging that "a Catholic novelist, if he's serious about his religion, can't help but see the world in a certain way," he insists that he does not aim to edify: "That is not the business of the novelist."

In the early 1950's, Percy had hardly begun to publish philosophical and critical essays in magazines as varied as *Psychiatry, Commonweal* and the *Sewanee Review* before he started trying to write fiction. He supported his family with a modest inheritance from his uncle. "I had a few years of grace, which was very lucky indeed, to be able to write as I pleased and what I pleased without worrying too much about bread on the table for a while." He spent most of a decade writing two never-published novels, though now he swears he never felt discouraged. "There was never a moment when I doubted what I wanted to do. It was always writing." In the mid-1950's, he began *The Moviegoer.*

"I can remember sitting on that back porch of that little shotgun cottage in New Orleans with a little rank patio grown up behind it, after two failed novels. I didn't feel bad. I felt all right.

"And it crossed my mind, what if I did something that American writers never do, which seems to be the custom in France: Namely, that when someone writes about ideas, they can translate the same ideas to fiction and plays, like Mauriac, Malraux, Sartre. So it just occurred to me, why not take these ideas I'd been trying to write about, in psychiatry and philosophy, and translate them into a fictional setting in New Orleans, where I was living. So I was just sitting out there, and I started writing.

"And it worked, just like that. I had this happy feeling that, this is it! The form was right, and the form fit what I had to say. Don't ask me how it happened."

Binx Bolling of *The Moviegoer* was an odd sock, as displaced and mocking as any number of young men in American fiction since World War II. Unlike them, Binx is funny. Like all of Percy's heroes, he sees the world with a deadpan eye. A 30-year-old stockbroker, he has removed to Gentilly, a sprawling faceless suburb where the only hint of New Orleans color is the wrought iron on the Walgreen drugstore. He is there to escape the Fine Old Family traditions on his father's side and the Catholicism on his mother's. Again, though, there is a difference in the quality of Binx's rejection: He wants to believe. There is scorn in him but no nihilism. For Binx, the world drained of meaning, there is nothing to do but go to the movies, "Where Happiness Costs So Little," according to the marquee on his neighborhood theater.

"Other people, so I have read," Binx says early in the book, "treasure memorable moments in their lives. . . . What I remember is the time . . . the kitten found Orson Welles in the doorway in *The Third Man.*"

Stanley Kauffmann, the film critic for *The New Republic,* was an editor at the publishing concern of Alfred A. Knopf when Percy's manuscript arrived in the late 1950's. Kauffmann worked with Percy for more than a year readying the book for publication, but he remembers that even in the initial draft "there was a clear sense of his own voice, of what he was writing about . . . you hear something unique and personal in the first paragraph."

As it turned out, the publisher Alfred Knopf did not like *The Moviegoer,* when he got around to reading it after publication. He had assumed that it would be like Will Percy's *Lanterns on the Levee,* which he had published years before. Perhaps as a result of his displeasure, the company did not promote the book. It remained for the journalist A.J. Liebling, searching for books with local color, to buy a copy in New Orleans, where he was researching a book about Earl Long. Liebling liked the novel a lot, and gave it to his wife, the fiction writer Jean Stafford. Stafford was a judge that year for the National Book Award, the year Percy won for fiction.

Binx Bolling earned for his creator a certain cult status. *The Moviegoer* has never gone out of print in hardcover or paperback. It is in its 14th hardcover printing. All of Percy's books, for that matter, are in print in hardcover and softcover, and each book sells better than the one before. According to Percy, the public response remains intensely personal. He averages three or four letters a day from readers.

For almost 40 years, the Percys have lived in Covington, a small town across Lake Ponchartrain from New Orleans. For the last three years, they have lived, with their Welsh corgi, Sweet Thing, in a trim, simply furnished, tin-roofed cottage on the banks of the Bogue Falaya River. Designed to the Percys' specifications, the house has but three rooms: a bedroom, Percy's book-lined study and a big living room and kitchen overlooking the river. The living room is full of furniture—a sofa, a large table, two chinoiserie lamps—from Will Percy's house in Greenville, long since demolished.

Until a few years ago, they lived next door, in a big French Provincial house now occupied by the family of one of their two daughters. Both daughters and their families live close by, there are young grandsons running in and out all day, and every Sunday everyone gathers for dinner at the Percys'. Once a week, Percy meets for lunch with a small group of old friends that includes the owner of a local automobile dealership, a doctor, and Percy's brother, a retired Tulane law school professor. Outside of that, "I don't have any social life," Walker Percy says.

His closest friend is the novelist and Civil War historian Shelby Foote. They went to high school and college together, but Foote lives in Memphis, so they meet only once or twice a year. "We correspond, talk occasionally." He sees other writers infrequently.

Percy admits that such isolation can make for eccentricity in a writer. "But," he adds, "it can also make for *The Sound and the Fury*."

He writes in the morning, and spends the afternoon retyping his handwritten drafts, listening to classical music, or reading, or walking, his principal exercise. At night, he watches television, pays bills and writes letters. He finds the routine congenial. "There's nothing else I want to do, or am fit to do," he says. "It may be my original Presbyterian morality. I would think it almost sinful to sit and read a book in the morning. I can remember my Presbyterian grandmother in Athens, Ga. She was strict Georgia Presbyterian, and I guess reading was all right, but on Sunday you didn't read, and I remember the strangest thing—you didn't cut out pictures. There's something to be said for the Protestant ethic. You're supposed to be working at what you're fit to work at. Nothing wrong with that."

In a Calm Setting, He Writes of the Whirling World Beyond

Timothy Dwyer/1987

From *The Philadelphia Inquirer*, April 19, 1987, 39, 41. Reprinted
with permission from *The Philadelphia Inquirer*.

COVINGTON, La.—Walker Percy steps out the door and onto the porch of
his tin-roof cottage. A visitor's arrival has been announced by the loud
barking of his dog, Sweet Thing, a spunky little Welsh corgi. Nearby,
there is a hand-painted sign nailed to a tree: "Bad Dog, Stay in Car,
Honk Horn."

Sweet Thing licks the visitor's hand. "Is this the bad dog?" Walker
Percy is asked.

"No," he says, with a kind, ironic smile. He shakes hands and
gestures toward a larger house visible through the trees. "My daughter
has a doberman up there," he says.

Sweet Thing has stopped barking. Once inside the house, Sweet
Thing jumps onto the couch and into the visitor's lap. "Take your coat
and tie off," Percy says, as he shoos the dog out of the living room.
"We don't wear coats and ties around here much."

Here on the banks of the Bogue Falaya is where Walker Percy lives
and works. The atmosphere is as slow and casual as the flow of the river
outside his living-room window. It is an atmosphere conducive to
reflection and writing. That is Walker Percy's vocation, and has been
for more than 25 of his 70 years.

I try to write in the morning," he says. "Ideally, I like to write
longhand, which is the way I write, a little scribble on three-hole paper
in a ring binder. Then I try to type it out in the afternoon. A lot of
writers have told me I really ought to get on the word processor. It
sounds great, but I just think I could be too old to change. This works
pretty well for me because I do a lot of revising. I can change things as I
type. I figure I'll stick with my old M.O. (modus operandi)."

His own way of writing has just produced a new novel, *The Thanatos
Syndrome,* his eighth.

"My novels start off, almost naturally, with somebody in a predicament and somebody trying to get out of it or embark on some sort of search, some sort of wanderings," Percy says.

In his latest novel, Dr. Thomas More, the alcoholic psychiatrist whom his readers first met in *Love in the Ruins* (1971), returns to life in Feliciana Parish, La., after a stint in the slammer for selling amphetamines to truckers.

Percy sets the scene for his novel in the introduction:

As pleasant a place as its name implies, it still harbors all manner of fractious folk, including Texans and recent refugees from unlikely places like Korea and Michigan, all of whom have learned to get along tolerably well, better than most in fact, who watch LSU football and reruns of M*A*S*H, drink Dixie beer, and eat every sort of food imaginable, which is generally cooked in something called a roux.

The downside of Feliciana is that its pine forests have been mostly cut down, its bayous befouled, Lake Pontchartrain polluted, the Mississippi River turned into a sewer. It has too many malls, banks, hospitals, chiropractors, politicians, lawyers, realtors and condos with names like Chateau Charmant.

Still and all, I wouldn't live anywhere else.

This is also More's South. In this book, Percy, a trained medical doctor, warns of the dangers of the dehumanization of science. The paroled hero, More, starts his practice again and notices that his patients and neighbors just don't seem like themselves. So he embarks on a search and discovers that some of his colleagues are secretly treating the drinking water with heavy-sodium coolant from a nuclear reactor. Already they have gleefully noticed a decrease in crime, teenage pregnancies, AIDS, suicides, violence and general anxiety. Even inmates at the state prison do their time peacefully, singing spiritual hymns while performing their hard labor, once under the influence of the treated water. The good people of Feliciana Parish are unaware of their aquatically induced psychosis. It is up to More to save them.

Percy, like More, is a social diagnostician. But instead of writing prescriptions to treat society's ailments, Percy writes novels.

"I was just trying to call attention to the fact, the danger of science— in spite of all of its beauty and elegance and that great good that it does—the danger and seduction of it. That is, it is easy to take a position of abstraction from the individual. . . . It is easy to forget the individual. I was trying to bring out the contrast of a humanistic

scientific view of society and one which overlooks what we would call
the sacredness of the individual."

In addition to being labeled a "Southern writer" by book critics, Percy
has been called the "moralist of the South" by such Eastern institutions
as the *New York Times*.

He does not consider himself a Southern writer "in the sense that I
was born and raised in the South, live in the South and am a writer. So
that makes me a Southern writer. My only objection to the term is that
in the minds of the rest of the country there is a kind of pigeonhole
classification called 'Southern writer,' you know, which doesn't apply
to any other part of the country. You don't think of Updike as being a
Northern writer or Saul Bellow as being a Midwestern writer. But that is
my only objection to the term."

He does object, though, to being labeled a moralist.

"I shy away from terms like moralist because if I ever got pigeon-
holed as a moralist or a religious writer, that would be the end of it.
People don't go to religious bookstores. I don't think it is a vocation of
a novelist to do any kind of preaching or edifying.

"Flannery O'Connor used to say that ladies around Milledgeville,
Ga., would complain to her: 'Flannery, you're such a nice girl, why
don't you write more uplifting books, edifying books?' And Flannery
would say something like, "Well, you get 50 ladies who want to read
edifying books and what you got is a book club.'

"I know what she means. She was a Catholic. So am I. The only way
that affects my writing is, I think, every writer or every person or every
novelist has a philosophy or a certain view of man. I call it an anthropology, really. . . . The way that affects my writing is, I see man as a
wayfarer or somebody in trouble. I consider my two main sources
Catholic theology and Freudian psychiatry, which are remarkably close
in some ways—although Freud would be horrified to hear it. Both start
out with the premise that man is born in trouble."

Percy was raised as a classic Southern gentleman on a delta plantation
owned by his uncle, Will Percy, in Greenwood, Miss. And with his
whitish-gray hair and calm-blue eyes, Percy still looks and acts like very
much the gentleman that his Uncle Will raised.

When Percy was 13, his father committed suicide. His mother died in
a car accident three years later. So Percy and his two brothers were
adopted by his uncle, who was a planter, a lawyer, a poet and writer

whose book *Lanterns on the Levee* has become "a minor Southern classic," in the words of his nephew. It was his Uncle Will who instilled in him the values and ways of the Old South. Percy, and most of his characters, live with one foot in the decaying society of the Old South and the other in the New South, with its shopping malls full of Tire Worlds, Shoe Towns, and Radio Shacks.

Percy says he transformed his Uncle Will into Binx Bolling's Aunt Emily in his first novel, *The Moviegoer* (1961). The lecture she delivers to Binx near the end of the book was one he heard from his Uncle Will, Percy says:

> I did the best for you, son. I gave you all I had. More than anything I wanted to pass on to you the one heritage of the men of our family, a certain quality of spirit, a gaiety, a sense of duty, a nobility worn lightly, a sweetness, a gentleness with women—the only good thing the South ever had and the only things that really matter in this life.

Percy smiles and laughs easily when he talks of his uncle. "I didn't know anyone like him. I didn't know anybody else who talked like him. He was right out of the 13th century."

The house where he grew up was a way station for intellectuals, writers and various characters who, upon receiving a grant to study race relations in the South, would head straight for Will Percy's house, where they would conduct their research by interviewing the maids, cooks, and butlers while mixing martinis. Perhaps that accounts for the ironic tendencies of most of his characters.

The Moviegoer was published when Percy was 45 years old. He had graduated from Columbia University's medical school and worked as a pathologist in the chest division at Bellevue Hospital on the East Side, where he contracted tuberculosis in the process. His "rest cure" lasted several years, during which he read profusely and began to write seriously. After a stint teaching pathology at Columbia, he turned to writing full time, producing two novels without seeing them published.

Those two works were failures, he says, because he was trying to write like someone else, first like Thomas Wolfe, then like Thomas Mann. Then he decided to write like himself. One day on the back porch of his Uptown New Orleans house, the beginning of *The Moviegoer* came to him.

"What happened was, I just hit a kind of despair. I bottomed out and I thought, well, I got nothing to lose, why don't I just write what I feel like writing. That sounds simple, like what anybody ought to do, but it was very difficult for me to write, to find my own voice. I don't know what happened, good fortune or whatever. . . . I knew right away. The first sentence."

Percy has the same detached, fresh-eyed view of life that his characters do, but without their malaise. He, too, notices and hears "certain things," usually after probing for details from whomever he is talking to. For example, a high school teacher recently told him that her students were not interested in reading.

"That is high school, which is depressing, and I think it is probably true all over the country. I asked her: 'Why is this? Why aren't the kids interested? Are they not intellectually stimulated by anything? Why is that, because they're watching the tube eight hours a day? Are they drinking beer or what?' She didn't know. I don't know. Maybe it's the damn tube. Maybe—they all drive cars in high school. That's something else. They are hanging out in cars. I didn't get a car until I was in medical school. A small Ford."

It's obvious to Percy that something is wrong here. Is another search about to begin? Maybe the sign on the tree in front of his house should be changed to something like, oh, "Stay In Car, Honk Horn, The Doctor Is In."

A Visitor Interview: Novelist Walker Percy

Robert Cubbage/1987

From *Our Sunday Visitor*, 76, (November 1987). Reprinted by permission of *Our Sunday Visitor* and Robert Cubbage.

Walker Percy is the only Catholic novelist of our time who might be considered in the first rank of American writers. In 1962, Percy's first novel, *The Moviegoer,* won the National Book Award. His second novel, *The Last Gentleman,* was a runner-up for the same award. His latest novel, *The Thanatos Syndrome,* was published last April. ("Thanatos" is the instinctual desire for death.) The book is his greatest commercial and critical success, bolting within two weeks of its publication into the top ten of national best-seller lists. *The Thanatos Syndrome* demonstrates how easily decent people fall into evil while attempting to do good. In the first of a two-part interview, the 71-year-old author talks about themes in his recent novel that are of particular concern to fellow Catholics. The interview was conducted for the *Visitor* by Robert Cubbage, who freelances from Spokane, Washington.

Part 1, 1 November 1987

Visitor: Do you believe we are living in the age of thanatos—in the century of death?

Percy: I guess I do. I have referred to that in past books and essays. In *The Thanatos Syndrome,* a character states the death century began with the Battle of Somme and Verdun, where in two months two million young men were killed—all from the same civilization of Western Christendom. At the end of these two horrendous battles, I think the lines changed a few hundred yards. That's as good a place as any to begin this dreadful post-modern age, this century of death.

You see, our tremendous advances in science are a great paradox in this century. Medical advances have saved many lives and the tremendous increase in the welfare system has taken care of millions of poor people, but at the same time, our present civilization has killed more people in 50 years than all other civilizations put together. Beginning with Verdun and Somme, and World War II—about 20 million people have been killed just in combat; and the Nazi Holocaust, what?—six million, seven million—and a million and a half were Catholics, but you don't hear about the Catholics. Stalin killed millions of Ukranian Catholics, too.

Visitor: What are the signs of death that you see in America in the 1980s?

Percy: Last night, I was listening to an interview between Bill Moyers and Associate Justice Harry Blackmun, who wrote the Supreme Court's decision that legalizes abortion. Obviously, Blackmun is a decent man, a thoughtful man, who was trying to do the right thing. Yet, what did he do? He helped to legalize the murder of 30 million unborn human beings. That, by the way, is not a theological, Catholic statement. Any doctor can tell you that an unborn child is fully human. There is no difference between a child five minutes before birth and five minutes after birth. What about a month before birth? Same. How about eight months? How about one day after conception? Sure, it's a separate organism. Any doctor will tell you that it's all standard biology: the fetus is a separate genetic structure, a separate immune system, a separate organism, a separate creature. So, we have this great situation where for the most humane reasons we kill more people than the Nazis did in all their death camps. In times like these, that is enough to give a novelist a cause to write.

Visitor: Do you see other signs of death?

Percy: Of course. I just saw on television a couple who gave birth to their second baby. The first baby was born three years ago, the other was born from a fertilized egg that had been frozen for the past three years. It had been unfrozen and implanted in the mother's uterus so that their second child could be born three years later. Okay. So, what's next? So, why not intervene in the genetic apparatus of the unborn child? Certainly, it's okay to correct defects. But why not make a better child? Why not make a blue-eyed child? Or why not get rid of unde-sirable, asocial children? In *The Thanatos Syndrome,* I have Father Smith say, "Tenderness leads to the gas chamber." Doctors and statesmen start changing life, intervening in life for "quality of life" reasons, and they end up killing Jews.

Visitor: In your novel, the U.S. Supreme Court hands down a decision that permits "pedeuthasia," which is the killing of "infants facing a life without quality." Do you think pedeuthasia might actually be sanctioned some day?

Percy: Sure, why not. That idea comes from my studies on linguistics. You can certainly make a case that until a child acquires language, utters sentences, names things, listens and talks that he is not human. Pedeuthasia is simply extending the argument of Justice Blackmun, who says if a child is not viable, then it is expendable. If a (born) child is not human yet, why not say it is expendable. Eighteen months might become a convenient cutoff date. Usually, a child starts uttering one-word sentences somewhere between 12 and 18 months.

Visitor: No one seems outraged in our society anymore. Where do you find your outrage?

Percy: I suppose through God's grace, I am a Catholic, and if you are a Catholic, you take these matters of life and death a little more seriously. Again, I recall Father Smith in *The Thanatos Syndrome* when asked why he became a priest or even stayed a Catholic, he simply answers that in the end one has to choose between life and death. And whatever else Catholicism is, it is certainly life-affirming.

Visitor: You converted to Catholicism in 1947. What motivated you to embrace the Catholic faith?

Percy: I have to give you a very trite answer. I read Scripture one day and discovered that the Lord had founded a Church on a man named Peter. I investigated the historical basis of that Scripture and sure enough there is such a Church and it goes all the way back. The Church even has St. Peter buried in the basement of a Cathedral in Rome. Other churches can't produce evidence like that.

Visitor: Was it solely an intellectual decision?

Percy: No. There is no way I can explain it. Because in the end, faith is a gift. It's a grace, an extraordinary gift. One day I found myself walking up to a rectory door of a Jesuit church in New Orleans, knocking on the door, and asking to see a priest. I had never said a word to a priest in my life, but I asked him, "How do you go about this? How do you become a Catholic?" He looked a little surprised, like I was crazy or something. (Next week Percy discusses suffering and horrors.)

Part 2: 8 November 1987

Visitor: You wrote in *The Thanatos Syndrome*, "We've got it wrong about horror. It doesn't come naturally, but it takes some effort." Have we really lost our sense of horror?

Percy: I think there is a sensitivity, almost a perverse sensitivity in ordinary civilian life. People are very much aware of horror and even actively seek it. For instance, people like wrecks. People will go out of their way to see wrecks and will even stop their cars to see the blood and the bodies. On the other hand, people are genuinely horrified by something happening in their neighborhood. Someone is murdered, raped, or a child is kidnapped. Horror does exist. But what people don't realize is how fragile horror really is; how easily it can be anesthetized. After the initial shock of combat, soldiers are no longer horrified by the gore. Even in the death camps, the inmates were not horrified after a couple of weeks.

The deadening of horror takes place very rapidly. Horror quickly becomes banal and routine. During World War II, Allied soldiers liberated a small hospital outside Munich. It was a simple, normal hospital except that children were routinely killed in its pediatric wing. These murdered children were undesirables for one reason or another: malformed, diseased, or whatever.

The nurses showed the soldiers the room where the doctor escorted and then killed the child. The room was tastefully furnished, complete with a geranium plant. After the doctor administered a poisonous gas to the child through a mask, the body would be disposed of through another door; the physician would leave, and the business of the hospital would go on as usual. What impressed the soldiers more than anything else was the ordinariness of the killing. The "special treatment" was no big deal to the nurses and other members of the hospital staff. There were no signs of horror in their eyes.

Visitor: What profit can we expect if we suffer the horror?

Percy: There is a positive side to horror. It can provide the turning point in one's life; it can even usher in a religious conversion. Any catastrophe, even death, or the nearness of death, can be an occasion for a kind of epiphany or revelation.

Horror penetrates the ordinariness of everyday life and opens one to mystery. This mystery often involves a religious opening to God. For example, Dostoyevsky's conversion happened in a prison in Siberia, among the most wretched of the earth.

Visitor: This ties into a recurring theme in your writings, which is "the recovery of the real through ordeal." Can you define that?

Percy: I believe you have to discover your true self through ordeal. Psychologists never tell people that. Instead, they give their clients pep-talks and avant-garde formulas for coping with life. God knows, it takes an awful lot of ordeal to come to a sense of self. It doesn't do any good to tell yourself how to live or what type of person you should be. You have to learn it yourself, through ordeal.

I take a Jungian point of view that maybe our neurotic symptoms, our depressions, our anxieties, and our dreams are worth investigating. We don't have to run from them. Carl Jung was right in encouraging his patients to believe that their anxiety and depression might be trying to tell them something of value. They are not just symptoms. It helps enormously when a person can make a friend with her terror, plumb the depths of her depression. "There's gold down there in the darkness," said Dr. Jung.

People can retrieve some beautiful things from their depressions and anxieties. It's true. They can. I tried to make this point in *The Thanatos Syndrome*. I had no interest in being polemical about it or even making too much of a point. But, I wanted to ask two questions. To what degree do we use chemicals and drugs to reduce symptoms? To what degree is it worthwhile to examine the symptoms and do old-fashioned psychotherapy—talking and listening? The trend today is away from talking and listening and toward chemotherapy. I don't know the answer. But one can imagine chemotherapy being so abused that everybody takes pills and feels better. It's not a new idea. After all, it was done by Aldous Huxley in *Brave New World*, everybody took a pill and felt fine.

Visitor: Some people would rather not face their ordeals. What then?

Percy: I have a theory that what terrifies people most of all is failing to live up to something or other. This terror is the result of television shows, movies, and bad books where things always work out. Even in tragic movies, things are rounded off pretty well; people suffer nervous breakdowns in style and form. But, after all, whenever a movie is filmed, serious moviemakers collect 40 or 50 outtakes or failures, scenes that didn't work, before they get one that works. So what the audience sees is the one that works. We should approach life that way. We should give ourselves permission to fail.

Visitor: Ordeals often produce the opposite: they destroy a person rather than reveal a true self. Why that?

Percy: I don't know. It is certainly easy to romanticize suffering. If

you have ever spent any time in a big hospital, especially a hospital like
Bellevue, suffering is an awful, awful thing. It is a terrible waste. There
is not much revelation or enlightenment there. It can happen. Sure it
can. An ordeal can become a sad, dreary loss of human dignity. It is not
a pleasant thing to see.

Why don't people make use of their ordeal and their suffering? I
don't know.

Century of Thanatos: Walker Percy and His Subversive Message

Phil McCombs/1988

From *Southern Review*, 24 (August 1988), 808–24. Reprinted by permission of Phil McCombs. [Copyright 1992 by Phil McCombs.]

Walker Percy's sixth novel, *The Thanatos Syndrome,* hit the best-seller lists immediately. It was widely and favorably reviewed in the mass media, though some critics found fault. "Eschatology made simple," complained Terrence Rafferty in the *New Yorker.* But, in fact, the book is far from simple: every paragraph, virtually every phrase, is crafted to mesh with the intricate thinking of the author. *The Thanatos Syndrome* is nothing less than a frontal assault on many easily imagined, or already current, ideas of social engineering and improvement. As the *Wall Street Journal*'s Edmund Fuller noted, it may be Dr. Percy's "most explicitly Catholic novel, and the author himself calls it his most political to date, his most "cautionary" tale. Dr. Percy was interviewed at his home in Covington, Louisiana.

I wish to thank Jo Gulledge for her help in preparing this interview for publication.

PM: In *The Thanatos Syndrome,* was the scene with the Nazi doctors real, with actual names?

WP: Yes, those are all historical characters, including Dr. Jung. I'm not saying he was a collaborator, but he wrote about Nazi Germany in terms of the archetypes and was not exactly condemnatory of it.

PM: Didn't you visit Germany in the 1930s?

WP: Yes, after my freshman year at UNC-Chapel Hill. My uncle, Will Percy, thought it would be great to go to Europe for a year, since he was a big Francophile. I went to Germany instead. I took a year of German from this old professor who was a German himself. He proposed to go to Germany in the summer of 1934 and take some of his students, so we thought it was a great idea. He was a funny old guy.

PM: So some observations in the book come from direct experience,

189

including the feeling of evil within oneself that Father Smith felt, or not?

WP: Well, yes, some observations, but nothing so dramatic as Father Smith's. I was only eighteen years old. But, as I think I mentioned in the book, no one thought much about the Nazis. Hitler had just come in during the early thirties; he had been elected, after all, and there was no great thought of the menace of the Nazis.

PM: William L. Shirer's book mentions that there was a great feeling of verve in Germany then.

WP: Yes, very true, but in this country all the interest was in Mussolini. Mussolini had been in Italy for quite a while and was making the trains run on time and so forth, so he was generally admired. And Hitler, well, who was Hitler? Well, maybe he'd be another Mussolini. So we went to Bonn with my professor, where his family lived. We stayed with him, his nephew, and his nephew's son, who was about fifteen and in the *Hitlerjugend,* and I got to know him real well. I got to know the family, and I'm not going to say the family Father Smith was talking about was drawn from them, but this youth was the one who made an impression on me. . . . I had been an ordinary Boy Scout, not very good, a second-class Scout—I never could make first class on account of the knots—but he was *not* like an American Boy Scout. He was dead serious, with this impressive uniform, and he was graduating from the *Hitlerjugend* and going into the *Schutzstaffel.* I remember he talked about the Teutonic knights, and taking the oath at Marienberg, the ancient castle. There was a tremendous mystique there. I don't remember Jews being mentioned the whole time. There was no particular thing about Jews. This was before *Krystalnacht,* when they began to beat up Jews.

PM: What about Father Smith's theory of the basis of the Holocaust, that is, the Jews are the chosen people, a sign from God, and the Nazis were anti-religious and wanted to wipe them out for that reason?

WP: Yes, Father Smith was very much aware of what Hitler was trying to do. Hitler was, if you read *Mein Kampf,* always talking about the purity of *das Volk.* It was not so much that the Jews were bad, but they, as Smith said, could not be subsumed under the idea of *das Volk,* no way! *(laughs)* The Jews were having none of it, and, of course, they were very bright, very intelligent, and very prominent in science. So they were a threat to Hitler's whole idea. So I guess I have to agree with

Father Smith. Of course the point Father Smith was making was that the Nazis didn't come out of nowhere, that they didn't just appear without progenitors. There were German doctors in the Weimar Republic who were very advanced scientifically and who had ideas about improving the quality of society. They paved the way for the Nazis more than one likes to believe.

PM: Are you talking about scientific humanism?

WP: Yes, I think it started with the psychiatrists who were getting rid of retardates and older people and various sorts of people who were ill, and for humane reasons, to put them out of their misery or to improve the general quality of life. So their motives were, as they saw it, humane. And I guess the point Father Smith was making was that it's a slippery slope to go from humane euthanasia to the removal of the unfit and undesirable. Once you ignore the uniqueness and sacredness of the individual human and set up abstract ideals of the improvement of society, then the terminus is the gas chamber.

PM: "Tenderness" leads to the gas chamber, as Father Smith says in the book?

WP: Tenderness leads to the gas chamber. *(laughs)* He could have said "abstraction," too, the idea abstracted.

PM: In the book you have the Supreme Court allowing the elimination of defective infants up to eighteen months of age.

WP: Well, why not? Yes, you could make out a case that you don't become a "person," properly speaking, until you acquire language. In a sense, I believe that. When you break through to learning things like names, which linguists recognize between the twelfth and sixteenth months of life, there's a sudden breakthrough into the human condition. So it's easy to imagine a scientist saying, "Well, what's the big deal? If a person by that definition is not properly human until he's eighteen months, what's wrong with getting rid of malformed infants or unwanted infants?"

PM: Sure, they're not going to have a quality of life anyway.

WP: No! *(laughs)* I wanted to avoid getting into this highly polarized pro-choice, pro-life, and anti-abortion thing because it's a lot more than that. We're talking about the thanatos, the death syndrome as the spirit of the times, which is a lot more than abortion. I think Dr. More said that the age of thanatos began with the Battle of the Somme and the Battle of Verdun in 1916 when we had this paradox of the flower of

European civilization, European science, European humanism, and European Christendom beginning to commit suicide. People were killed not by the millions, but by the tens of millions.

PM: But in your book Dr. More is shooting the evil guys. On the one hand you have the banality of evil, but on the other hand you have the American idea that if enough good men don't act, then evil will triumph. Where's the balance?

WP: Uncle Hugh Bob doesn't kill anybody. The most he does is shoot one guy's earlobe off; he's a crack shot with his Colt Woodsman. And Dr. More is terrified when he shoots another fellow with a double-barreled shotgun. And Uncle Hugh Bob says, "Don't worry about it, I just dusted him off, shot the seat out of his pants." So nobody was really hurt badly.

PM: Well, that's the Lone Ranger idea, that's in the American tradition.

WP: (*laughs*) Sure, but the point, and I must say it was the part I enjoyed most writing, was having these fellows—God, I can't even remember their names, Van Dorn, the coach, and the other scientists—having them administered their own medicine, heavy sodium. Dr. More quietly says, "No, I mean the real thing." He pours a glass out of the tube, and Van Dorn says, "This is molar, Na24," which means a concentrated solution. And More says, "That's right. Go ahead and drink that." I enjoyed having them regress on the spot. It's also a commentary, which some readers will recognize, about the whole cult of teaching language to chimpanzees, dolphins, and gorillas. (*laughs*)

PM: Right, some people think dolphins will talk and so on.

WP: For ten or fifteen years or so there was a tremendous effort among primatologists and psychologists to teach language to primates. It has all fizzled out. In fact, a guy named Terrace wrote a good book which blew up the whole enterprise. He adopted a chimp, which he named Nim Chimsky. He was a true believer—he thought he'd be able to teach language to this chimp and he was spending hours, more than he was spending with his own child. He finally came to the conclusion that these chimps were simply learning responses, just like a rat in a maze, responses which were rewarded and reinforced by bananas or whatever. So he wrote this book which was a devastating criticism of all the language experiments with chimps and gorillas. In fact in the end I

believe he said that no chimp had ever uttered a single sentence or
named anything.

PM: Jacques Cousteau is always looking for some real intelligence in
octopuses and so on.

WP: I'm sure there's a great deal of intelligence there, but all I'm
saying is that it seems to me that it's different. I remember when I wrote
this sad little thing, at the end of *The Thanatos Syndrome,* about Eve,
the gorilla, who was finally sent back to Zaire. She was last seen sitting
on the riverbank by herself; she had been kicked out by her human
friends and had not been picked up by the mountain gorillas of Zaire.
That has actually been tried—some of the primatologists have had to
send the primates back to where they came from. Or to zoos. Either way
it's tough on the gorillas.

PM: The ending of *Thanatos,* where Dr. More gets back with his
wife, is different from *The Second Coming* when he ends up with the
"new" woman.

WP: Dr. More wouldn't have worked out with Lucy. That's funny,
I was talking with a good friend, a woman writer, yesterday, who said
she liked the book all right, but she said it was too cerebral. She likes
The Second Coming better, a love story, you know. She said, "Why
didn't he take off with Lucy? Why did he have to come back to Ellen?"
It just seemed like the thing to do; it was kind of a repetition. Also, at
the end of *Love in the Ruins,* he's back with Ellen. Yes, I think he's
been to Mass, and he's had two or three shots of Early Times and he's
cooking and singing and cutting the fool like David in front of the Ark.
That's the way Thomas More is. And once Ellen gets off the heavy
sodium, she's all right.

PM: All of your novels are written around ideas; that is, that you've
got a message.

WP: True. For instance, Edmund Fuller, in the *Wall Street Journal,*
said this book was the most "Catholic" book I had written, the one in
which I'd come closest to talking about God and the sacredness of
human life. He didn't object because he felt it worked all right. My
response is much the same as Flannery O'Connor's, who would always
say something like, "You know, I am what I am, my writing is me. I
don't preach, but my writing is informed by my being a Catholic." This
means you don't preach; God knows she didn't preach, but it entails a

certain view of the way people are. In a technical sense, it entails an

certain view of the way people are. In a technical sense, it entails an anthropology, a theory of man—that man is a certain way, in traditional terms a fallen creature, or as both the Old Testament and Freud would say, he's born to trouble, as the sparks fly up. So there's something wrong with man. That's why Father Smith says the words are no good; the words have been deprived of meaning. (*laughs*) Words are like the original sin, the fall of man. Father Smith says you can't use the words anymore; the Great Depriver has deprived the words of meaning. But the novelist is a crafty and devious individual, so he has his own way of dealing with these things. One of his tasks is the renewal of words.

PM: Flannery O'Connor clubs us over the head with her views, but gets away with it. Kiekegaard hid his views carefully in some of his work. Are you sneaking up on the reader?

WP: Well, after all, where does this novel end? This novel ends where it began. It begins with a patient walking into Dr. More's office. She's a woman named Mickey LaFaye, from New England. She went to Bennington and then met a high roller at Amherst, a Creole, and she married him and is living happily ever after out there on a golf course somewhere. She has everything that her heart ever desired: husband, children, family, books, music, golf, bridge, everything. And yet she's in despair, suffering from anxiety and depression. Dr. More's been treating her and possibly getting somewhere with her. She begins talking about a dream she had when she was spending summers with her grandmother, dreaming about something that happened in the basement of her grandmother's farmhouse, which of course is a Jungian sort of dream. At least, it's more Jungian than Freudian. Her dream is about a stranger who was coming to tell her something, tell her a secret. She was looking through the dusty windows of the cellar up to the green hills of Vermont. There was the smell of winter apples. His approach there was more Jungian than Freudian because what she wanted to get at was the idea that all this is part of herself. And which part of herself was the little girl, and the green hills and the cellar? Of course, in the Jungian sense, the cellar would be extremely important; that would be the depths of the self, what's going on down there. The smell of the winter apples and the stranger would be part of herself trying to tell another part of herself. Then she blows up; she comes in dosed up on heavy sodium, feels fine. By medical standards she's all right. She's fine and seems to be completely cured with the sodium 24, which More is not aware of at the time. This fact comes out in the story.

PM: In the end, she's back feeling the terror.

WP: That's right, but earlier on he goes to visit her in the hospital, and he tries to get her to talk about the dream and she doesn't know what he's talking about. For a second she remembers the dream, but then she says, "Oh forget it. Come out and visit us. I'm a rich bitch now and I love horses and ride horses. . . ." But the point is that at the end she's off the heavy sodium, and her symptoms have all come back—she's got her old anxieties. The paradox, the scandal of the book, is that she's better off with her anxiety and depression than being without them. This is the proposition of the book. Without her anxiety, if you recall, she's happy as a chimp. In fact, she talks like a chimp.

PM: The stranger is the apostle she's hoping for?

WP: (*laughs*) I'm not saying. But the point is that Dr. More's listening and she's willing to talk about the dream. He says, "Well, okay, you want to talk about it." But she opens her mouth and starts to talk, and then he says, "Well, well, well," and that's as far as I go. There's no big conversion—there's no great light that appears to Thomas More like St. Paul on the road to Damascus. He goes back to practicing Jungian psychiatry. The only hint that's dropped is through his wife, who has followed Jimmy Swaggart, and she cannot stand Catholics. She can hardly bear to talk to Father Smith but she does transmit messages from him, and Father Smith calls them on the phone to give a message that somebody is going to make a contribution. You're to meet this person in the tower. This is Father Smith's way of telling More, and More gets the message, namely, that Smith wants him to serve Mass for the Feast of the Epiphany. Here's the Jewish girl, and baby, and rich people, kings who are bearing gifts. The trick which I try to pull off in the novel is that Thomas More gets the message from Father Smith, filtered through his slightly nutty wife who doesn't know what she's telling him. So he says okay, so obviously he's agreeing to serve Mass at the Feast of the Epiphany, to celebrate this ordinary looking Jewish girl, her son, and the Magi who are bringing gifts. That's as close as the reader is allowed to come to Dr. More's spiritual state. In fact, I'm not sure exactly what More's spiritual state is.

PM: He isn't in the religious stage, though he's trying to be.

WP: Well yes, it starts out at the beginning of the book that he's given up his religion. It means nothing to him. He said he hadn't been to Mass in two years but he still remembers Father Smith. More says he doesn't know what God is. He went to Mass when he was in the minimal security country club jail in Alabama, but only to get out of jail. He was tired of being cooped up in the Quonset hut, and cutting grass at the country club, and he was allowed to go to Mass at Father Smith's, but it didn't mean anything to him. So there's a kind of hidden conversion—I wasn't primarily interested in More's conversion—that wasn't the main thing. I was more interested in Father Smith, and in what he had to say at the end.

PM: Father Smith is in the religious stage. He's in it.

WP: Sure. And he's a little deranged, of course. He's trying to repeat what St. Simon Stylites did in the fifth century—climbed up and actually stayed on top of a column for twenty years.

PM: All of this is about how do you act in the world. You believe in God, and then what do you do? He goes up in the tower because he doesn't know what to do?

WP: No. You can make what you like out of it and you can be as right or as wrong as I am, but the parallel is what St. Simon Stylites who went up as an act of penance and to escape the sinful world—to do penance and to worship on top of the tower, which admittedly is a little odd, odd behavior. And he comes, the saint comes down after twenty years, and the bishop wants him to work in a parish for a while. It doesn't work out, and the bishop in effect says, "Well, you're not good down here, you can go back up," so he goes back up in the tower. That's his vocation, and, of course, there's a deliberate play on the semiotics of being in the tower. In a fire tower you look for signs, for signs of fire. The first thing that happens when Thomas More goes up to see him is that Smith says, "Why don't you line up that smoke over there?" Smoke, the classic example of sign process when you read any textbook of psychology or semiotics is, smoke is a sign of fire. That's the one you always read about. (*laughs*) So Smith is onto signs, and I use that as a classic example. He sees a column of smoke, and Thomas More lines up his azimuth and locates the fire. They call up the gal in the other tower and get the triangulation and they locate the fire. I don't think most readers picked up on "signs" but the underlying, very lightly stressed, idea was that the present day world is almost without signs. The signs have, as Smith would say, been evacuated, or deprived, devalued, and the words are worn out by the Great Depriver, that is, the great prince Satan. So naturally Father Smith is in the sign business— in a fire tower you look for signs.

PM: Your book is very cautionary about "do-gooding," especially if done in a secular environment. Yet Dr. More does good, goes to work in the hospice. What about Robert Coles and the whole question of do-gooding? Coles teaches his affluent students at Harvard to try to do some good in the world. What influence has Coles had on you?

WP: Well, we're good friends and I'm a great admirer of his. He's a very caring sort of person. He's not content to be a Harvard professor, which he is, and give lectures and so forth. He'll go out and spend six months with Navajo Indian children, and he's a deeply religious man in the Judeo-Christian tradition. I've never asked him what religion he is. He's not a do-gooder in the pejorative sense in this novel. I guess his great breakthrough was when he was down here as a psychiatrist and working at Keesler Air Force Base and he saw blacks being attacked on the beach in Gulfport. Then he got to know a little black girl named Ruby. Here's a Boston Yankee, who's probably never talked to a black before, and he actually wanted to know what it was like to be a young black person, and he really found out! And I would hold him up as a true example of what psychiatrists ought to be up to—talking to people in the best intersubjective mode—not trying to apply this or that theory, or not trying to fit them into a Freudian or Jungian mold, just trying to see what's going on and to help out. After all, Dr. More, in the end, is trying to do the same thing.

PM: Coles comes out of a liberal tradition of scientific humanism, and yet somehow he broke with the liberal intellectuals, or went beyond them.

WP: Coles doesn't have much use for them if you want to know the truth. You should hear him talk about them, about those professors at Harvard. Yes he is, he's remarkable. I don't know how he does what he does. I couldn't do what he does. He looks frail, but he's tough—he's really tough and so productive. He spent all this time with black children, Navajo Indian children, Belfast children, Catholics, Protestants, trying to figure out what's going on in Ireland.

PM: *Thanatos* is probably your most political novel.

WP: Yes . . . to date, that is.

PM: Well then, back to this question of how far do you go. Your idea is that you've got to have a caring heart. But doesn't there come a moment when you've got to pick up a gun and kill the bad guys—the Nazis? Where's the line?

WP: I guess so, as I told some interviewer when she asked if this was a cautionary novel. I said yes, but novel writing is a rather humble vocation, that is, making up stories to give people pleasure. That's the main business a novelist is doing—he's making up a story to divert the reader. And if he can do that he's succeeded, but even a novelist has a right to issue a warning. It's in a noble tradition, going back to Dostoyevsky. When Dostoyevsky wrote *The Possessed,* he was talking about these young nihilists who didn't believe in God and man, and were simply out to bring on revolution. They were the pre-Communists. They were out to revolutionize Russian society. And I guess the great saying of Dostoyevsky he put in the mouth of Ivan Karamazov. Ivan was arguing with his younger brother Alyosha, who was a young monk. Alyosha was trying to convert Ivan. Alyosha says, "You don't believe in God" and Ivan says, "If God does not exist, all things are permitted." So there's no reason not to use technology to improve society, even if it means killing people. Anything is permitted in order to achieve these goals. The shocker here is that the enemy is the present state. I don't know whether I should be telling you this or not. *(laughs)* A novelist ought to keep his mouth shut. It's supposed to be picked up in the book, but anyway the subversive message is the danger to the present state of the scientific community and the medical community in this country. The comparison is not with the Nazi doctors, but with the Weimer doctors, who were just before the Nazis. The doctors I name here were real doctors in the Weimar Republic. They were not Nazis; they would have no use for the Nazi brutality and the killing of Jews and the Holocaust, but they were saying what's wrong with these humane ideals, the abstract ideal of improving society, improving the quality. They were qualitarians—improving the quality of life—either by trying to cure people, or if you can't cure them, you get rid of them. It's better for society. So that is the subversive message, the comparison of our scientific community with the pre-Nazi doctors. So far the doctors haven't picked up on it.

PM: If this is understood, people will be jumping all over you.

WP: Well, I'm not telling them anything they don't already know. Like Father Smith, I'm not talking. I'm just the writer. I'm not talking about my own convictions at all. Who cares?

PM: What about the concept of active evil? Of course, what you're talking about is what Hannah Arendt was talking about, the banality of evil.

WP: Sure.

PM: Flannery O'Connor brings out active evil in her work.

WP: Active evil?

PM: Well, in "A Good Man Is Hard to Find," you have the idea that everything is permitted so let's have some fun and kill people and so on. And Whittaker Chambers drew on the same concept of everything is permitted, it's the whole rationale of these totalitarian societies. . . .

WP: I know, but if you ever talked to anybody who was in Germany, on the German side, or even on the American side, or as Father Smith was saying, before he became a priest he was in the American army—it was not killing for fun. It was killing for an idea. General Patton's army crossed the Rhine but Father Smith's outfit didn't liberate Dachau— they didn't see the concentration camps—what they saw was a hospital in Munich. That hospital exists: Eglfing-Haar. A nice tender-hearted humane hospital. He saw evidence that they were getting rid of children, either malformed, or unfit, or Jewish, or whatever, and it was all done in a decent, humane way. There was a little room. Incidentally, I read about it, it actually existed. The room was done in good taste— there was a beautiful geranium plant there.

PM: Where did you read about it?

WP: In the introduction of this book I talk about the source: "I am indebted to Dr. Frederic Wertham's remarkable book, *A Sign for Cain.*" That's where I read about this, the hospital at Eglfing-Haar. It was a beautiful little room, and the nurse would bring in the child, and they had the new lethal drugs then, Zyklon B, which had just been invented by I.G. Farben Industries, the great German chemical complex, which was a kind of cyanide, I think. Then, the child would simply disappear. There was one door to enter and a small door to exit, through which the child's body would be removed after the Zyklon was administered, so the other children wouldn't get upset. Father Smith could never disassociate the smell of the geranium plant from the lingering smell of the cyanide. So . . . what we were talking about was the banality of evil. He said he saw Dachau after that, and he said, "The funny thing was that we were not horrified. War was horrible, but you get used to it. And so they were doing this, and the nurse told me about it, and so what?" I don't think soldiers are horrified. I think they're curious and they suffer a great deal, like in the movie *Platoon,* but who's horrified? You could be horrified for ten minutes. The twentieth century might be described as a century of horror in which no one is horrified.

PM: You get sort of hardened. I remember that happening to me when I was a soldier in Vietnam.

WP: Then you know better than I do what I'm talking about. Horror is something that's cultivated. Horror takes an effort. People are horrified for a while. That's what impressed Father Smith. He had to think for a long time before he realized what had happened in Germany.

PM: A Kierkegaardian "repetition" is what you're talking about there.

WP: Yes, and the point was he was telling this to his friend Thomas More and More had the conventional American reaction, "Well, yes, the Germans were doing these terrible things, and are you suggesting that we are like the Germans?" and I think Smith said something like, "Are you suggesting that we are any different?" I mean, what's different? Does anyone imagine that we are not capable of doing what the Germans did, or what the Russians did—given the proper circumstances?

PM: It all goes to scientific humanism. Binx, with his *merde* detector, says that people are dead, dead, dead. And *Thanatos* embraces spiritual death, too—the way people are closed off to one another. . . .

WP: Well, "thanatos" is a big term. It covers the twentieth century, and the main thing is the peculiar paradox. The twentieth century is without a doubt the strangest century that I've ever heard or read about, what little I know of history. We have the apposition, the coming together of these two extraordinary occurrences—this is the most humanitarian century in history—more people have helped other people, more money has been spent, more efforts have been made, all the way from tremendous missionary efforts, the foundations, the hospitals, to helping the Third World, FDR's New Deal to help the poor people. But at the same time it is the century in which men have killed more of each other than in all other centuries put together, and this before the atom bomb.

PM: And your idea is that there's a connection between those two opposites.

WP: Yes, when, in 1916 in the Battle of the Somme and the Battle of Verdun two million young men, from the three or four most civilized nations in the world, the French, German, and English, were killed in one summer. Here they were, people who were from the same culture, even the same kings, royal families, kin to each other, the same science, the same backgrounds, same Christendom. Something had happened. Something new was happening in the world. So you have this, two things happening—a humane science which was improving the lot of mankind, and tremendous humane efforts from Albert Schweitzer on up, or on down, helping poor people, at the same time you have what Freud would call the "spirit of thanatos." He said you have eros and thanatos going together. I guess the implicit warning is that Father Smith says the American medical profession is, in many ways, the most admirable in all the world, yet he is attacking Thomas More. He says, "Look you guys, for the last 2,500 years you have taken the Hippocratic oath never to perform an abortion, and now nobody thinks anything of it. Two million abortions a year and you guys haven't turned a hair, with a couple of exceptions. Not one single letter of protest in the august *New England Journal of Medicine.*" That's the only time abortion is mentioned in the book. So the comparison is there to be drawn, which I don't draw—it's just not my place as a novelist. Father Smith hints at it, says there's a certain similarity between the American medical profession now and the German Weimar Republic medical profession, who did what they thought was the best thing for mankind.

PM: What is the "spirit of thanatos"?

WP: I guess originally the idea came from Freud, who made the polarity, eros and thanatos. I changed the context. He certainly would have disregarded any Judeo-Christian background, and he certainly had no use for the idea of the great prince Satan.

PM: What about moral courage? What's the message? The way to keep scientific humanism from becoming Pol Potism is to draw the line somewhere, have moral courage? Is that what appeals to you about Thomas More?

WP: I'm not so sure how much moral courage he had. It's very difficult to do such things in a novel now. You know what Flannery O'Connor said—she said beware of writing edifying novels. She was always saying, "These ladies are coming up to me and saying why aren't your novels more uplifting?" And Flannery said something like if you get fifty women who read uplifting novels what you've got is a book club. So the novelist is very limited in what he or she can do. The most that I ventured to do here was to have Thomas More serve Mass with Father Smith on the Feast of Epiphany on top of his tower. He doesn't experience any great return to religion. Maybe there's a hint there.

PM: So you have your somewhat ambiguous ending that you seem to like so much.

WP: Well, I was content to have Dr. More end up where he started off, getting a patient to talk about herself, back with her old anxieties, back with her depression, back with her dislocation which is where she should be, dislocated. They're both more human and he is trying to help her. Like I say, the novelist's vocation is a modest one.

PM: So you mean if you're not crazy, and you look around at how things are and see things clearly, it will make you crazy.

WP: That's right. Better to be a dislocated human than a happy chimp. That's the only message I have. The question is always raised who's crazy, whether "normal people" are normal, or deranged people are the ones who know something's wrong. It's not new with me—the psychiatrist R. D. Laing raised this question quite a while ago, but it's just explicit here. This could be read partially as an attack on the present trend in neurology and psychiatry to trace all symptoms to genetic disturbances and to treat symptoms with drugs which will remove the symptoms. And, as a matter of fact, this could be read as a Freudian novel. This guy's a practical Freudian and Jungian, who talks and listens. Just recently I read that some guy had claimed to have discovered the gene responsible for manic depressive psychosis. Well, maybe he did, maybe it's true, which would be good. But what I'm saying is that a good deal of the anxiety, the alienation, and the depression in the modern world is not due to any gene. It's due to something wrong with the modern world and something wrong with the way we live.

PM: So what's the next age, the new age, going to be?

WP: I'm not in that business. (*laughs*) I'm not a prophet. The most I attempt to do is to say this is the way it could be, this is what could happen. I'm not getting into any debate about pro-life or pro-choice. I'm not getting into media polemics. But in the novel I am uttering a

warning. Look what happened to the Weimar doctors and to Germany.
I will admit the idea came not from me; it's Dostoyevsky's idea. He
said even a novelist can raise a warning flag and say this is what can
happen. Ivan Karamazov says without God all things are permitted. But
not even Dostoyevsky imagined what man without God is capable of.

PM: Father Smith calls himself a spiteful man; that's an echo from
Notes from Underground.

WP: He was a terrible guy, rotten, mean to his mother and his father.

PM: You converted to Catholicism when you returned from Santa Fe.
Why did you convert?

WP: Right. These things are both mysterious and commonplace. Of
course, the technical answer is always that faith is a gift, a gratuitous
gift. But there I was living in New Orleans, married, happy, had two
little girls. Who was the philosopher, was it Nietzsche, who said, well,
what do we do next? (*laughs*) What do we do now? So I decided well.
. . . And my Uncle Will was a Catholic, a lapsed Catholic; he didn't go
to church but he was always talking about the great Catholic tradition.
I was brought up Presbyterian. So I don't know except to say that I
decided to do it. I remember walking up to the rectory door, I'd never
even spoken to a Catholic priest in my life, walking up to the rectory
door of the Jesuit church on St. Charles Avenue, and asking for a priest
and saying, "I'd like to be a Catholic, what am I supposed to do?"

PM: You did that? Just like that?

WP: (*laughs*) And said, "What do I do next?"

PM: How did you get to that decision?

WP: Kierkegaard, if I had to blame it on somebody.

PM: He wasn't a Catholic.

WP: He certainly was not. Karl Barth said that he had to rule him out
of the great Protestant theologians because if he'd lived long enough he
would have become Roman. (*laughs*)

PM: You made that, if not a leap of faith, you somehow got up
to it. . . .

WP: Sure, and this astonished priest took a look at me; he couldn't
figure out what I was up to, and we went through regular instruction. It
worked out all right.

PM: Well, you and Kierkegaard don't agree on the idea of the hero
getting the girl and God both. You broke with him on that.

WP: Well, you see if he'd been Catholic he would have known

better. He had this Protestant thing about sex. The Catholics are a little
bit wiser than that, maybe a little bit more sinful, I don't know.

PM: You don't get out and about much?

WP: As little as possible. For instance, I was invited to go to France
a couple of months ago. Strangely enough, the French have a fairly
centralized educational system so that in the French universities it
appears that for all courses in English or American literature, required
reading is *The Moviegoer*. That means thousands of students are forced
to read *The Moviegoer*. (*laughs*) In France! So they asked me to come
over on some exchange program and go around to different universities,
provincial universities like Lyons, Marseilles. I didn't want to do it, so
we settled for my going to New Orleans and talking via satellite to three
or four French scholars about *The Moviegoer*. So I did that. I've got all
I can do to handle what I'm thinking about and trying to work on. I just
don't need to go anywhere.

PM: What's your next book?

WP: I usually alternate from fiction to non-fiction, and right now I'm
thinking of something in the line of semiotics, something about human
communication, about language, in connection with literature, with
maybe Scripture. My own theory is that even after all these years and all
the linguistics, all the behavioristic psychology, nobody knows what
language is. Nobody knows how it works. As I have said before, I think
Charles Peirce, the American philosopher, maybe had the best clue
about it, which has not been pursued or developed. So what I would like
to do is something like J.D. Salinger did, that is, go into absolute
seclusion, become a recluse for the next four years and work on Charles
Peirce's triadic theory of language. That may come to nothing at all, I
don't know. I should live so long. But anyway you asked me what I was
thinking about.

PM: You've said your predominant mood is one of mild depression
punctuated by bouts of transcending when you're writing.

WP: I come from a long line of manic depressives, and my wife kids
me. She says, "Why, you're not manic depressive. A manic depressive
has his highs and you're depressed all the time." (*laughs*) Which is her
way of saying that I'm not really depressed. I've lived long enough so
I've gotten used to a very sort of low-keyed existence and take pleasure
in certain experiences—for instance, in writing a book, in this last
book. A book's a failure, I mean, novels are always failures, a failure

of some idea—and so is this novel, and I think every other novel. I can
only think of two or three novels that ever really succeeded. So this
book mostly failed—I only got a couple of things right. And I just
remember feeling good when everything fell out right.

PM: And those were . . .

WP: I just remember one line when I think Van Dorn has been
regressed by heavy sodium into a kind of pre-human, say a pongid,
state, and he was almost like a gorilla. He was up on the balcony with
one elbow hooked over his head, and playing the part of the presiding
bachelor gorilla who was running the group. And the only way they
were keeping him at bay was by Dr. More throwing him Snickers bars.
There was a machine in the back with Snickers bars and he told Uncle
Hugh Bob to go shoot up the machine and get the candy bars out.
(*laughs*) So Thomas More was feeding him Snickers, and Van Dorn was
peeling back the candy wrappers like bananas. When he ran out of
Snickers he came down to attack the women or God knows what, and
there's Tom More without any more to give him. So More says to Hugh
Bob, "Give me your Snickers" and Uncle Hugh Bob says, "Shit, he's
got his own Snickers!" I liked that line, I enjoyed that. (*laughs*) The
point is that once in a while you do something right. Mostly you don't,
but it makes it worthwhile once in a while when you get things right.

PM: You have a different flair of humor than, say, Flannery
O'Connor—just out of curiosity, did you ever meet Flannery O'Connor?

WP: Yes, I did. She was amazing. It was shortly before she died.
She discovered she had lupus erythematosus before she published
anything. In other words, during her whole publishing life she knew she
had a fatal disease because her father had died from it. She lived with a
literary couple, Robert and Sally Fitzgerald in New Haven or some-
place, who were very good to her. I think the diagnosis was made when
she was staying with them, so during her whole writing life, which I
think was very short, ten or twelve years, she had lupus the whole time.
And she was much more active than I am. She would accept lectures.
Somebody would ask her to come lecture at Southwestern Louisiana in
Lafayette or wherever and she'd go . . . very apostolic. She thought she
ought to spread the good news. The only time I met her was when she
was invited to Loyola in New Orleans. I had corresponded with her, so
we went in to see her. I remember we were going into this lecture hall,

and she came in from a side entrance. Somebody was with her from the
university and helped her. She had crutches and they helped her up to
the podium, where she sort of hung on and delivered a stunning lecture.
I think the lecture, as a matter of fact, is part of her collected essays, in
Mystery and Manners. Then she answered questions and was just
extraordinary. I could recognize the symptoms of advanced lupus,
which means destruction of connective tissues. For instance, she had
lost most of the tissue of her chin. You could see it, her face was very
strange, but her voice was clear, her mind was clear, and we invited her
to meet with us afterwards. We were with friends, so we picked her up,
took her to an apartment house, and I can remember a flight of steps
that my daughter bodily carried her up. We spent an evening with her,
with some friends, and that's the only time I ever saw her. A few
months later Caroline Gordon, who was a good friend, I mean a really
good friend, wrote or called me to say O'Connor was dying. She was in
an Atlanta hospital and wouldn't I like to come see her. I didn't want to
go see her—I didn't think she wanted to see me. Maybe I should have
gone, but I didn't go. Anyway, that's the one and only time I ever saw
her.

PM: Your novel is comic.

WP: Thank you. It's supposed to be. I was aware of the risk of
having comedy juxtaposed with high seriousness. There's nothing funny
about what Father Smith is talking about, but I hope the two work
together. My justification is that Sören Kierkegaard said that true comedy is deeply related to religion. He didn't quite explain why, but I
think I understand what he means. The comic condition is the last stage
before the religious condition or religious stage he called it. People have
the wrong idea about comedy. People think the comic is the opposite of
the serious, but that's not true at all. The comic can also be part of high
seriousness.

PM: Is anger a motivation for you to write? How'd you get the idea
for *The Thanatos Syndrome?* After all, you said getting angry at Carl
Sagan had something to do with writing *Lost in the Cosmos.*

WP: *Thanatos* was a sequel, or came out as a sequel, to *Love in the
Ruins*. I decided instead of writing a far out sci-fi piece like *Love in the
Ruins* with all sorts of futuristic gimmickry like More's ontological
lapsometer which measures the defects of the cortex in the brain and
also treats it, I decided to do something much more contemporary, to

turn things around. Instead of relying on the technology, I wanted to have a fellow who was somewhat old-fashioned, a practical psycho-analyst. Instead of using the lapsometer, he had gone back to his roots of Freud and Jung, and he had gone back to talking and listening to people, mostly listening. I wanted to use that as a device to view current technology, which is actually going on. Most psychiatry, more and more, has to do with the use of drugs, endorphins to treat emotional disorders. Of course, what I want to do is use this as a statement about the search for oneself, or the quest for selfhood, the idea being that no technology, however designed, however advanced, can aid one in the search which I figure is integral to the human condition.

At Court with Walker Percy

Michael Swindle/1989

From *New Orleans Magazine*, 23 (January 1989), 38–42, 76–77.
Reprinted by permission of *New Orleans Magazine* and Michael
Swindle.

Walker Percy. This man's name has been burned into the soul of
Southern literature and has become enmeshed in the fabric of New
Orleans history. He lives at the apex of the Southern storyteller
hierarchy, along with Sydney Lanier, Thomas Wolfe, William Faulkner
and Robert Penn Warren. In the wake of Walker Percy's works, a cult
has formed and the cult numbers admirers, if not worshippers, in the
hundreds of thousands.

Writers often become the objects of cults, small groups of people who
idolize the writer's work because the writer, unlike the movie star or the
singer, must have some view of the world, of existence, of life, that the
remainder of us somehow haven't the sight or the temperament to see or
feel, much less communicate.

And Walker Percy, the frail, 72-year-old writer who lives in
Covington is certainly the kind of figure around whom cults can form.
Hardly a giant in literature, as measured by the sale of books, Percy is
reclusive and deep. His mind is his playground, but mere thoughts
aren't his only reason to go to work. Money has always played a major
role in his career, a career that has spanned six novels and two non-
fiction works that cover topics from arcane Catholic theology and
existentialism to psychology and semiotics. And while the pinnacle of
raw book sales has alluded him, Percy remains one of the most honored
writers living, a giant above all in the rarified air of America's literary
circles. This year he won the coveted T.S. Eliot Award for his complete
body of works and he is the first American to be so honored. This
spring, he will deliver the Jefferson Lecture in Humanities, the highest
award a person of letters can receive in this country. But for all his
name recognition, for all his attraction to admirers around the world,
the man the South created and New Orleans calls its own remains an
enigma wrapped up in a small Louisiana town.

Walker Percy was born in Birmingham, Ala., on May 28, 1916, and lived in a very well-to-do southside neighborhood at the corner of Highland and Arlington avenues. He still remembers falling off a stone retaining wall in his yard when he was four years old. His family later moved to Number 3 Country Club Rd., next to the country club golf course in Mountain Brook, the wellest-to-do suburb in Birmingham.

Here, in this gracious haven of wealth and privilege, where he rode his bike over Red Mountain to attend the exclusive Birmingham University School and learned to love the game of golf, the walls of 13-year-old Walker's world would come tumbling down. His father, a prosperous businessman, Episcopal Sunday school teacher and (unknown to everybody) a manic depressive, committed suicide.

After spending a year in the stately Milledge Avenue Victorian home of his maternal grandmother in Athens, Ga., Walker, his brothers Leroy and Billips, and their still grief-stricken mother moved to Greenville, Miss., into the home of his father's first cousin, the lawyer/poet/planter William Alexander Percy.

Tragedy struck again in young Walker's life, however, when shortly after moving to Greenville his mother was killed in an automobile accident.

Although his Uncle Will adopted the Percy boys and provided not only security but also an enviable cultural atmosphere—he was an accomplished classical pianist as well as a writer, and noted houseguests such as William Faulkner, Carl Sandburg and Vachel Lindsay were commonplace—Walker felt adrift, "outside," dependent on his wiles to make it in an alien and hostile world, despite the economic and social privilege accorded him.

Coming to grips with his mother's death, though difficult, was at least tempered by the fact that hers was accidental. His father's suicide presented young Percy with a whole new set of problems and would occupy him the remainder of his life. Perhaps that is why the protagonists of his novels are invariably people to whom "much has been given" and who are always engaged in one way or another in a quest for meaning or a struggle against chaos (the death force). Like young Percy, his characters are concerned with their sense of impoverishment in the midst of plenty, seeking the answer to the riddle of why they feel so bad in such a good environment.

Yet while Walker Percy was sorting all this out best he could for himself, he lived up to his family's expectations and earned a medical degree at Columbia University's College of Physicians and Surgeons, after finishing undergraduate studies at the University of North Carolina. He specialized in pathology and psychoanalysis, but his medical career ended during his internship at New York's Bellevue Hospital in 1942, when he contracted tuberculosis. By the time he had recovered from the illness at the end of World War II, he had made his decision to be a writer.

At about the same time, Walker made two other decisions that were to have a major impact on his life. The first was to marry Mary Bernice "Bunt" Townsend, a young nurse he'd met in Greenville. The second, which he made in tandem with his bride and after a year of study and contemplation at his Uncle Will's home in the hills outside Sewanee, Tenn., was to convert to Catholicism.

Walker's conversion was emotional, intellectual, and total. Writes Linda Whitney Hobson, in her recently published book, *Understanding Walker Percy,* his faith "is at least partly a form of knowing and, as such, his important cognitive effects on the believer. This means that the believer—an existentialist as well as a Catholic—can choose to believe or not; can choose to perceive God's abundant grace or not; and thus can take control of his spiritual life and, following that, his daily life. Percy's is an optimistic or 'comic' view of life, one which he has never abandoned since his decision to become a Catholic."

Equal to his faith, Walker's wife Bunt has been a tremendous asset to him during these last 40 years. More outgoing than her modest and reclusive husband, she was always supportive of his writing ambitions and has served as a kind of buffer between the demands of the real world and the writer's need to take nourishment from his own world.

And his own world is in Walker Percy's mind, though he also considers New Orleans part of his own world. He and Bunt moved to the Crescent City in 1947 where he chose to take up writing as a career, living in the meantime in the Garden District on a small inheritance. Some years later, however, Percy moved out of the city over to Covington because, he says, he was concerned that he and Bunt would be too caught up in the social swirl of Uptown New Orleans. It was in Covington in 1961 that he saw his first novel, *The Moviegoer,* published. It was also in Covington that Bunt took more control in guiding her husband's public life, if not his career. Remembers longtime family friend and

Covington car dealer Lawrence "Chink" Baldwin: "When Walker first
came over here, his health was still very delicate. Bunt would see to it
that he got his nap every afternoon. She would shield him from phone
calls and things like that and she wouldn't let him go out two evenings
in a row—though he does now, if he's inclined to. She saw to it that
Walker took it very easy. She was very concerned and very efficient at
keeping Walker tied down to a normal, quiet routine."

The idea of routine plays a big part in Percy's life. Though it is a
good thing insofar as it leads to productivity, routine can also lead to
alienation, the dullness of the everyday, which is to be avoided if we are
to lead a full life.

Walker is a man of the mind, not so much from his life as a writer,
but because of the frailty of his health. In his mind, he sees dullness
warded off by two processes. The first is "rotations," or the seeking of
new experiences. The other, the more sublime, perhaps the more
fulfilling for a 72-year-old semi-recluse, is what he calls "repetitions,"
literally the re-experiencing of past emotions, events, places. And few
things in Walker Percy's life are better for repetitions than his weekly
lunch with Chink Baldwin, his brother Billips Percy, and one or two
other close friends. As with almost everything else in Percy's life, even
here the business of religion has some influence. Then again, so does
almost everything else—everything else worth discussing, that is.

"Even though I'm the only non-Catholic in the group," smiles brother
Billips, who recently retired from the law faculty at Tulane, "they call
me the Pope. I'm in charge of whose time it is to pay and, if you want
to bring someone extra along, you're supposed to check with me.
Several times, Walker has had people visiting and they're surprised
about how little literature or serious matters were discussed and about
how Walker could hold his own about sports or sex or politics—
whatever six guys sit around and talk about. There's no feeling that a
celebrity is in the group."

Ben C. Toledano, an attorney, writer and former candidate for mayor
of New Orleans and U.S. Senator from Louisiana, occasionally attends
these weekly lunches. He met Percy over 20 years ago, when a friend
was attempting to put together a movie based on Percy's first published
novel, *The Moviegoer*.

"Over and over again," Toledano says, "I've heard people talk about,
'Oh yeah, I know Walker Percy. I had a drink with him; I had lunch

with him.' If you feel mean enough to pursue it with them, you find out they really don't know Walker Percy. They may have met him or made small talk with him on occasion, but they don't really know him. Getting to know him would be sort of tough anyway because then they may have to say something. It's part of this cult situation in our society, where people are more interested in knowing about the artist than they are about knowing the art.

"My observation is that Walker is a very kind and generous person with his time, where he feels that person is worthwhile helping and spending time with. I think this is true with a lot of thinkers and writers. The role of the sensitive, feeling person is a difficult thing. On the one hand you want to give of yourself and, on the other, you're a little timid and frightened about it because you don't want people walking all over you. I've always been impressed by the time Walker was willing to spend with people certainly not equal to his accomplishments. He's a very giving person.

There is no doubt that Percy is a warm, caring, generous and self-effacing person. His most publicized act of generosity was helping John Kennedy Toole's mother publish her dead son's manuscript, *Confederacy of Dunces* (the book subsequently received the Pulitzer Prize for Literature), but in talking to those close to him one hears of many other instances of his kindness. (During the time I was writing this piece, he took time to come into New Orleans to meet with a friend of mine who was a stranger to him and offer what guidance he could for dealing with the grief brought on by the recent suicide of her stepson.)

On the other hand, he doesn't let people take advantage of his good nature (especially interviewers) and there are times when his anger flares.

He was strongly in favor of President Reagan's contra aid legislation that was defeated in Congress earlier this year. Lindy Boggs was the only member of the Louisiana delegation to vote against the bill and Percy wasted no time in personally registering his displeasure with the congresswoman. An avowed conservative, Walker, as well as his brother Billips, is a regular letter writer to the daily newspapers in New Orleans. On the other hand, Walker isn't quick to take an active role in politics, to wit his short-lived tenure last year in state government.

It all began with an early morning telephone call from Gov. Buddy Roemer, who urged Walker to accept a post on the 18-member

Louisiana State University (LSU) Board of Supervisors. The persuasive Roemer, having caught Percy, according to press reports, "before his head had cleared," talked him into a seat on the august body.

Although his ever-protective friends warned Percy that it was a "political" board, Percy stood by his word, though both he and Gov. Roemer should have seen that Walker, as a writer accustomed to working in solitude and with total control over the subject at hand, was especially ill-suited to get work done in committee. Even so, in early July, he traveled to Baton Rouge for his first committee meeting. It lasted five hours, during which time, according to a close friend of Percy's, "nothing he considered worthwhile took place." He resigned from the board the next day.

Although Percy, characteristically, could not be reached for comment, it was reported that he had resigned for "health reasons." While it's true that Percy's health has been fragile since his bout with tuberculosis in the 1940s, and that his family and friends have been genuinely worried about him since he underwent prostate surgery last year, another more important factor in his decision to resign from the board could be that his mail "quadrupled, or more," after his appointment to the board was announced. It seems that each member of the LSU Board of Supervisors can award up to 20 scholarships a year to the university, a fact that filled his mailbox with requests from scholarship hopefuls. Too much reading for a writer and, besides, Percy is conscientious about these kinds of things and, after seeing the volume of mail the appointment produced and the lack of meaningful work the committee did, he decided that rotations would be better found elsewhere.

At his age, says writer Linda Hobson, "while he's not obsessed with his own mortality, he's very conscious of his time, using it for his work. You know, not going to lunch with people. Certainly no more interviews, no more talks. He will deliver the Jefferson Lecture next year, which is pretty special, but mainly, I think he's really concerned with getting his work done."

And so here we were, Walker Percy, recluse writer, and I mouth to ear in a rare interview. To say he is jaded is not fair. To say he approaches success with a low energy level certainly is. For example, the coveted T. S. Eliot award and being tapped to deliver the Jefferson Lecture. Big deals? Not really, he says. "I never write with prizes or awards in mind; that is a fatal goal. But, of course, I'm very pleased to get them, especially when money is involved. But it's a pain to go up and get the things, but the T.S. Eliot Award is especially gratifying because I'm the first American to receive it."

Is there another book in the works?

"I'm working on a book of essays," he says, "some lectures I've given over the years, on semiotics—the study of signs and symbols. I've always been interested in the startling fact that no one knows what language is. I'm fascinated by the nature of language. There is a gap between the scientific view of man as an organism, which approaches language from the point of view of stimulus/response or quantitative conditioning and the linguistic approach, which sees language as an innate characteristic of man and begins its studies with the earliest speech patterns—naming, two-word sentences. There's a huge gap between these two approaches to the nature of language and I'm interested in what's in the gap.

"I've always alternated my made-up stories—my novels—and semiotics, which I never tire of brooding over. When I finish a novel, which for me entails a great deal of re-writing, I'm sick of it. I never re-read them. I never want to talk about them. Oh, I'll answer questions about them, but only under pressure. You know, much of a writer's life is spent dealing with despair and depression."

How does he deal with those feelings?

"Oh, there are all kinds of ways. Travel is one, though it's not very satisfactory. It only works for two or three weeks for me. There's re-entry into the commonplace, like going to the symphony or to the movies, or just enjoying being with my grandchildren. One recent example I can give you, I seldom get to the French Quarter anymore. It's been 20 years since my wife and I have gone down to Jackson Square. But we were there a couple of weeks ago for a wedding in St. Louis Cathedral. Afterward, we were sitting out on the benches there and it was a beautiful autumn day. Children were playing and the throngs of people were milling about. It was the same scene we remembered from 20 years ago. I got hungry and the only thing I could find to eat was a Lucky Dog, so I sat there eating one and thinking of Ignatius in *Confederacy of Dunces*. It was a wonderful repetition."

On that note, Walker Percy had to go. Enough interviews. Enough questions about what it is that makes him tick. You hang up the telephone somehow admonished for calling him up in the first place. He did the talking, but you feel somewhat short changed at not getting more, but the toughest question in the world to ask of a writer is, "How do you write?" You ponder on his answers, his Southernness, his own need to ask the questions and then you go back to his books and read his characters and think of his life and his friends and weekly lunches and his interest in the language and you ponder again his fame, his cult, his power in the world of letters.

The answer is, in the final analysis, perhaps much more simple than his admirers might think. He is Walker Percy and he has shared his life and his thoughts and we are richer for it, as he is richer for it. But like the intimacy of a marriage, the writer and reader can only share so much. After that, each is left to his own devices. The reader continues his study. Walker Percy just goes to lunch. That is exactly the stuff cults are made of.

Southern Semiotics: An Interview with Walker Percy

Rebekah Presson/1989

From *New Letters Review of Books*, 3:2 (Winter 1990), 12–13, 17 1990. Rebekah Presson's interview with Walker Percy was conducted in April 1989 for "New Letters on the Air." It was originally published in the *New Letters Review of Books* (3:2, Winter 1990). It is reprinted here with the permission of *New Letters* and the Curators of the University of Missouri-Kansas City.

Walker Percy has adapted the Southern tradition of writing to the philosophical discussions more common in European fiction. His training as a physician and deep reading in philosophy guide an exacting technique, but one supported by poetic and emotional assumptions.

His first novel, *The Moviegoer* (1961), with its microscopic examination of the nature of reality, survives with Joseph Heller's *Catch 22* as one of the most influential novels of the 1960s. More recent work flirts with the techniques of science fiction to comment on our modern malaise; in his nonfiction particularly, Percy has shown a concern for how symbols influence behavior, with semiotics. Percy takes the high ground, but in many ways his popularity can be explained by the fact he tells a compelling story and is often extremely funny.

Rebekah Presson interviewed Percy in April of 1989 in Chattanooga, at the Fellowship of Southern Writers' Fifth Biennial Conference in Southern Literature.

NL: A reviewer once quoted you as having said that one of the things that keeps you going as a writer is the promise of the potential big one. And that critic seemed to think that *The Second Coming* was the big one. But the book that people make the most of is *The Moviegoer*, right?

WP: I guess I was lucky with *The Moviegoer*. It seemed to hit at the right time and I was doing something which had not been done in this

216

country so much. It was more the European style than the American style.

At the time, which was 1960 or 1961, there was a great popularity of the existentialists, the European writers and philosophers. And they were distinguished from American writers by translating their ideas and convictions into fictional form. Usually, the traditional American novel is a story about people, about characters and what happens to them: war, peace, love, death. But I'd been reading European existentialists like Kierkegaard and particularly the French writer Albert Camus, and Jean Paul Sartre. And I was excited by what they had done. They had taken the ideas of philosophers, which are usually very abstract, and incarnated them in novel form. They created living characters who illustrated the themes of the philosophy. So I said, why not do that in the South? Why not do that in New Orleans? I was living in New Orleans at the time.

Why not have a young man with a good background and a good education who finds himself in a certain predicament, and see what he does with himself? This is a typical existentialist beginning. He's fed up with education. He's fed up with his own background, he's fed up with the books he's read and the courses he's taken and the people he's known—so what does he do with himself? I said why not take a young man of a certain background, in Louisiana, in the South, put him down in a kind of middle class suburb in New Orleans, a suburb called Gentilly, and see what happens to him?

He was a moviegoer. His main diversion in life was going to the movies. In fact, he suffered a strange dislocation of reality. He found the movies more real than the people he saw, the life he lived. To answer your question that's what it's about: what happens to a young man in a certain situation with no beliefs in particular, what happens to him in the end. How he gets more in touch with life; how he goes from moviegoing to living.

NL: Do you suppose that your decision to write a novel of ideas, about a sort of spiritual journey, rather than a more narrative-type novel, also had to do with your own lack of activity over many years? That is, in addition to reading the existentialism?

WP: I guess so.

NL: I should clarify. You were ill with tuberculosis.

WP: I think we all write about ourselves more or less. To summarize my own experience. I was headed for medicine. I went to pre-med, in college, at the medical school at Columbia, New York, interned at Bellevue in New York. I was working with tuberculosis patients and contracted the disease. Not seriously, it was called a "minimal lesion," but in those days, unlike now where we can treat tuberculosis with a couple of shots, it was a serious disease. In those days one took the classical "rest cure" just like Hans Castorp in *The Magic Mountain* and my experience was like his. The crisis of his life occurred in the two years he spent in a sanitarium. What happened to me was I got interested in reading and writing. I read everything that I hadn't read before, as I was studying science, medicine, and chemistry. I got turned on by the reading and started writing and one thing led to another. So I decided I was cut out for writing more than medicine.

NL: When you were recovering and fighting for your own life, did you feel, like your protagonist, that this was the time when you were most alive?

WP: I wasn't fighting for my life. As I saw it was a very minimal lesion. It was not a confrontation with death, although that was there. I had friends who died. It was not that so much as simply the enforced inactivity. Two years. First, on your back, total bedrest. Then getting up, walking 15 minutes once a day and gradually up until you're walking twice a day for an hour. It was much more the enforced idleness— what am I doing here, is the rest of my life going to be like this? So maybe Binx Bolling's moviegoing was something like my lying in a bed in upstate New York for two years. It was a crisis in life in the sense of what to do with one's life.

You raise an interesting question, though, whether the background of death has something to do with it. You could, after all, die of it. And it was wartime too, and people were getting killed and people were dying of TB, so that does make things a little more vivid. It makes you appreciate life a little more.

NL: You've described yourself as being not driven, that you lead a pretty simple life.

WP: I don't like to travel very much. In fact, the only reason I'm up here is to see some writer friends that I want to see, but I'd just as soon stay home. We live a very quiet life, my wife and I, and I know exactly what I want to do for the rest of my life. I know the books I want to write and how I want to spend my time, and I have enough to do right there.

Somebody asked me how much I work. I said, I work three hours a day in the morning. He looked at me like I was goofing off. But I reminded him what Flannery O'Connor said when somebody asked her the same question. She said, "I work three hours a day in the morning and spend the rest of the day getting over it." What she meant, of course, is true—if you are a serious writer, it's hard work. I'd rather dig a ditch. You sweat and you feel tired. Then the rest of the day we take walks and work in the garden and read. I'm perfectly happy doing that.

NL: What do you like to do the most?

WP: This seems paradoxical, but if I'm writing well I'd rather write than anything else. It's both the worst and the best of all possible worlds. The worst of it is getting up in the morning, going into the study and looking at a blank sheet of paper. At that period, I envy every other man in the world: a guy selling Electroluxes, any salesman, anybody, a garbage collector. At least he's doing honest work, and here I'm looking at this stupid piece of paper and wondering what's going to happen, what am I doing here, this is a bad way to spend your life.

But, sure enough, things begin to happen. What you do is—all writers are different. Mine is an exercise in despair. Some writers go in all juiced up, they know exactly what they're going to write and they take off right from where they left off full of juice. I can only operate from despair. I look at the paper and say, "Oh, this is hopeless. Let's give up, this is the end." Once you admit that it's hopeless there's only one or two options: suicide or total depression, a wasted life: once you admit that you say, "Oh, well, I have nothing left to lose. The only way from here is up." Then you say, "If nothing's left to lose, why not write down a word or two—what have I got to lose?" So I write down a couple of words and then maybe something will happen. Then I say, "Why not write a paragraph—write a couple of things more."

And then if you're lucky—you never know how this works—either through an act of God or through luck or body chemistry or something, but once in a while things happen just right. That's what makes it worthwhile. I'd rather do that than most anything I can think of. Those are the good times. There are a lot of bad times.

NL: Does this happen most days?

WP: No, no. A lot of people like my writing—like the way I do it—but the thing that pleases me, that's what counts. And I've gotten about two or three things right in my life, where I thought, you finally did it right.

NL: What are they? Do you mean whole books or parts of a book?

WP: Parts of a book. A character falls out just right. Maybe Binx Bolling gets tired of going to the movies and he hires a secretary. His romantic life consists of hiring a series of secretaries. He's looking for the right girl. Finally, he hires one who looks and acts like a certain movie star and things happen just right. He takes her out to meet his family, his nephews, whom he likes very much. And the first secretary, Tiffany somebody, she was no good, she just stood around lumpy-looking and didn't know how to do anything, how to talk to the nephews. The second secretary squatted down—she was too gracious. She was like Joan Fontaine visiting an orphanage. Finally, the third secretary does it just right.

Well, that worked fine. He was watching the way these girls reacted to his family. That was the way he was picking his girlfriend, future wife, whatever. Just a little thing like that, to get a line on a character through somebody's eyes. The little things are what count.

NL: He's still resistant to that interaction, isn't he? He doesn't want to admit that he's falling for her.

WP: Right. And, of course, he doesn't in the end. He gets tired of her and he finally takes up with his sick cousin, who is schizophrenic and God knows what. He comes out of his life-long trance of moviegoing and sees somebody who needs something. For the first time in his life he gets out of himself.

NL: You told me that your current project is nonfiction. Could you talk a little bit about it?

WP: My younger daughter was born deaf, so I'm very much interested in her education, how she learns language. And I know about the experience of Helen Keller and how she discovered language even though she was blind and deaf. She had been responding to language in a certain way. Somebody would touch her hand in a certain way and they would spell out "water" and she thought it meant "Go get water" or "I'm thirsty." Or "ball" meant "Go get the ball" or "Where's the ball?" She would respond like a good animal.

Of course, the famous scene was when Miss Sullivan was trying to

teach her that words mean something, there in the pump house in
Alabama. They go to the pump house and Miss Sullivan is showing her
the water, she's pumping the water and the water is flowing over
Helen's hand. And then Miss Sullivan writes the word water in the other
hand. She's trying to get over the idea, "This is water." This word is
this stuff, flowing water. And Helen Keller described it in her auto-
biography. All of a sudden it dawned on her, "This is water." This
symbol means this stuff. She said it was the beginning of her life, the
beginning of her consciousness.

You could say all my writing and philosophizing about language
comes from this extraordinary realization that the human has a different
way of understanding signs than any other creature. The fact that words
can mean things, that sentences can be asserted. Even the smartest
chimp, or the smartest gorilla or dolphin cannot do anything like it. So
our whole philosophy can be derived from a philosophy of language.

I don't think the specialists of language have explored this. The
linguists, most semioticians, who study signs—or the behaviorists, the
psychologists who study behavior. Most behaviorists think human
language and understanding of language is the same as a chimpanzee's
or a gorilla's understanding of signs, only more complicated. My point,
and what other semioticians say, is that it's totally different. There's a
qualitative difference. I've been writing and talking about a whole new
way of looking at language, and how so much about human beings and
their relationships can be understood by our study of language.

NL: And are you dealing with other cultures, or just ours?

WP: I'm interested in the generic nature of language. I don't care
what the culture is. There are two things in common with all languages.
I know this from being told, not because I know all languages. And that
is: all languages have symbols which name things, different kinds of
things, clouds, different cloud structures. And all languages have sentences which are asserted. I declare something to you and you
understand that it is an assertion, not a question. I don't care how
complicated, how different the language is, the two things are the same.
There's the symbolic structure and there's the assertion.

NL: It sounds to me like this is more of an essay than a research
book.

WP: A series of essays. I've done two books like that. One was
called *The Message in the Bottle,* which talks along the same lines. And

the other is called *Lost in the Cosmos,* which was a kind of satire of Carl Sagan's book. Carl Sagan tries to explain human beings as part of the cosmos and not really different from other creatures and things in the cosmos. I'm showing how human beings are different. That a human being can maybe best be described as being lost in the cosmos, particularly now. So it's partly funny and partly serious and partly satirical.

NL: Do you have a name for the new book?

WP: I'll tell you the present working title. My publisher asked me and I said, "The title I'm thinking of now is *Contra Gentiles.* It's a title I stole from St. Thomas Aquinas," and he said, "Yeah, Walker, that's fine. But do you know how people are going to read it? They're going to read it, first, 'contra'—that means the people that are fighting in Nicaragua. And they're going to read 'gentiles' as gentiles—they're going to think you're talking about gentile contras in Nicaragua." But it's borrowed from St. Thomas and there are certain resemblances between what St. Thomas was doing in the 13th century and what I'm doing.

NL: Will this be Farrar, Straus & Giroux again?

WP: I hope so. If I ever finish it, and it's any good.

NL: So it might be a ways away.

WP: Well, I'm hard to please. I'm much harder to please than Farrar Straus. But if I like it, they probably will. So, I don't know, maybe this year, maybe next. It all depends on what happens to that page when I look at it.

NL: Do you go to anyone else for advice?

WP: My wife's a very good reader. She'll pick up things that I missed and I have a very good publisher and a good agent. They'll see things. I don't show it around, if that's what you mean.

NL: But your editor does work with you some. Sometimes editors are afraid of a highly established writer, and don't want to say anything.

WP: I've got a very established publisher, Bob Giroux. And he has an uncanny knack for seeing where something went astray, where something didn't mesh. Thank goodness. I'm lucky to have him.

NL: Let's talk about this business of being a Southern writer. Can you tell me why a group of 26 writers want to get together and call themselves the Fellowship of Southern Writers?

WP: That's a good question. I don't know that I know the answer.

Most of us don't like to be described as a Southern writer. I don't like to
be described as a Southern writer. Would you describe John Cheever as
being a Northern writer? No, you don't think of John Cheever or John
Updike as a Northern writer. So why should I be thought of as a
Southern writer?

The danger is, if you're described as a Southern writer, you might be
thought of as someone who writes about a picturesque local scene like
Uncle Tom's Cabin, Gone with the Wind, something like that. If you're
a serious writer you do the same sort of thing in the South as you do
anywhere else.

Most of us know each other, like each other and have a good time
getting together. And maybe the best thing about it is we're trying to
figure a way to encourage younger writers who are coming along in the
South. The strangest thing about the South is, in this century, particularly in the last 40 or 50 years, how many very good writers it's
produced and how little they are appreciated.

William Faulkner's read much more in France than he is in Mississippi, where he comes from. This is less true now than a few years ago
but, if a young person, man or woman, comes along in high school and
college in the South and wants to be a writer, he or she is likely to have
a pretty hard time of it. If he comes from a typical small Southern town
there's apt not to be a great deal of encouragement. So we're trying to
think of some way to make ourselves known and establish scholarships
or some kind of endowment or grants, to help young writers get started
and maybe get their stories published.

NL: I've heard the complaint that Southern writers don't want to be
called Southern because they don't want to be thought of as regionalists,
but don't you think that, of all writers, Southern writers are considered
to be in the mainstream?

WP: I think so. But I also think there's no contradiction between
being extremely regional and being universal. Nobody was more
regional than William Faulkner. Nobody was more immersed, in fact
saturated, by the atmosphere of a certain rural part of Mississippi. And
yet from this postage stamp of a fictitious county, which he made up
and populated very much like the place he came from—from this small
group of people in this tiny place come the most universal themes from
Shakespeare on down.

NL: That's what you said you were trying to do in your writing, to take an intellectual movement from Europe and place it in a different location.

WP: That was the fun for me because I was more interested in philosophy at first than I was in fiction. Maybe one of the reasons I was picked up on by some people was this combination which Europeans have done for years. If you're interested in ideas and philosophy, and you want to do fiction, why not do both in the same form? Somebody can read my novels simply as story and be entertained—I know that, people tell me—and miss the whole subtext. That's fine, but the more serious reader understands that something is going on. What I'm talking about is the deepest kinds of issues which man addresses: spiritual issues, ideological issues, issues of life and death, of being authentic or not being authentic, and what does that mean. So it's a very nice balance.

On the one hand, if your issues become too predominant, then you write a bad novel. Because the message will become too evident. You cannot preach in a novel. Take Flannery O'Connor again, one of our best fiction writers, a very strong Catholic, and she said something like, "If you write an edifying novel it may be edifying, but it ain't no novel." It's a bad novel. A lot of people are confused about this.

Of course, whatever you believe, whatever you think, is the way you are, and what you are informs your novel. I suppose my model is nearly always Dostoyevsky, who was a man of very strong convictions, but his characters illustrated and incarnated the most powerful themes and issues and trends of his day. I think maybe the greatest novel of all time is *The Brothers Karamazov,* which, written in the latter part of the 19th century, almost prophesies and prefigures everything—all the bloody mess and the issues of the 20th century. These three brothers, incarnate in themselves very deep religious themes, atheism. Ivan Karamazov says, "If God does not exist, all things are permitted." And that explains so much of what has happened in this century. Dostoyevsky forecast communism and what would take place with the rise of all the ideologies.

Earlier, you mentioned the big one. You always think about the big one. Always when you're writing a novel, even when you're doing as well as you can and you get lucky, everything works out fine—you're always disappointed. You always say, "I could have done better than that. Maybe next time." If you didn't have that feeling of both dissatisfaction and hope it wouldn't be worthwhile, you wouldn't be motivated to do it again.

Out of the Ruins

Scott Walter/1989

From *Crisis*, (July-August 1989), 12–18. Reprinted by permission of *Crisis* magazine, Notre Dame, Indiana.

Conversions have figured prominently in Walker Percy's life. He trained as a physician, but contracted tuberculosis during his internship and found himself confined to bed for three years. While convalescing, he read widely and, as his friend and admirer Flannery O'Connor put it, "he and St. Thomas became friends." His reading converted him first to philosophic reflection, then to Catholicism, and finally to his new vocation as a writer.

His conversions to Catholicism and to the craft of writing have borne considerable fruit: Percy has just been awarded the nation's highest honors in both categories. First, Notre Dame honored him with the Laetare Medal, the most prestigious award given American Catholics for contributions to the arts and sciences. Then the National Endowment for the Humanities named him the 1989 Jefferson Lecturer, the highest national honor for distinguished achievement in the humanities.

In Washington to deliver the Jefferson Lecture, Percy spoke with *Crisis* editor Scott Walter in his hotel suite. Dressed in khakis and a plaid shirt, the 72-year-old author spoke leisurely and laughed often, belying his claim that his profession is "a very obscure activity in which there is usually a considerable element of malice." Slouched in his chair—"I don't ever stand if I can sit, and I don't ever sit if I can lie down"—Percy proved once again that though he may deplore the urge to edify, he cannot avoid pricking the consciences of men and women late in the twentieth century.

There is tremendous intellectual opposition in the Church to Pope John Paul II. What do you make of that?

The poor man. I think he's getting a bum rap. On TV, they usually say: This pope is a nice man, but he's a Pole and just by nature reactionary. Yet if you look at his encyclicals, he's quite liberal politically.

He's almost as critical of free-wheeling capitalism as he is of Marxism.
He certainly doesn't come across as a "conservative" in the usual sense.
What his critics mean, although they won't admit it, is that he is an
orthodox Catholic, that he's bound and determined to maintain the
magisterium.

I was talking to a priest the other day who said he was leaving the
Church. Why, I asked? Because nothing had changed, he said. Changed
how? Well, the bishops should be more independent, the *magisterium* is
too strong, it should be up to the bishops to determine the nature of the
Eucharist, and so forth. I said, If you do that, what you've got is
another Episcopal Church—just another church on the street: a Roman
Episcopal Church, next to the Protestant Episcopal Church, and so on.

*A couple of years ago you were asked what you thought of Cardinal
Ratzinger. You said you didn't know his work that well, but the right
sort of people hated him, so he couldn't be all bad.*
[laughter] I guess I'll go with that.

*Cardinal Ratzinger recently said that sometimes bishops ought to be
martyrs.*
I'm sure he'd like to assist some of them.

What do you think of the Catholic press?
I think it's all over the place. It's extremely pluralistic, which is
good, and some of it I like, such as *Crisis,* which I like considerably
better than the *National Catholic Reporter.*

*Your writings embody a critique of many of the philosophies of people
who now praise you extravagantly. What do you think of this paradox?*
Who praised me extravagantly?

*Well, when your last book came out, it was surprising to see your
face splashed across the front page of the Washington Post "Style"
section and the front page of the New York Times Book Review. All of
these publications which ought, philosophically, to dislike you, seem to
like you, while the mainstream Christian press, which ought to like you,
has begun to complain that you don't care enough about women, the
poor, and so on.*
Well, that may be a good place to be—misunderstood both by one's
fellow Catholics and by the secular press. For instance, I remember *The*

Moviegoer was well received, and for the wrong reasons, I think. The Catholic novelist has to be very careful. He has to be underhanded, deceitful, and damn careful how he uses the words of religion, which have all fallen into disuse and almost becomes obscenities, thanks to people like Jimmy Swaggart.

I remember that *The Moviegoer* was well received and reviewed favorably by the New York *Times* and other papers. One reviewer said that the reason he or she liked it so much was that at the end of the novel Binx Bolling says something like, "When the word God is mentioned, a curtain comes down in my head; I can't think about it. What I really believe is that a kick in the ass, in the right place, is the only thing a man can do." That was read by non-believers to mean, a kick in the ass to the Church, you see, instead of to the non-believers. That may be my fault.

On the other hand, if the subject of religion comes up in a novel, or any hint of any kind of conversion or revelation, it's disapproved of. The secular reviewers say: the author did a good job, his characters are well drawn, and the plot moves along, but his religion shows. It's a game you can't win. What you do is, you tell the story. As Flannery O'Connor said, the worst thing the novelist can do is be edifying. She kept most specific references to the Church out of her work, yet God knows she was as powerful a Catholic as I ever knew.

If Miss O'Connor popped out of the grave today, what would surprise her most about the Church?
I think probably the disunity, the near-sundering of the American Church. I think she would be horrified, and probably most of all by the nuns, by what happened to the Georgia nuns, to the Louisiana nuns, and I guess to most of the others. They completely fell apart. They were seduced, not by feminism—which the pope approves of, in the sense of the right of women not to be discriminated against—but by radical feminism. Many of the nuns I know were completely seduced by it, to the point of rebelling against any sort of discipline. They began to mix up the *magisterium* with macho masculinism, as if the Pope were Hemingway. I think that would horrify O'Connor more than anything else.

Speaking of Flannery O'Connor, how did you happen to use as the leitmotif of The Thanatos Syndrome *a passage from one of her essays: Tenderness leads to the gas chamber.*

Did she say that?

It's at the end of her Introduction to A Memoir of Mary Ann.

I'm amazed. I would happily admit that I did that consciously because I'd love to give her the credit.

Could you explain what "tenderness leads to the gas chamber" means?

I don't know what exactly Flannery said, but I was thinking of the Nazis and of my experience of the Germans, whom I liked very much. I was in Germany in 1934, the year after Hitler came into power. The Germans seemed to me extremely likable people, extremely sentimental people; they had tremendous tenderness in their conversations. After all, the romantic *Gefuehl,* openness to feeling, comes from the Germans. God knows they did great things with it: the great German composers from the nineteenth century, for instance. The apposition of German feeling, German tenderness, and the gas chambers struck me as a great mystery at the time. Yet is it a paradox? If *Gefuehl* or tenderness is all you have, it can lead anywhere. The opposite of tenderness is not cruelty.

That passage from O'Connor about the gas chambers is, in a way, the most political thing she ever wrote. It begins: "In the absence of faith, we govern *by tenderness" (emphasis added). Similarly, it seems that your last novel is, in one sense, the most political work you've written: the subject matter is Tom More foiling a plot against the public weal. Then there's your recent, unsuccessful effort to publish a letter in the New York* Times *warning about the danger of taking innocent life by abortion, euthanasia, etc.*

The *Times* was offended. Nothing offends the American liberal more than being compared to the German liberals of the Weimar Republic. There's a book—not by Nazis, in fact long before the Nazis—advocating abortion and the elimination of life "without value." It was written by German doctors of the Weimar Republic, which was probably the most liberal democracy in Europe. Not only did large-scale abortions start in the Weimar Republic, not under the Nazis, but euthanasia did, too, as did the elimination of the malformed and "unfit." All these practices were justified in a book by two liberal Weimar physicians: *The Defense of the Destruction of Life Without Value.* The whole notion is very reasonable without the Christian ethic—no, it's got to be more than the Christian ethic, it's got to be an article of faith. We talk about the sacredness of life as if it's a democratic swear-word, but unless you really mean it, what's more reasonable than doing what the Weimar scientists did? Why bother with people whose "quality of life" is inferior?

Why are abortion rights so central a feature in the ideological canon of groups who are usually committed to what we would call compassion or tenderness?

That's a very good question. If I had anything to say to the liberals, in the usual sense of that word, it is that I agree with them on almost everything: their political and social causes, and the ACLU, God knows, the right to freedom of speech, to help the homeless, the poor, the minorities, God knows the blacks, the third world—their hearts are in the right place. It's actually a mystery, a bafflement to me, how they cannot see the paradox of being in favor of these good things and yet not batting an eyelash when it comes to destroying unborn life.

They also pride themselves on being scientific, yet the scientific consensus is, in the matter of *Roe* v. *Wade,* how wrong Blackmun was when he said there's no scientific agreement about when human life begins. That's absolutely untrue, scientifically. It was a stupid statement, and I've heard indirectly that he knew better. To get back to the liberals, I feel a great sorrow that this tremendous energy that goes into all the other causes with which I agree is not going into the protection of life.

Would the disregard of the spiritual have something to do with that? Many criticized the character Father Smith in your last book because he keeps leaving the world and going up into the firetower to wrestle with his God. Spiritual life, it seems, is unimportant; only good works matter.

Absolutely. That's the Christian scandal: the emphasis on individual human life. Absent that, what's wrong with improving the quality of life? What's wrong with getting rid of people who get in the way? What's wrong with putting old, miserable people out of their misery?

What's wrong with getting rid of badly handicapped, suffering children? Once you're on that slippery slope, where does it end? It ends in the gas chamber. If the consensus is that the Jews are bad for the polity, what's wrong with getting rid of Jews? How do you make the argument that we shouldn't get rid of Jews, or gypsies, or Catholics, or "anti-social blacks"?

A novelist you admire, Saul Bellow, recently endorsed Allan Bloom's book The Closing of the American Mind. *But it's not as well known as it ought to be that you stated Bloom's thesis almost 20 years ago. Tom More in* Love in the Ruins *complained that "Students are a shaky dogmatic lot. And the 'freer' they are, the more dogmatic. At heart they're totalitarians: they want either total dogmatic freedom or total dogmatic unfreedom, and the one thing that makes them unhappy is something in between."*

That's not bad, is it? [laughter]

What did you think of Bloom's book?

I just finished Bloom's book about two weeks ago. I was curious about this book, which was extremely popular—a one-million best-seller. I thought it would be something like Will Durant, a history of Western thought. It was instead a very heavy book, very formidable, and very mysterious. I'm still not sure what he's getting at. He's certainly not suggesting a Christian or Jewish solution. He covers his tracks very well. I suspect he is a nihilist.

What in the world made it a bestseller? I think the title has a lot to do with it. You go to a bookstore in a small town in Louisiana and you see the damned thing piled up. It turns out that a lot of parents are buying it for their kids in college. It struck a nerve with parents who think that those damn professors are screwing up their kids.

There may be something to that.

I didn't say there wasn't. [laughter]

Apparently the publisher concocted that title. Bloom's original title was Soul without Longing. *Father James Schall quips that it ought to have been called* Longing without Soul. *There's a paradox: many souls now go along without any natural longings, but if you do see someone brimful of longing, it's probably a housewife who's into EST.*

Yes [laughter]. Of course, publishers probably know more than we do about what works. My publisher asked what I was working on, and I said another collection of essays. He said, What's the title? I said, *Contra Gentiles*. He laughed and said it'll be read as being about the contras in Nicaragua, and not just any old contras but *gentile* contras. Who knows; maybe that will work.

The American stereotype says that the North is the land of industry, while the South is the home of culture, manners, and belief. Is that true?

It used to be, I think. Maybe most of all in the so-called Southern Renaissance with people like Robert Penn Warren, and Allen Tate, and Andrew Lytle. I don't know about culture in the antebellum South. It's hard to think of a first-class novelist or poet in the antebellum South. Even if the stereotype were true a few years ago, the country is so homogenized now through the media, particularly television, that my grandchildren in southern Louisiana are probably much more like the kids in Dubuque, Iowa, or Springfield, Massachusetts, or San Luis Obispo, than they were like each other a hundred years ago on isolated plantations.

What now provides the subject matter of literature, then? It used to be regional experience—what was distinctive about my small town or this big city. If everyone has the same narrow body of experience, what becomes the great topic for a writer?

Well, I can speak for myself. I'm not interested in the South except as a backdrop, a setting. To over-simplify vastly, I work on a couple of premises. One is that twentieth-century man is deranged, literally deranged. In this society, which is post-Christian, post-modern—the era doesn't have a name yet—there is no coherent theory of man, as I say in my Jefferson lecture. The only theory of man in the air is what comes from the popular media, which is a kind of a pop scientific idea which I say is fundamentally Cartesian and incoherent.

Tocqueville—an amazing fellow—said it 150 years ago: All the Americans I know are Cartesians without having read a word of Descartes. He meant that an educated American believes that everything can be explained "scientifically," can be reduced to the cause and effect of electrons, neurons, and so forth. But at the same time, each person exempts his own mind from this, as do scientists. I see this endemic

Cartesianism, and my criticism is that it leaves us without a coherent theory of man. Consequently, modern man is deranged.

I write from that premise and ask, What are the options for characters living in a deranged world in which the Church is no longer regnant, no longer even terribly important in many places? I find it very useful to array the possible options, the different ways of human existence, first described by Kierkegaard and later by the phenomenologists—different ways of inserting oneself into the world. There's a difference between the environment, which we hear a great deal about, and the world, which is actually where one lives, in a named, symbolized world. The phenomenologists—or existentialists, as they used to be called—say that one is obliged to insert oneself into this world in some mode of being. Even if you don't know you do it, you do it by default. I find it useful for my characters to be living out these various modes of being. I first did it in *The Moviegoer*: Binx Bolling lived out the various Kierkegaardian modes of existence: aesthetic, ethical, and religious. *Love in the Ruins* is really an exercise in Cartesianism. I think Thomas More had something called a Qualitative Quantitative Ontological Lapsometer that measured the distance between Mind and Body. The problem then became finding a technique of getting the two back together. Why not use heavy sodium to heal the split psyche?

The same sort of insidious program that he later fought against in Thanatos Syndrome.

Yes. [laughter]

In these books you seemed to have solved a problem that Tocqueville and Flannery O'Connor both worried about, namely, What will writers have to write about as modern life becomes ever more prosaic, safe, and comfortable? It seems that a safe and comfortable existence can produce more than enough turmoil in a soul to provide a writer with drama.

Yes, Will Barrett in *The Second Coming* had it made, did everything, accomplished everything, then had a mid-life crisis and started falling down in the sandtraps on the golf course. This fits in well with a recent discovery called the "Florida Syndrome." A psychiatrist in St. Petersburg studied a lot of people, good people, who did the right American thing: worked hard for 30 years, saved their money, retired, and went to

live in this American Eden in Florida (or Southern California or
Phoenix). They feel entitled, and are entitled, to be rewarded for a life
of toil, usually pretty dreary. After 30 years they go to Florida, and a
very large percentage, according to this doctor, get depressed, get
disoriented, feel terrible, so bad that a lot of them move back to their
little house in Dubuque. I was pleased to hear that. [laughter]

I like one thing that Einstein said—I couldn't understand much else
that he said. Somebody asked him, How did it happen that you got into
nuclear physics, this extraordinarily theoretical work? He said, I did it
to escape the dreariness of ordinary life in this world. He said, I mean
dreary. He was living an ordinary middle-class, German, Jewish life.
From what I observe, even with the huge consumption in this country,
an awful lot of people are very unhappy, find life very dreary, and move
a lot—all the time. I know a couple—both of them over 70—who
move from one condominium to another, looking for a different golf
course. [laughter]

*You mentioned the absence among people of a shared view of life.
The conventional view seems to be: Who needs that? Everyone should
come up with his own philosophy. Why bother with an overarching,
teleological point of view? What's wrong with this commonplace
privatization of "values"?*

Well, I can't do better than quote Mother Teresa. She said about
abortion: "If a mother can kill her unborn child, I can kill you, and you
can kill me." The privatization of values could lead to that, couldn't it?

*You once said you converted because of "Christianity's rather
insolent claim to be true." What can the Church do to reap converts?*

Well, that's the answer. The only chance the Church has of ever
making converts, or even getting vocations within her own people, is to
remain true to herself. God knows, it's hard. The Holy Father is trying
to cleave to these very unpopular teachings on monogamy, abortion,
contraception, and all the others. The poor man is having the hardest
time in the world. He's going squarely against the entire *zeitgeist* of the
modern world. But if he doesn't do it . . . well, what's happened with
so many religious orders? They've become so "liberal," so unrecogniza-
ble as religious orders, that they're not getting any people coming in.
Why bother? Vocations are down dramatically. Why not? They were
not down when I became a Catholic; we had a flourishing Benedictine

community right in the little town where I lived. The nuns have disappeared, folded. They've gone in all kinds of different directions, every kind of feminism.

Vatican II, of course, was the opening of the Church to the modern world. The idea was precisely to make Catholicism more relevant, to attract more converts. Was Vatican II in any sense a mistake, or at least imprudent tactically?

I don't think so. I think the Church will weather that. There was nothing unorthodox about Vatican II; it is no abridgement of dogma or doctrine. I think a lot of people use Vatican II as an excuse to chuck the whole thing, to throw out the baby with the bath water. They talk about Vatican II, but what they really want to do is get rid of the *magisterium*, get rid of the Eucharist, and you know what Flannery O'Connor said about that: "If it's only a symbol, the hell with it."

Didn't you once tell an interviewer who asked about the "heroic role" of the writer: "Hell, I can't think of any writer who was heroic, except maybe Flannery O'Connor"?

That's true for me. Writers are a pretty sorry lot, to tell you the truth, a bad lot altogether.

Your work often makes one think of Chesterton: both of you make so much use of paradox and comedy. Why do authors with Christian concerns use paradox and comedy?

Kierkegaard said that the comic is of the same essence as the religious. Even though they appear to be bipolar, one springs from the other. Only a true believer can see how funny it all is. It just seems so natural to me, maybe I can't even analyze it.

To get back to your question about the Catholic media, if I had one wish for Catholic journalism, it would be to have something like the Jews have in *Commentary*. It doesn't matter whether you agree or disagree with *Commentary*; if you want to find out about current Jewish thought, *Commentary* comes to mind right away. It's extremely well done. I wish there was a journal like it for Catholics. Maybe *Crisis* can do something like that.

Walker Percy Talks about Science, Faith, and Fiction

Brent Short/1990

From *Sojourners,* 19, (May 1990), 27–29. Reprinted by permission from *Sojourners,* Washington, D.C.

Diagnosis comes as second nature to Walker Percy. Trained as a physician, Percy's own confinement as a tuberculosis patient during his medical internship was instrumental in his second career as a writer.

His first novel, *The Moviegoer,* follows the restless ponderings of a young stockbroker living in a suburb of New Orleans. The winner of the 1962 National Book Award, *The Moviegoer* (and Percy's novels to come) describes the spiritual malaise of the 20th century against the backdrop of the passing experience of the old South's mystery and manners.

A convert to Catholicism, Percy is a 20th-century writer serving witness to this century's intellectual life as well as its grim chapters of history. Combining his avocation as a scholar of semiotics (the study of symbols) with his use of the novel form, Percy's work has continued to reflect his critique of scientific progress as it infiltrates into an increasingly homogenized, technologized popular culture.

Readers of Percy novels can look forward to each story being characteristically rendered in a unique ironic voice, filled with droll commentary as well as political, religious, and social allegory, and an unending search to name the age in which we live. As an allegorist, Percy possesses such a penetrating sense of satire, social critic Robert Coles declared simply: "Walker Percy is a gift."

In *Lost in the Cosmos,* a 1984 collection of non-fiction essays, Percy takes on the conventional wisdom of the day—a meld of media, New Age philosophy, and superficial scientism—producing a thought-provoking and often hilarious antithesis to the euphemistic answers of the television age.

In Percy's most recent novel, *The Thanatos Syndrome,* the character Dr. Thomas More stumbles on a plot among local scientists to cure the social ills of the commonweal by tech-

236

nological means—loading the water supply with the chemical heavy sodium. In More's struggle to penetrate a
conspiracy of silence and at the same time discover his own
rightful place as a scientist, the author posits a most challenging thesis about genocide in the modern age and contemporary scientific mores.

In an unending search to diagnose the dangers of our age,
Percy's last two novels, *The Second Coming* and *The
Thanatos Syndrome,* have specifically concerned themselves
with the post-Christian West as a culture of death. Percy's
protagonists' encounters with other wanderers provide comic
relief as well as a way to open up to a more serious antidote.
To the discerning reader, hidden within Percy's powerful
critique are subtle and allusive signs of grace.

Sojourners: In your novels, you seem to render a diagnosis for the age
and the people in it. How has your medical background influenced you
as a writer?

Walker Percy: Some people think that the two vocations—being
first a physician, then ending up as a novelist—couldn't be more
different. I find it very useful to use the same stance. The stance of the
physician is that of a diagnostician. The premise, the presumption, is
that when you see a patient, something is wrong. The question is,
What's gone wrong, and how do you find out to make a diagnosis?

I find that extremely useful in dealing with the present age. Something's clearly wrong, maybe even worse than usual in civilizations. I
find it a natural stance from which to write both novels and non-fiction.

Sojourners: Your novels and essays contain a great deal of comic
satire of science, but a great love of and respect for science come
through as well. Would it be possible to separate you as a novelist from
Walker Percy the scientist?

Percy: Well, I hope not. I don't think the two are mutually exclusive.
I don't have any quarrel with science. What the sciences do, they do
very well.

The trouble is, the sciences for the last 200 years have been spectacu-
larly successful in dealing with subhuman reality—chemistry and
physics of matter—with extraordinary progress in learning about the
cosmos, but also extraordinary lack of success in dealing with humanity
as humanity. I think it's very curious that the scientist knows a

tremendous amount about everything except what he or she is. Despite
the extraordinary successes of science, we do not presently have even
the rudiments of a coherent science of humanity.

Sojourners: In *The Thanatos Syndrome,* the forces of death seem to
be masquerading in the guise of social betterment. Do you think by
naming or describing those forces, one comes closer to coming to grips
with the contemporary predicament?

Percy: The old, addled priest who is holed up in a firetower says it in
his own peculiar way. He observes that the society has learned a great
deal, everything seems to be going pretty well, some guys have
discovered that heavy sodium seems to cure the contemporary ills—
reduces the number of teen-age pregnancies, reduces depression and
anxiety, and seems to help people get along better. The trouble is,
people are beginning to act more and more like subhuman primates.

The priest goes back to the fact—and this is the central point of the
book—that the evils of the Nazis did not begin with the Nazis. The
Nazis didn't come out of nowhere. They came out of the German
Democratic Republic, the Weimar Republic—one of the most democratic in Western Europe. The Weimar doctors, not the Nazi doctors,
wrote a book called *The Defense of Destruction of Life Without Value.*

The criterion became what you hear so often now—"quality of life."
If the quality of life is not good, why not get rid of it? This is quite
reasonable, absent the Judeo-Christian ethic. If one can dispense with
the scandalous Christian proposition that each human being is created by
God, and accordingly sacred, one can quite reasonably use the criterion
of the quality of life for all people.

First, get rid of malformed children, then get rid of old people, anybody. If the quality of life is bad, what is wrong with terminating it for
the benefit of the person suffering, for the benefit of the family that is
going through a lot of trouble, for the benefit of the state because it's
extremely expensive?

I was making a not-too-subtle suggestion that once you cross the
barrier of the destruction of human life, you're on the slope. I don't see
how it ends short of how the Weimar Republic ends. The Nazis come
in, and if the majority of the people come to believe that the Jews—or
the gypsies, or the Hispanics, or the blacks—are bad and undesirable,
then what is wrong with getting rid of them? Once the barrier is crossed,
I don't see what hinders what the Germans called "the final solution."

It was a somewhat shocking thesis for a novel—and not really picked up by a lot of people, because you can't do that in a novel. A novel had better not be caught preaching or edifying. It's okay to be satirical and funny. But if there's a heavy message, it better be concealed. So I conceal it in the mouth of a nutty old priest.

Sojourners: Your novels are often described and discussed as novels of ideas, but most novelists find that their fictional characters take on a life of their own. Has this been your experience?

Percy: That's the best thing that could happen to a novelist. If the characters are vehicles, mouthpieces for your own ideas, you're in trouble, you're going to write a bad novel. The best way to create a novel is to create a character. Naturally, if you create characters, they're going to be "informed" by the way you see life and the nature of human beings. But then you turn them loose, and you find them doing all sorts of things. That's the freedom the novelist hopes for.

Sojourners: You seem to present the signs of grace in your work in a way that leaves it up to the reader as to how to take them, and what exactly to discern from them. What is your intention by doing it that way?

Percy: Trying to get away with it. If you get caught writing a "religious" novel—about God, Judaism, Christianity—you are dead. You'll be read by a few people. As one of my characters, Binx Bolling in *The Moviegoer,* says, "Whenever anyone says God to me, a curtain goes down in my head."

I have to be careful when I talk about grace. I have to be extremely allusive. I think Caroline Gordon said, "The novelist is entitled to use every trick of deceit and underhandedness at his or her control."

Sojourners: How does one go about writing about Christian faith in a culture in which the language of faith has been discredited and devalued?

Percy: That is *the* problem. And it's getting worse, because the language of Christianity is increasingly discredited—mainly by the media and the TV preachers. They've given us all a bad name. You do the best you can with it, usually by avoiding the words or using other words.

Sojourners: In your background, there was a bout with tuberculosis during medical school?

Percy: Yes, I was interning at Bellevue, a big charity hospital in New

York City. I was working with tuberculosis cases, doing all the autopsies in pathology. I just picked it up that way. It was noticed on a routine X-ray; I never had any symptoms.

I had to take the classic rest cure. That was before there was chemotherapy. I had the classic experience of Hans Castorp in *The Magic Mountain,* which was a turnaround in his life. It was certainly a revolution in mine. If it hadn't been for that, I'd probably be a second-class psychiatrist in Birmingham.

Sojourners: How did that time of recovery affect the "cure" you allude to in your novels?

Percy: It was valuable to me, and I used it later in various ways. Most of the time we are not what we really are. We are some distance away, not really ourselves. There is a paradox: One is most one's self usually not when one's needs are satisfied, but under conditions of catastrophe.

My character in *The Moviegoer*, Binx Bolling, said the time he was most himself was when he had been shot in the Korean War; when he was that close to death, all of a sudden he was most alive. Actually, I think I swiped that from Tolstoy, when he had his character Prince Andrei at a Napoleonic battle about to get killed, maybe badly wounded. All of a sudden he realizes for the first time what it is to be human, what it is to be alive, what it is to be himself.

In Louisiana we have hurricanes. My theory is that people enjoy hurricanes, whether they say so or not. In a hurricane terrible things are happening, but there is a certain exhilaration. It comes from a peculiar sense of self, the vividness.

As Einstein said, "Life is dreary as hell." Somebody asked him why he went into quantum mechanics. Well, to get away from the dreariness of life. Louisianans enjoy hurricanes, if they're not too bad.

Sojourners: Despite their outward appearance of success as doctors, lawyers, scientists, all your protagonists—all Southern gentlemen— seem unsatisfied with life in conventional society. Would you say that is one of the central dilemmas you try to address?

Percy: Yes. And it relates to your question about the relationship between being a Christian and being a novelist. Some people would think of the two as antithetical. But I find it extremely valuable being a Catholic. (It can also apply to any Christian church or to Judaism.) The peculiar Christian notion of humanity as wayfarer, as pilgrim, in search, in quest, is of course the very essence of the novel. The novel is about somebody in trouble, in a predicament.

As Binx Bolling says, he undertook the search when he came to himself on the battlefield and realized who he was, with this very vivid sense of being human. The rest of his life was devoted to the search, and not to the standard secular practice of satisfying one's needs or achieving one's life goals—or "growing as a person" (a favorite expression these days).

I wonder how many books have been written about growing as a person. That may be useful, but it doesn't work very well in a novel. But the idea of humanity in quest, humanity in search, doesn't have to have any great revelation, any great conversion. It doesn't have to end up like St. Paul knocked off his horse. It's the idea of the quest which is very useful to a novelist.

So, the two backgrounds have been so useful—the background as physician, diagnostician, recognizing that something's wrong with the world; and the anthropology of Christianity, seeing humanity as the creature something has gone wrong with. If humanity has any sense and comes to itself, we will spend our time searching for what happened, searching for the answer.

Sojourners: What kind of impact and influence do social planners and theorists, who measure society in quantifiable terms, have on contemporary culture? Does that create its own ethos?

Percy: The practice is easy to criticize, but it's certainly not bad. A social planner is trying to plan some way that the state and society can take care of, or better the situation of, those who are in a terrible situation, terrible trouble—the deprived, including minorities and the homeless. There's certainly everything to be praised about planning for betterment.

The danger is from the point of view of the individual. Our culture is informed by a kind of popular scientific notion of "the experts." They are those who know—not only know, but owe it to us to make things better. If you come to the point where you are relying on "the experts" —on the scientists to give you the answers to your life, or the social planners to get you out of the mess you're in—that's unfortunate to the degree that it destroys one's own initiative.

Sojourners: You seem to make a distinction between science and scientism.

Percy: Oh, yes. It's not my distinction, but I think it's quite true. Science is fine for what it does; for what it does, it's magnificent.

The idea of scientism is a cultural transmission of a notion of science for the popular mind in which they—"the experts"—have all the answers. Of course, the answers are abstractions. As Kierkegaard would say, they cannot utter one word to me about what it is to be born, to live or die.

Scientism has been called a misplacement of reality—from the reality of one's self and individual things to the notion of abstractions where things or selves are simply exemplars of this or that theory or abstraction.

Sojourners: You've been quoted as saying, "If the first great intellectual discovery of my life was the beauty of the scientific method, surely the second was the discovery of the singular predicament of humanity in the very world which has been transformed by science." Does that still hold true?

Percy: You don't have to be a sage or a prophet to point out the fact that the 20th century, which should have been the greatest triumph of civilization of all time—the triumph of science, technology, consumership—has been the most murderous century in all of history. More people were killed by each other—20 million in the first big war, and I think 40 or 50 million killed in the second—than from all other causes since then. It's an interesting paradox for a writer to think about.

Index